INTERFERENCE

The Inside Story of Trump,
Russia, and the Mueller Investigation

By Aaron Zebley, James Quarles,
and Andrew Goldstein

With a Preface by Robert S. Mueller, III

SIMON & SCHUSTER
New York London Toronto Sydney New Delhi

100 YEARS
SIMON & SCHUSTER

1230 Avenue of the Americas
New York, NY 10020

First Simon & Schuster hardcover edition September 2024

SIMON & SCHUSTER and colophon are registered trademarks of Simon & Schuster, LLC

Simon & Schuster: Celebrating 100 Years of Publishing in 2024

For information about special discounts for bulk purchases, please contact Simon & Schuster Special Sales at 1-866-506-1949 or business@simonandschuster.com.

The Simon & Schuster Speakers Bureau can bring authors to your live event. For more information or to book an event, contact the Simon & Schuster Speakers Bureau at 1-866-248-3049 or visit our website at www.simonspeakers.com.

Interior design by Wendy Blum

Manufactured in the United States of America

10   9   8   7   6   5   4   3   2   1

Library of Congress Cataloging-in-Publication Data has been applied for.

ISBN 978-1-6680-6374-3
ISBN 978-1-6680-6376-7 (ebook)

*To public servants everywhere
who stand up for the rule of law.*

CONTENTS

CONTENTS

GLOSSARY

SPECIAL COUNSEL INVESTIGATIVE TEAMS

Team F: Team responsible for matters involving Michael Flynn, President Trump's first national security adviser.

Team M: Team responsible for matters involving Paul Manafort, chairman of the Trump campaign from May to August 2016.

Team R: Team responsible for matters involving Russian interference in the 2016 election and contacts between Russia and members of the Trump campaign (other than Flynn and Manafort).

Team 600: Team responsible for investigating President Trump's conduct toward the investigation of Russian election interference.

PEOPLE

Ahmad, Zainab: Lawyer working on Team F in the special counsel's office.

Andres, Greg: Lawyer working on Team M in the special counsel's office; lead trial counsel in *United States v. Manafort* in Eastern District of Virginia, resulting in Manafort's conviction.

Assange, Julian: Founder of WikiLeaks, which in 2016 posted on the internet documents stolen by Russian military intelligence (GRU) from entities and individuals affiliated with the Democratic Party.

Atkinson, Rush: Lawyer working on Team R in the special counsel's office.

Bannon, Stephen: White House chief strategist and senior counselor to President Trump (January 2017–August 2017); chief executive of the Trump campaign (August 2016–November 2016).

Barr, William: Attorney general (November 1991–January 1993; February 2019–December 2020); deputy attorney general (May 1990–November 1991); assistant attorney general, Office of Legal Counsel (January 1989–May 1990).

Boente, Dana: Acting attorney general (January 2017–February 2017); acting deputy attorney general (February 2017–April 2017); US attorney Eastern District of Virginia (December 2015–January 2018).

Carr, Peter: Department of Justice press officer assigned to the special counsel's office.

Clinton, Hillary: 2016 Democratic presidential candidate; secretary of state (2009–2013); Democratic senator from New York (2001–2009).

Clovis, Samuel, Jr.: Chief policy adviser and national cochair of the Trump campaign.

Coats, Dan: Director of national intelligence (March 2017–August 2019).

Cobb, Ty: Attorney in the White House who served as counsel to the president (July 2017–May 2018).

Cohen, Ben: FBI security officer assigned to the special counsel's office.

Cohen, Michael: Former vice president of the Trump Organization and counsel to Donald Trump before his presidency. Pleaded guilty in the Southern District of New York to federal charges related to campaign finance, tax evasion, and making false statements to a bank; pleaded guilty to federal charges brought by the special counsel's office for lying to Congress. Sentenced to three years in prison.

Comey, James: Director of the Federal Bureau of Investigation (September

4, 2013–May 9, 2017); deputy attorney general (December 2003–August 2005); US attorney Southern District of New York (January 2002–December 2003).

Daniels, Stormy: Pseudonym for Stephanie Clifford, adult film star who allegedly had a sexual encounter with Trump in 2006 and received a "hush money" payment from Michael Cohen in 2016 in exchange for not revealing her alleged relationship with Trump.

Deripaska, Oleg: Russian oligarch with ties to Vladimir Putin; hired Paul Manafort for consulting work between 2005 and 2009.

Dowd, John: Personal attorney for President Trump (June 2017–March 2018).

Dreeben, Michael: Deputy solicitor general at the Department of Justice; leader of the legal team and member of Team 600 in the special counsel's office.

Durham, John: US attorney for the District of Connecticut (February 2018–February 2021), special counsel who investigated the origins of Crossfire Hurricane.

Engel, Steven: Head of the Office of Legal Counsel at the Department of Justice (November 2017–January 2021).

Flood, Emmet: Attorney in the White House who served as counsel to the president (May 2018–June 2019); replaced Ty Cobb.

Flynn, Michael: National security adviser (January 22, 2017–February 13, 2017), director of the Defense Intelligence Agency (July 2012–August 2014), and Trump campaign adviser. Flynn pleaded guilty to lying to the FBI about his communications with Russian ambassador Sergey Kislyak in December 2016. Pardoned by President Trump in 2020 before he could be sentenced.

Gates, Richard (Rick), III: Deputy campaign manager for the Trump campaign (March 2016–August 2016), Trump inaugural committee deputy chairman, and longtime employee of Paul Manafort. Gates pleaded guilty to federal charges related to a tax scheme and the Foreign Agents

Registration Act. Cooperated with the US government in the cases against Paul Manafort. Sentenced to forty-five days of incarceration and three years probation.

Giuliani, Rudolph: Personal attorney for President Trump beginning March 2018, mayor of New York City (1994–2001).

Hicks, Hope: Press secretary for the Trump campaign; White House communications director (August 2017–March 2018).

Jackson, Robert H.: Attorney general of the United States (January 1940–June 1941); US Supreme Court justice (July 1941–October 1954).

Kelly, John: White House chief of staff (July 2017–January 2019).

Kilimnik, Konstantin: Russian-Ukrainian political consultant and longtime employee of Paul Manafort; assessed by the FBI to have ties to Russian intelligence.

Kislyak, Sergey: Russian ambassador to the United States (2008–2017).

Kushner, Jared: President Trump's son-in-law and senior adviser to President Trump.

Lavrov, Sergey: Russian minister of foreign affairs (2004–) and former permanent representative of Russia to the United Nations (1994–2004).

Manafort, Paul, Jr.: Trump campaign member (March 2016–August 2016) and chairman and chief strategist (May 2016–August 2016). Convicted in the Eastern District of Virginia for federal charges related to his work in Ukraine for Russia-aligned politicians; pleaded guilty in DC to federal charges related to the Foreign Agents Registration Act. Sentenced to 7.5 years. Pardoned by President Trump in 2020.

McCabe, Andrew: Acting director of the FBI (May 9, 2017–August 2, 2017); deputy director of the FBI (February 2016–March 2018).

McGahn, Donald: White House counsel (January 2017–October 2018).

McGarry, Beth: Executive officer for the special counsel's office.

Meisel, Omer: Lead FBI special agent for Team M in the special counsel's office.

Meisler, Scott: Lawyer working on the legal team in the special counsel's office.

Mifsud, Josef: Maltese national and London-based professor who, immediately after returning from Moscow in April 2016, told George Papadopoulos that the Russians possessed "dirt" on Hillary Clinton in the form of "thousands of emails."

Miller, Stephen: Senior adviser to President Trump (January 2017–January 2021); senior policy adviser (January 2016–January 2017).

Monteleoni, Paul: Assistant US attorney at the Southern District of New York.

O'Callaghan, Edward: Principal associate deputy attorney general at the Department of Justice (April 2018–December 2019).

Page, Carter: Foreign policy adviser to the Trump campaign (March 2016–September 2016).

Papadopoulos, George: Foreign policy adviser to the Trump campaign. Received information that the Russians had "dirt" on Hillary Clinton in the form of "thousands of emails," and that the Russians could assist the Trump campaign with the anonymous release of information damaging to Clinton. Pleaded guilty to lying to the FBI about contacts with Josef Mifsud. Sentenced to fourteen days of incarceration. Pardoned by President Trump in 2020.

Podesta, John, Jr.: Clinton campaign chairman whose email account was hacked by Russian military intelligence (GRU). WikiLeaks released his stolen emails during the 2016 campaign.

Polonskaya, Olga: Russian national introduced to George Papadopoulos by Joseph Mifsud as an individual with connections to Vladimir Putin.

Pompeo, Michael: US secretary of state (April 2018–January 2021); director of the Central Intelligence Agency (January 2017–April 2018).

Prelogar, Elizabeth: Lawyer working on the legal team and Team 600 in the special counsel's office; United States Solicitor General (October 2021–).

Priebus, Reince: White House chief of staff (January 2017–July 2017); chair of the Republican National Committee (January 2011–January 2017).

Priestap, Bill: Head of the FBI's Counterintelligence Division (December 2015–December 2018).

Prigozhin, Yevgeny: Head of the Russian companies Concord Catering and Concord Management and Consulting, which supported and financed the Internet Research Agency's "active measures" social media campaign to interfere in the 2016 US presidential election. Also head of Wagner Group. Deceased.

Putin, Vladimir: President of the Russian Federation (2000–2008; 2012–).

Raskin, Jane: Defense lawyer, personal attorney for President Trump. Married to Marty Raskin.

Raskin, Marty: Defense lawyer, personal attorney for President Trump. Married to Jane Raskin.

Rhee, Jeannie: Lawyer who led Team R in the special counsel's office.

Rogers, Michael: Admiral, US Navy; director of the National Security Agency (April 2014–May 2018).

Rosenstein, Rod: Deputy attorney general (April 2017–May 2019); acting attorney general for the Russia election interference investigation (May 2017–November 2018).

Sanders, Sarah Huckabee: White House press secretary (July 2017–June 2019).

Schools, Scott: Associate deputy attorney general (October 2016–July 2018).

Sekulow, Jay: Personal attorney for President Trump beginning in June 2017.

Sessions, Jefferson, III: Attorney general (February 2017–November 2018); Republican senator from Alabama (January 1997–February 2017); head of the Trump campaign's foreign policy advisory team.

Starr, Kenneth: Independent counsel who investigated President Bill Clinton and the Whitewater-Lewinsky scandal (August 1994–October 1999).

Steele, Christopher: Former British intelligence officer; compiled an unofficial report during the 2016 presidential campaign on candidate Donald Trump's activities in Russia; this was dubbed the "Steele dossier."

Stone, Roger: Adviser to the Trump campaign. Convicted in 2019 for federal charges related to lying to Congress about his conduct with respect to WikiLeaks' release of stolen emails damaging to Hillary Clinton during the 2016 election; sentenced to forty months of incarceration. Sentence commuted by President Trump in July 2020; pardoned by President Trump in December 2020.

Strzok, Peter: FBI special agent and deputy assistant director for counterintelligence who led the FBI's Crossfire Hurricane investigation.

Taylor, Michelle: Lead FBI special agent for Team 600 in the special counsel's office.

Timofeev, Ivan: Director of programs at the Russian International Affairs Council; communicated in 2016 with George Papadopoulos; attempted to arrange a meeting between the Russian government and the Trump campaign.

Trump, Donald, Jr.: President Trump's eldest son; trustee and executive vice president of the Trump Organization; helped arrange and attended the June 9, 2016, meeting at Trump Tower between Russian lawyer Natalia Veselnitskaya and Trump campaign officials.

Van Grack, Brandon: Lawyer who led Team F in the special counsel's office.

Veselnitskaya, Natalia: Russian government lawyer who was the principal speaker at the June 9, 2016, meeting at Trump Tower with Trump campaign officials.

Weissmann, Andrew: Lawyer who led Team M in the special counsel's office.

Yanukovych, Viktor: Former president of Ukraine who had worked with Paul Manafort. Forced from office by popular uprising and exiled to Russia in 2014.

Zelinsky, Aaron: Lawyer who worked on Team R in the special counsel's office; nicknamed "AZ2."

ENTITIES AND ORGANIZATIONS

Concord: Umbrella term for Concord Management and Consulting LLC and Concord Catering, Russian companies formerly controlled by Yevgeny Prigozhin and which funded the IRA.

CrowdStrike: An American cybersecurity technology company that investigated the Russian hacks of the Democratic Congressional Campaign Committee and the Democratic National Committee.

DCLeaks: Website registered and operated by Russian military intelligence (GRU); released documents stolen by the GRU during the 2016 US presidential campaign.

Guccifer 2.0: Fictitious online persona operated by Russian military intelligence (GRU); released documents stolen by the GRU during the 2016 US presidential campaign.

Internet Research Agency (IRA): Russian entity based in Saint Petersburg; engaged in an "active measures" social media campaign to interfere in the 2016 US presidential election.

Main Intelligence Directorate of the General Staff (GRU): The Russian Federation's military intelligence agency.

Opposition Bloc: Ukrainian political party that incorporated members of the defunct Party of Regions.

Party of Regions: Ukrainian political party of former President Yanukovych; generally understood to align with Russian policies.

WikiLeaks: Organization founded by Julian Assange in 2006 that posts information online, including data stolen from private, corporate, and US government entities. Communicated with and released data stolen by Russian military intelligence (GRU) during the 2016 US presidential election.

ABBREVIATIONS

AAG: Assistant attorney general

AUSA: Assistant US attorney (federal prosecutor)

CIA: Central Intelligence Agency

DAG: Deputy attorney general (number two official at the DOJ)

DCCC: Democratic Congressional Campaign Committee

DNC: Democratic National Committee

DOJ: Department of Justice (aka "the department" or "Main Justice")

EDVA: Eastern District of Virginia (a judicial district with a US attorney centered in Alexandria, Virginia)

EDNY: Eastern District of New York (a judicial district with a US attorney centered in Brooklyn, New York)

FARA: Foreign Agents Registration Act (US statute)

FBI: Federal Bureau of Investigation (aka "the bureau")

FSB: Federal Security Service (Russia) (the Russian Federation's domestic security service, akin to the FBI)

GRU: Main Intelligence Directorate of the General Staff (Russia) (the Russian Federation's military intelligence agency)

HPSCI: House of Representatives Permanent Select Committee on Intelligence (aka "House Intelligence Committee")

IRA: Internet Research Agency (Russia)

JCC: Justice Command Center (facility inside Department of Justice headquarters, Washington, DC)

NATO: North Atlantic Treaty Organization

NSA: National Security Agency

ODNI: Office of the Director of National Intelligence

OLC: Office of Legal Counsel (part of the Department of Justice)

SCIF: Sensitive Compartmented Information Facility (a specially designed room where classified information can be safely stored, processed, and discussed)

SCO: Special Counsel's Office (operated by Special Counsel Robert S. Mueller, III, May 2017–May 2019).

SDNY: Southern District of New York (a judicial district with a US attorney centered in Manhattan, New York)

SIOC: Strategic Information Operations Center (facility inside FBI headquarters, Washington, DC)

SSCI: Senate Select Committee on Intelligence (aka "Senate Intelligence Committee")

PREFACE

Since 2021, my colleagues Aaron Zebley, Jim Quarles, and Andrew Goldstein have taught a class at my alma mater, the University of Virginia School of Law, on the role of the special counsel. I have attended many of their seminars and listened as the students wrestled with some of the difficult decisions we faced throughout our investigation of Russian interference in the 2016 presidential election. Should we have subpoenaed the president? How should we have interacted with the attorney general? How can a special counsel, working under the president as part of the executive branch, investigate the president and potentially hold him accountable for criminal misconduct? The students weighed in thoughtfully, with some supporting the decisions we made, others being more critical, and several more unsure of their positions until they had to sit down and write their final term paper.

At one point while teaching the class, Aaron, Jim, and Andrew raised the possibility of writing a book that would address many of these same questions. I was dubious. I have always maintained that the work of the special counsel's office should speak for itself. Our report contains our findings and analysis and the reasons for our decisions—that still stands. But five years have passed since we issued the report, and recent events have persuaded me that there is value in identifying lessons learned from the decisions we made and how we made them, mistakes and all.

Since our office closed in 2019, the country has faced several new special counsel investigations into current and former presidents. What had been a once-in-a-generation appointment is becoming more commonplace. Perhaps our experience can help Americans better understand both the value and the limitations of special counsels, and the difficult decisions they make. As this book demonstrates, there are often competing interests at stake: independence, credibility, thoroughness, speed, and accountability. How to balance them is not always straightforward.

It is also evident that Americans have not learned the lessons of Russia's attack on our democracy in 2016. As we detailed in our report, the evidence was clear that the Russian government engaged in multiple, systematic attacks designed to undermine our democracy and favor one candidate over the other. We were not prepared then and, despite many efforts of dedicated people across the government, we are not prepared now. This threat deserves the attention of every American. Russia attacked us before and will do so again.

It is for these reasons that Aaron, Jim, and Andrew have my full support. I am grateful for this book. They are the right people to tell this story. They were with me at every major decision point. They care deeply about the rule of law and know the importance of making decisions with integrity and humility. These qualities matter most when some refuse to play by the rules, and others are urging that you respond in kind.

I am also grateful for the devotion and work of our entire special counsel team—the agents, analysts, professional staff, and attorneys—who spent nearly two years helping conduct this investigation. Public service is a contribution to something bigger than oneself. It is essential for people to find ways to serve, and to do so with integrity.

Robert S. Mueller, III

AUTHORS' NOTE

We are donating our proceeds from this book to the Karsh Center for Law and Democracy at the University of Virginia School of Law, which sponsors the course we have taught since 2021 titled "The Mueller Report and the Role of the Special Counsel." The Karsh Center is a nonpartisan legal institute whose mission is to promote "civil discourse and democratic dialogue, civic engagement and citizenship, ethics and integrity in public office, and respect for the rule of law."

This book tells the inside story of the decisions we made during our two years working with Bob Mueller in the special counsel's office. It is not an exhaustive account of every detail of our investigation. Instead, we have tried to capture the complicated issues at play and the principles that guided us. We also fill in and, where necessary, correct the historical record.

This book shows how Bob steered our office through the many obstacles we faced. He led the office by example and made clear that while the facts we uncovered and the conclusions we reached were important, so was the manner in which we conducted ourselves. Bob insisted we take the long view of what is ultimately most important for the country. We think much can be learned from the way he put principle and integrity first.

As this book was going to press in July 2024, the Supreme Court issued its opinion in *Trump v. United States*, which granted the president broad immunity when exercising "core constitutional powers" or engaging in other "official" acts. The Court's opinion would have limited—if not eliminated—multiple lines of our investigation. We might never have learned all that we did about Russia or Trump.

We hope this account of the efforts we undertook, the decisions (and mistakes) we made, and the information we uncovered will be useful in determining whether, and if so how, it is possible to hold a president accountable in the future.

Aaron Zebley, James Quarles,
and Andrew Goldstein

INTERFERENCE

One

NINE DAYS IN MAY

Tuesday, May 9, 2017

Robert S. Mueller, III, was in a cab when the news hit. It was a Tuesday in Washington, DC, the evening sun breaking through a bank of clouds, and the former FBI director wore his usual dark suit and white button-down shirt. His gray hair was parted on the side with military precision, and his plastic Casio watch faced the inside of his wrist, a common practice among Marines so they can check the time without wasting a fraction of a second rotating their arm. A Vietnam War veteran who had been wounded in action, Bob had become a prosecutor and risen to the highest ranks of the US Department of Justice (DOJ), including heading the Criminal Division and leading the FBI, where he oversaw the transformation of the bureau following the 9/11 terrorist attacks.

Bob was widely regarded as a person of integrity known for conducting his business—whether in government or in private practice—without fear or favor. His thoroughness and impartiality had earned him overwhelming bipartisan support during his time in government. Bob, a Republican, had

1

been appointed FBI director by President George W. Bush and started his term just one week before 9/11. After Bob had served the statutory maximum ten-year term, President Obama asked Congress to pass special legislation allowing him to serve for an additional two years. The Senate passed that legislation by a vote of 100–0.

When Bob finally left the FBI on September 4, 2013, he was replaced by another Republican, James Comey. Both men had famously intersected in 2004, when they and other senior Department of Justice officials objected to President Bush's reauthorization of a secret surveillance program that DOJ lawyers had concluded was unconstitutional.

Now, two presidents later, Bob and Comey were about to intersect again.

The news that hit that evening came from Bob's longtime colleague, Aaron Zebley, who was also in the cab. Aaron had started his career in the trenches as an FBI counterterrorism agent, investigating al-Qaeda's bombings of the US embassies in Kenya and Tanzania in 1998. A year later, Aaron was on the arrest team that found and captured one of the bombers in South Africa. Aaron went on to become an assistant US attorney in Virginia in the terrorism and national security unit, and he later returned to the FBI as Bob's counsel for national security. Bob then made Aaron his chief of staff and they later became law partners. By May 9, 2017, the two men had been working together nearly every day for eight years.

Bob and Aaron were now starting a new assignment involving, of all things, automobile airbags. Specifically, airbags manufactured by Takata, a Japanese auto parts maker. The company had pleaded guilty to selling faulty airbag systems, and Bob had been asked to manage the disbursement of nearly $1 billion in victim compensation funds.

Bob and Aaron were on I Street, just north of the White House, on their way back to their firm after a meeting with Takata's lawyers. Aaron stared at a news alert on his phone as the cab drove west. "Trump just fired Comey," he said, and showed Bob the screen.

Bob read the headline and then looked out the window for a moment, considering the news. Then he turned back to his notes from the meeting they had just left. Bob had seen a lot during his life and was almost always even-tempered. He spoke only when necessary—something often attributed to his years as a Marine. He made no comment on Comey's firing.

Aaron scrolled his phone for more updates, trying to understand what had happened. Comey, a towering figure at six feet, eight inches tall, was well liked at the FBI but had become a political lightning rod in the summer of 2016. On July 5 of that year, Comey had announced at a press conference that there would be no criminal charges against Hillary Clinton, who, at the time, was running for president against Donald Trump. Clinton had used a private email server for government business while she was secretary of state. During Comey's press conference, he announced that Clinton had been "extremely careless" in handling what he called "very sensitive, highly classified information," even though no charges would be filed against her.

Comey's announcement infuriated people across the political spectrum. For some, it was hard to understand why Clinton hadn't been prosecuted. For others, it was hard to understand why, if there were no charges, Comey had said anything at all. Typically, the FBI says nothing when it closes an investigation without charges. And the FBI, which is part of the DOJ, almost never holds press conferences unless it is announcing criminal charges alongside DOJ prosecutors. The public rebuke of Comey had been fierce, and since that time he had been criticized both for not recommending a charge against Clinton and for the perception of helping tilt the election in Trump's favor. Another round of criticism came when Comey announced the FBI was reopening the Clinton email investigation in late October, mere days before the 2016 election.

After Trump's inauguration, Comey continued to assert his independence. He testified before Congress in March 2017 that the FBI had an open investigation into Russian interference in the 2016 election—a foreign-interference campaign that had been designed to help Trump beat Clinton. In his testimony, Comey said he had been authorized by the Department of Justice to publicly confirm that the FBI was "investigating the nature of any links between individuals associated with the Trump campaign and the Russian government and whether there was any coordination between the campaign and Russia's efforts."

Now, nearly two months later, President Trump had fired Comey. As Bob and Aaron pulled up to the corner outside their firm's office, Aaron wondered why Trump had fired Comey when the FBI was in the middle of an investigation into the Trump campaign; the firing would surely spark questions. Of course, the president could have fired Comey for any number of other reasons. Maybe Trump didn't trust Comey, or perhaps he thought the bureau needed a change, or maybe Trump simply didn't like him.

Whatever the reason, Comey's dismissal felt unprecedented. Only one other FBI director had been dismissed—William Sessions in 1993—and that had to do with internal matters at the bureau.

That evening, the *New York Times* reported that Democrats on Capitol Hill were calling for a special counsel—a unique kind of prosecutor that is part of the DOJ but with some degree of independence from it—to take over the Russia inquiry.

Aaron wanted to know how the White House would explain the decision to fire Comey.

The administration soon claimed that Trump had acted "based on the clear recommendations" of both Attorney General Jeff Sessions and Deputy Attorney General Rod Rosenstein, the two most senior officials at the Department of Justice. The White House released letters from both officials, each dated May 9, that same day. Sessions's letter was a single paragraph that stated, in part, "A fresh start is needed at the leadership of the FBI." Rosenstein's letter ran several pages and was titled "Restoring Public Confidence in the FBI." It was much more detailed, and it mostly focused on Comey's announcement about the Hillary Clinton investigation.

Aaron knew both Rosenstein and Comey. Why would Rosenstein urge

Trump to fire Comey? And why would Trump fire Comey for his Clinton press conference, which had taken place nearly a year earlier and had been a blow to Trump's political opponent?

Wednesday, May 10, 2017

The next morning, Bob and Aaron took an early flight to San Francisco on other firm business. They were overseeing the resolution of the Volkswagen "Clean Diesel" case, which involved the rigging of diesel-powered vehicles to defeat government emissions tests. Bob had been appointed as the settlement master and, after eleven months, had brokered a $14.7 billion deal that had to be finalized in California. Traveling with them was Jim Quarles, who had been friends with Bob since 1993. Jim had spent most of his career as a trial lawyer at the same firm, most recently on technology patent cases. But he had not always been in the private sector. He'd started his legal career as one of the youngest assistant special prosecutors in the Watergate investigation, headed by Special Prosecutor Archibald Cox, whom Jim had studied under at Harvard Law.

After the plane landed, Jim turned on his phone and quickly found the latest news from the White House. He leaned closer to Aaron and said, "Whoever makes the president's schedule might want to rethink strategy." Jim pointed to a *Bloomberg* article titled "Russia's Lavrov Visits White House after Trump Fires Comey." "Lavrov" referred to the Russian foreign minister, Sergey Lavrov, who had been Putin's top diplomat since 2004.

It was jarring. President Trump had taken his first-ever meeting with a senior Russian official in the Oval Office less than twenty-four hours after firing the man whose agency was investigating whether the Russian government had helped bring Trump to power. Also present at the meeting: Russian ambassador Sergey Kislyak, whose interactions with Trump's former national security adviser, Michael Flynn, had led Flynn to resign less than a month after Trump's inauguration. Kislyak's communications with Flynn were known to be part of the FBI's investigation, so it was especially strange to see the Russian embassy post a photo on Twitter of a beaming Trump shaking hands with Kislyak in the Oval Office. The *New York Times* reported that US media outlets were kept out of the meeting; only the Russian state-run news agency TASS had been allowed inside.

Bob, Aaron, and Jim quickly disembarked, and as Bob stepped into the terminal at San Francisco International, he found an empty gate with few passengers for a private call.

The call was with Deputy Attorney General Rosenstein, a man Bob had known for years, but only at arm's length. Rosenstein was a career prosecutor, a Republican who had served under presidents on both sides of the aisle. George W. Bush had nominated him to be US attorney for the District of Maryland in 2005, and he had been one of the few US attorneys retained by President Obama in 2009. Tall, with rimless glasses, Rosenstein had been sworn in as the deputy attorney general (DAG) only two weeks earlier, on April 26, 2017. His superior, Attorney General Jeff Sessions, had been the junior senator from Alabama during the presidential campaign; Sessions had been the first senator to endorse Trump. Because of Sessions's role in the 2016 campaign, he had recused himself from any involvement in the investigation into Russia's efforts to influence the election. His recusal meant that in these matters Rosenstein was the acting attorney general and in charge.

The call between Bob and Rosenstein was quick. Rosenstein said he had tried to reach Bob that morning and asked if they could meet once Bob was back in DC. "I'm on the one forty-five flight back tomorrow," Bob said. "Can I come by Friday morning?"

Rosenstein said yes, thanked him, and hung up.

When Bob met up with Aaron and Jim near the taxi stand (Bob never checked luggage), he revealed that he had spoken with Rosenstein. Without missing a beat, Jim said, "They're screwed. He's going to ask you to come back as director."

"No way," Bob said.

"No way they'll ask, or no way you'll say yes?" Jim asked.

"No way," Bob repeated without elucidating.

"Can't happen anyway," Aaron pointed out. "He's term limited."

"You think Congress wouldn't change the law to let Bob Mueller come back?" Jim asked.

Bob knew the job of director better than anyone alive, but he had already served as the longest-tenured director since J. Edgar Hoover. A return to the bureau seemed out of the question.

That afternoon, Bob, Aaron, and Jim met with the judge in charge of the Volkswagen settlement. When they were finished, they decamped to a restaurant near their hotel in Nob Hill. At one point during dinner, Bob said, "If the department does ask me to come back in some capacity, I would want both of you to come with me."

"Whatever post they might ask you to fill—and I really do think it's going to be director—it'll be frickin' intense," Jim said. "But hell, I'm in."

Aaron paused, then said, "I would do it."

"But I will have to clear it with my wife," Jim said.

"I will likely need to do the same," Bob said.

Thursday, May 11, 2017

Bob, Aaron, and Jim spent the morning at the courthouse finalizing the Volkswagen settlement and then flew back to DC. That evening, Jim sat in his living room and watched NBC's Lester Holt conduct a wide-ranging interview with President Trump. Among many topics, Trump tried to explain why he had fired Comey, and brought up Russia: "Regardless of [the] recommendation [from Sessions and Rosenstein], I was going to fire Comey. Knowing there was no good time to do it! And in fact when I decided to just do it I said to myself, I said, 'You know, this Russia thing with Trump and Russia is a made-up story.'"

When Holt pressed him, Trump responded, "Look, let me tell you, as far as I'm concerned I want [the Russia investigation] to be absolutely done properly. When I did this now I said, 'I probably, maybe, will confuse people, maybe I'll expand that, you know, I'll lengthen the time [of the investigation]'—because it should be over with, it should—In my opinion it should've been over with a long time ago, because all it—all it is, is an excuse. But I said to myself, 'I might even lengthen out the investigation.'"

Jim found his comments perplexing. Was Trump admitting that the investigation into Russia's election interference was the real reason he had fired Comey, and not the letters from Sessions and Rosenstein? Or did his assertion that the firing might lengthen the investigation mean he fired Comey *despite* the FBI's Russia investigation and not *because* of it?

Friday, May 12, 2017

On Friday morning, Bob drove to Main Justice, just across Pennsylvania Avenue from FBI headquarters, for his meeting with Rosenstein. Officially known as the Robert F. Kennedy Department of Justice Building, Main Justice is a sprawling neoclassical trapezoid whose facade consists mainly of Indiana limestone. Bob parked his blue Subaru Forester and made his way to Rosenstein's office. He knew the building well, if not as well as FBI HQ. Bob was greeted by Rosenstein's executive assistant, who immediately ushered him through the outer office to the DAG's conference room.

Rosenstein was alone. He said he wanted to know if Bob would accept an appointment as special counsel to take over the Russia investigation. But he also said there was some possibility that Bob might be asked instead to return as FBI director, and that Bob should be prepared for that contingency. Most urgently, Rosenstein wanted to know whether there were any professional reasons that might prevent Bob from coming back to the DOJ more or less right away.

Bob said, "I'll need to check. Our firm might have some clients involved in the matter, but I have nothing to do with them."

Rosenstein said he understood. The meeting ended not long afterward.

As Bob returned to his car, he was struck by Rosenstein's demeanor. Rosenstein was a respected prosecutor who had spent nearly his entire career at the DOJ. But he seemed rattled. He was under pressure from all sides—the White House, Congress, the FBI, and the public—and Bob could tell it was taking a toll. Without saying as much, Rosenstein indicated that Bob's presence—either as a special counsel or as director—would convey calm and assure Congress and the country that the Russia investigation would continue.

Bob went straight from Main Justice to his firm's office, only a few blocks west of the White House. Once there, he met with the firm's general counsel to review any potential conflicts. The main concern was whether Bob—as well as Aaron and Jim—would be ethically allowed to work on the investigation.

The general counsel told Bob he would take the weekend to go over everything, but that on the face of it he saw no conflicts, because Bob, Jim, and Aaron had no personal involvement in representing these clients. He would give Bob a full report first thing Monday morning.

Bob then met with Aaron and Jim, describing his meeting with Rosenstein. Aaron was beginning to think through what it would mean to take on such a sensitive investigation. He had been one of two lead FBI case agents for 9/11, which involved nearly 170,000 interviews in dozens of countries. There was no doubt this case would also be complicated, but he didn't find its prospect daunting.

Jim's mind went to his Watergate days. He had lived through the Saturday

Night Massacre in 1973, when Nixon ordered Attorney General Elliot Richardson, and then–deputy attorney general William Ruckelshaus, to fire Special Prosecutor Cox. Richardson and Ruckelshaus refused and resigned immediately. The next-highest-ranking DOJ official—Solicitor General Robert Bork—agreed to fire Cox. (It was later revealed that Bork meant to resign as soon as he'd fired Cox, but that Richardson and Ruckelshaus convinced him to stay for the sake of the department.) Given this history of obstructive acts by a sitting president, Jim was particularly interested in Comey's firing and the reasons behind it.

Comey's dismissal was the action that had precipitated this whole series of events. If Trump had fired Comey with the intent of improperly stopping or trying to curb the FBI's Russia investigation, then it had resounding echoes with Watergate. The primary turn in that case had occurred when the "smoking gun" tape emerged, revealing that President Nixon had tried to use the CIA to shut down the FBI's investigation into the Watergate break-in.

Jim stepped out to speak with his wife. This was all getting more real.

When he returned, Aaron asked, "What'd she say?"

"She didn't say no," Jim responded.

"That's good," Bob said.

"But she didn't say yes, either," Jim deadpanned. "I was supposed to retire this December." He took a deep breath. "Heading home early to talk it out. I'll let you know what the verdict is over the weekend."

Saturday, May 13, and Sunday, May 14, 2017

In the end, the verdict from Mrs. Quarles was "OK."

Throughout that weekend, Bob, Aaron, and Jim spoke often. It looked increasingly possible that the DOJ would push to get Bob back at the FBI in the director's seat, even if it were in an acting capacity.

On Saturday, Rosenstein called Bob. He had Attorney General Sessions on the line. They asked whether Bob would consider coming back to serve as FBI director. Sessions said they could get sixty votes in the Senate to change the law and make it possible. Bob was polite and gave some thoughts about the future of the FBI but said he didn't want to be interviewed for director.

On Sunday, which was Mother's Day, Aaron stepped away from his wife and daughters to speak with Bob. He had been mulling over the issue of Bob's returning to the FBI and had arrived at one question: What would it mean to serve as director under President Trump?

As soon as Bob came on the line, he asked Aaron, "Should I consider this?"

After a pause, Aaron said, "If that is the ask, could you serve in that role, under this president?"

Ideally, a president serves as a steward of the office. The same goes for FBI director. In both cases, the office is what's important, not necessarily the person in it. In nearly any other circumstance, if a president had asked Bob to serve, he would accept without hesitation. But this time?

The circumstances here were more complicated. If Bob were asked to be director again and he accepted, then he would ultimately be in charge of the Russia investigation. He would draw on his decades of experience in law enforcement, he would trust the agents and prosecutors involved, and he would make sure the investigation ran without interference. But the role of director requires interaction with the president, a person who was within the scope of the Russia investigation. Bob was wary of this arrangement.

Serving as special counsel, on the other hand, would separate Bob from both the president and the FBI. In this position, Bob would be the one taking incoming fire, not the bureau. And in the event that Bob were fired, the bureau would not be taking another direct hit.

"No," Bob finally said. "I don't think I could return as director."

Aaron agreed.

Monday, May 15, 2017

By Monday morning, Bob knew he would decline a request to return as director, but he would agree to serve as special counsel if asked. He went to the firm and met with the general counsel. "I see no ethical reason why the three of you can't move into government," he said. "If that's what comes to pass."

There was some vanishingly small part of Bob that had hoped this wouldn't be the case, but there he was. "Thanks," Bob said.

Bob heard nothing from Rosenstein that day.

Tuesday, May 16, 2017

Bob was due to fly to Boston on Tuesday to meet with the most recent honorees of the Princeton Prize in Race Relations, a group of distinguished high school students from all around the country working to advance racial equity in their communities. But just as Bob was about to leave for the airport, he had to postpone his flight.

The president wanted to see him in the Oval Office.

Bob phoned the folks in Boston and told them he would have to meet with the students remotely. "Things are too busy here," Bob said. "Please tell everyone I'm sorry I can't be there in person."

That afternoon, Bob went to the White House, as he had so many times before as FBI director. Back then, he would pass through the far west entrance that led almost immediately to the Situation Room. This time he was asked to enter via a warren of passages beneath the Eisenhower Executive Office Building, just west of the White House. It was an odd approach, especially for someone who had been summoned by the president, but the White House did not want the press to see him enter.

The meeting was short. Vice President Mike Pence, Sessions,

Rosenstein, and several White House staffers were present. President Trump did most of the talking. Bob was asked what it would take to do the job as FBI director. He spoke about the role, the importance of the institution, and his respect for the men and women of the bureau. When some of the staff said they were willing to push Congress to pass a new law to make his reappointment possible, Bob told the president he was not the best person for the post.

The president would later claim that Bob had come to the meeting asking to be FBI director, and that the president had turned him down. This was false. Bob did not come to the White House looking to be director. The president never turned him down. Instead, Bob made it clear he didn't want the job.

The unspoken result of the White House meeting for Rosenstein: he was now ready to appoint Bob as special counsel.

Soon after Bob got back from the White House, the *New York Times* reported that in February 2017, less than a month into his administration, President Trump had asked Comey to shut down the FBI's investigation into Michael Flynn, the former national security adviser. In late December 2016, Flynn had spoken with Russian ambassador Sergey Kislyak about US sanctions imposed by President Obama against Russia for interfering in the election. The *Times* also said Comey had documented the entire encounter in a memo he wrote shortly after the meeting and had created similar memos about other calls and meetings he'd had with the president. "I hope you can see your way clear to letting this go, to letting Flynn go," Trump told Comey, according to Comey's memo. "He is a good guy. I hope you can let this go."

Within hours of the *Times* report, Congressman Jason Chaffetz—the Republican chairman of the House Oversight Committee—wrote a letter to the FBI demanding copies of all of Comey's memos documenting his interactions with the president, commenting that the memos raised questions as to whether Trump had tried to obstruct justice.

Wednesday, May 17, 2017

The next morning, Aaron received a draft of the appointment order from Rosenstein. Bob would be named special counsel that day. There was some back-and-forth between Aaron and Scott Schools, Rosenstein's most senior career deputy. Schools had earned his position through a sharp intellect and long experience in the department; his involvement in this matter was reassuring to both Bob and Aaron.

The order was short—just one page. The special counsel would indeed take over the investigation into Russian interference in the 2016 election. As a special counsel, Bob would be overseen by the attorney general. Since Sessions had recused himself, this meant that for Bob, Rosenstein would be the acting attorney general. Rosenstein would be both accountable for the investigation and the buffer between the special counsel's office and the president. At one point that day, Jim said, "I do not envy that guy."

Once Bob decided to accept the post of special counsel, there was never any question that Aaron and Jim would accompany him. It was settled. All that remained was to sever ties with the firm that had become home—for Bob and Aaron, for the previous three years; for Jim, for more than forty-two years. There were clients to inform, handoffs to be made, and goodbyes to colleagues who had become close friends.

By five o'clock, the resignations were complete.

We would now be known as the SCO—the special counsel's office.

Two

CROSSFIRE HURRICANE

No one likes to be investigated. Presidents in particular do not like to be investigated. Nixon didn't like it, Clinton didn't like it, and Trump wouldn't like it either.

The order appointing Bob authorized him to investigate any links or coordination between the Russian government and people associated with the Trump campaign; any other matter that arose or may arise from that investigation; as well as any general matters detailed in the special counsel regulations—such as possible obstruction of justice, witness tampering, or destruction of evidence, among others. If we found evidence of criminal wrongdoing and we determined it necessary and appropriate, we could bring indictments. (Whether we could indict the president, if it came to that, was another matter.) Even if we brought no indictments, the regulations governing a special counsel required that we write a confidential report to the attorney general explaining our decisions at the conclusion of our investigation.

The first thing we needed to do was get up to speed on the FBI's ten-month-old investigation. The intelligence community, including the FBI, had concluded that the Russian government had interfered in the 2016 election—but the details and the proof had not been fully developed or publicly disclosed. We also knew the FBI had been focused on the numerous touchpoints between Russia and members of the Trump campaign while Russia was running its interference operations.

The other thing we needed to do was set up an office. Ours would require a SCIF—a sensitive compartmented information facility—so we could safely store and review classified materials, as well as sufficient space for our team, which in a matter of weeks would comprise nineteen lawyers, forty FBI agents, and various professional staff.

But first, the FBI. What had it already done? What did it already know?

We traveled to FBI headquarters on the morning of May 18 to meet with Acting Director Andy McCabe, a career FBI agent who was liked and respected throughout the bureau. Bob knew him well, and so did Aaron. Both were confident McCabe would be helpful, buttoned up, and aboveboard.

We arrived at the FBI's J. Edgar Hoover Building—a Brutalist structure widely regarded as one of Washington's ugliest. We were headed to the seventh floor, where the FBI's senior leadership worked. Their offices were arranged along a hallway called the Zero Corridor. As we moved through the building it was plain to Jim, who had never walked these halls with Bob, that Bob was returning home. Everywhere he went, he was met with a congenial, "Hello, Director," or "Hi, Director," or simply "Director!" At the firm, Jim was accustomed to hearing "Hi, Bob"—that was never the case at the FBI, not before, and not now. Bob quietly returned every greeting, but just as when he was director, he kept moving. He was all business.

This reception underscored how unusual this was—because of course Bob was *not* director. McCabe was. Comey's firing nine days earlier had clearly affected morale. And now here was Bob, the much-respected former director who had led the organization through the post-9/11 years, returning to his home turf, but now as special counsel. His presence appeared to provide some measure of comfort to the agents and professional staff who saw him walking by.

After ten minutes of navigating the building, we entered the Zero Corridor. Bob and Aaron exchanged a few more hellos before we all finally entered the director's suite of offices.

First came the director's waiting room, followed by the edge of the inner sanctum, where two executive assistants were stationed. After this was the director's massive conference room, which was a SCIF, followed by the director's personal office. Normally, only the director and his closest colleagues ever went into this last office.

We paused for a minute in the executive assistants' room to sign interim security clearance documents and then walked into the conference room.

We were greeted by McCabe and members of his team: Bill Priestap, head of the FBI's Counterintelligence Division, and Carl Ghattas, head of the National Security Branch; as well as a few additional bureau employees.

The director typically takes the head of the table for meetings, but out of deference to Bob, McCabe left that seat open and took a chair along the far side of the conference table. Bob sat opposite McCabe.

Priestap began the briefing. A former football coach with a brown crew cut, Priestap was known by Bob and Aaron to be a highly capable agent. Jim would later come to recognize that Priestap was a careful thinker who could see around corners. The FBI's investigation was code-named Crossfire Hurricane. (Case names are usually generated randomly by a computer. Sometimes these are awful, but on rare occasions humans get involved; this one, taken from a Rolling Stones lyric, had been picked by an FBI agent.) From the outset, we realized this was a sprawling counterintelligence operation. There were Russians and Americans, Ukrainians and Brits, and dozens of contacts between Russians or their associates and people involved with the Trump campaign. This sounded like a lot of contacts, but we could not tell how meaningful they were. Up until then, the investigation had a distinct counterintelligence bent and had not been pursued in the manner of a criminal investigation.

Counterintelligence operations are concerned mainly with gathering information in order to understand possible threats to the United States. Sources for intelligence can be humans, bank records, travel records, text messages, emails, photos, videos, receipts, location data, browsing data, call logs, and more. If material touches on the investigation, then it may well be worth noting and could be added to the file. Generally, agents and officers who gather this data—this is especially true at places like the CIA—do not appear in court or sit before a judge. Their task is not to build a case that can go to trial but to paint a picture, which can then be used to aid in making decisions to safeguard the national security of the United States.

At bottom, counterintelligence investigations produce data, and lots of it—some of it from exceedingly sensitive and obscure sources.

Criminal investigations also can produce reams of data, and they too have to paint a picture. But the ultimate audience for this picture is not an agency deputy or head or the president, but rather a judge or a jury. Criminal cases require evidence that can be presented in court and tested. Agents and prosecutors always have the courtroom in mind, as well as the statutes of the US criminal code, which by necessity must be used to charge and try defendants.

None of this is to say that there is always a bright line between counterintelligence and criminal investigations—an investigation is an investigation. Criminal cases can produce information that is highly relevant to intelligence judgments and recommendations. One of the most powerful tools for generating intelligence is plea bargaining in criminal cases. Prosecutors and agents often use this to incentivize cooperation that can produce significant, timely, and accurate information. At the same time, counterintelligence investigations can produce information that can potentially be proved in court during a prosecution.

Bob was the expert in this area. He had led the transformation of the bureau into a national security organization in the wake of 9/11. The attacks precipitated a shift in how the FBI used its investigative and intelligence resources—whether for counterintelligence or criminal matters—to understand threats before they resulted in any subsequent attacks. Bob described this as the FBI shifting to be an "intelligence-led, threat-focused organization." Bob often attributed this realignment to a simple question from President Bush during a briefing on September 12, 2001: "What are you doing to prevent the next terrorist attack?" From that moment forward, the FBI would still develop cases, charge wrongdoers, and take cases to trial—President Bush fully expected the bureau to continue its core criminal work—but it would also do everything in its lawful power to *prevent* terrorist attacks against American interests.

At that day's meeting, McCabe and his team told us about the main aspects of Crossfire Hurricane, which had mostly resulted in the gathering of information without a focus on building a criminal case. At one point, one of the FBI officials mentioned that the bureau had accumulated tens of thousands of pages of material. Priestap added that, following the meeting, we would head down to the Strategic Information Operations Center (SIOC) to have a look. "It's a lot," the official said, as if to prepare us.

The briefing made clear that Russia had interfered in the 2016 election. Russian operatives had hacked into Democratic campaign computers, stolen private emails and other electronic data, and then released the stolen information throughout the campaign. At the same time, Russian entities had engaged in a social media campaign aimed at influencing American voters. The briefing also covered dozens of contacts between members of the Trump campaign and Russians or Russian intermediaries. But there was little talk of potentially prosecutable crimes.

Right before the meeting wrapped, a knock came at the conference room door. Bob and McCabe both turned to the noise with perplexed expressions. People hardly ever knocked on this door when a meeting was in progress, and certainly not when a meeting like *this* was in progress. McCabe called the person in. A young-looking agent entered holding a folder. He crossed the room, handed it to McCabe, and told him it was urgent he review it. McCabe opened the folder and drew out a letter, placing it in front of him.

After taking a few moments to read it, he jabbed it with an index finger and slid it across the table to Bob.

Bob spun the letter around, scanned it, and said, "Makes sense." He then handed it to Aaron. "What do you think?"

Aaron read the letter carefully. It was a preservation order on FBI letter-head, and it was addressed to the White House. It said, in essence, that no one there was to destroy or move documents or material from the White House complex that related in any way to Comey's termination, and that everything must be preserved in case any of it was needed in the FBI's—now the special counsel's—investigation. Sending the letter meant the FBI believed there was evidence on the White House premises, and that it must not be tampered with in any way.

The letter was extraordinary. Not because it was an order to preserve documents—these are as common as any other procedural item in an investigation—but because it was directed to the White House.

Aaron joked that he knew only enough about the case to say that the letter was punctuated correctly, but then read it one more time and said, "I think we send it."

"Send it," Bob said, passing it back to the agent. The agent placed the letter back into the folder and disappeared as quickly as he'd arrived.

(We later learned that when White House Counsel Don McGahn received the letter, he ordered that day's "burn bags" brought back to the White House. Burning bags of documents is a normal housecleaning task every administration does regularly, but that would no longer be the case in the Trump White House. As all good lawyers know, the only thing worse than destroying potential evidence is doing so *after* having received a preservation order from the FBI.)

The briefing ended shortly after that. Priestap took us down to SIOC, a massive windowless command center in the very heart of the Hoover building. We were led to SIOC's largest workspace, and here we finally confronted the sheer volume of the FBI's material. Tens of thousands of pages may have been an undercount. It would take weeks to process all of it and find whatever might be in it that warranted a closer look. Notably, a substantial volume of material in the room was marked "Top Secret," designated with an orange blaze on the cover sheet.

The next day, Friday, May 19, we had a meeting at Main Justice with Dana Boente, the US attorney for the Eastern District of Virginia (EDVA), and Brandon Van Grack, the lone prosecutor assigned to the FBI's Russia investigation. Boente, a blond-haired Eagle Scout from Illinois, had briefly served as acting attorney general earlier in the Trump presidency and was now serving as the acting head of the DOJ's National Security Division, along with being a US attorney. Van Grack was a bright and committed prosecutor who had served for years in the National Security Division.

We met both men in the Justice Command Center (JCC)—Justice's counterpart to the FBI's SIOC—a large, wood-paneled space reminiscent of an out-of-date college reading room. Like SIOC, JCC was a giant SCIF, and was also located at the heart of the building. The central room was surrounded by smaller offices replete with monitors, computers, and people working at them 24-7.

Boente and Van Grack told us about their investigation into Michael Flynn, Trump's first national security adviser, for his possible role in FARA violations. FARA—the Foreign Agents Registration Act—was a World War II–era criminal statute originally passed to identify Nazi propagandists working in the United States. In essence, FARA required anyone lobbying or performing certain other activities in the United States on behalf of a foreign principal to register with the Department of Justice. At the time, Flynn was being investigated for lobbying on behalf of Turkey without having registered. The investigation was still in its early stages, and no subpoenas had been issued.

Boente and Van Grack also told us about Flynn's interactions with the Russian ambassador, Sergey Kislyak, in the days after the Obama administration imposed sanctions on Russia for interfering in the 2016 election.

The media had reported on that episode in the early part of the Trump administration, revealing that Flynn had discussed sanctions with Kislyak. Flynn, however, falsely denied that he had spoken about sanctions with the Russian ambassador, telling Vice President Pence, other administration officials, and the FBI that sanctions had not been discussed. On February 13, 2017, President Trump asked Flynn to resign. The next day, the president had a one-on-one conversation with Comey in which he said, "I hope you can see your way clear to letting this go, to letting Flynn go." This was one of several potentially obstructive acts we would end up investigating.

During our visit, Jim, ever the trial lawyer looking to piece together the story behind it all, asked Boente and Van Grack, "Have you asked anyone who Flynn spoke with just before he talked to Kislyak?"

Van Grack's answer was telling: "You know, no one has ever asked me that question." By his tone, he wasn't so much saying that this had been an oversight, but that he had been laboring alone and welcomed the help along with any fresh insight into the issues.

It was clearly time for a new approach. Subpoenas would need to be issued, some sooner than others. We would need to ask who Flynn had spoken with and when, particularly surrounding his interactions with the Russians.

The next stop after the Command Center was to get fingerprinted in another section of Main Justice. Despite their prior government service, Bob and Aaron had to be fingerprinted along with Jim. This was standard procedure for securing clearances and becoming properly credentialed. It was, however, an unusual scene. Bob was still thought of as the boss. (Months earlier, when he was traveling through Grand Central Terminal, a similar scene had occurred when three unsuspecting New York City police officers chose Bob at a random checkpoint and patted him down. Bob played it straight and readily complied. Aaron pulled one of the officers aside to joke that his partners were patting down the former director of the FBI. The officers would have a tale to tell.)

Jim tried joking with the fingerprint technician. "This to identify the body?" he asked.

The technician didn't laugh. "No, sir. Just need your prints to differentiate them from others. We also run them against the database."

"Got it," Jim said. He didn't try any more humor.

The next day was a Saturday. Bob, Jim, and Aaron met at their firm mainly to discuss logistics—where the SCO would be located, who would procure the furniture, where the SCO's IT team would come from, when the office would receive computers, what the budget would be for the remainder of the year, and what it would be for the following year, if it came to that.

Bob also talked more about the need to stay focused on our mission. Under no circumstances were we to replicate Ken Starr's sprawling independent counsel investigation into President Clinton, which started with the "Whitewater" real-estate project in Arkansas and ended up examining Clinton's relationship with White House intern Monica Lewinsky. That had gone on for years, and at times appeared to be a boundless investigation.

When prosecutors start at the Justice Department, they often are given the text of a speech delivered in 1940 by then–attorney general Robert H. Jackson, seen as a kind of bible for prosecutors. "[T]he most dangerous power of the prosecutor," wrote Jackson, "[is] that he will pick people that he thinks he should get, rather than pick cases that need to be prosecuted." Bob was clear: he wanted nothing to do with an investigation that was cut loose from its mooring of Russian election interference and possible links to or coordination with the Trump campaign—this was never going to be about getting any one person.

Bob was unlike Starr in another respect: "We will not be holding press conferences." Our investigation would be about the facts we uncovered and our assessment of the law, not the individual responsible for looking into them. This was not going to be about Bob. For our part, this would not devolve into some sort of contest that appeared to pit Bob or the SCO against President Trump or anyone else we might investigate.

After speaking some more about logistics, Bob went to his office down the hall. Aaron and Jim reflected on all that had happened in the last few days. It had been a whirlwind. Yet Aaron was matter-of-fact about what might be in our future. He could see a path for the investigation and he believed that Bob's ability and reputation would help us weather any storm.

For Jim, the future was less clear. It wasn't only that we'd been torn from our busy but comfortable lives in private practice, but that all of this was happening in the first place. Did Comey's firing really have to do with the Russia investigation? Had Trump pressured people to get the FBI to drop the case, as Nixon had tried to do during Watergate?

While going over Monday's agenda, Aaron's desk phone rang. He answered. "Hello?"

"Is this Aaron Zebley?" The man was clearly outdoors, calling from his cell phone.

"It is."

"I'm an FBI special agent assigned to the investigation. I've been told that if I want to do anything, I have to call you."

"OK. What do you have in mind?" Aaron asked.

"I have a subpoena I'd like to serve today."

"Who's it for?"

"It's for the White House, sir."

"The White House?" Aaron wasn't sure he'd heard correctly.

"Yes, sir."

"What's it for?"

"Documents, sir. I'm just a few blocks away. Can I serve it?"

Aaron politely asked the agent to explain his thinking about the timing and whether this was the moment to serve a subpoena on the White House, which would require, under penalty of law, that the White House provide documents for use in a grand jury investigation. In this regard, it was a substantial escalation from the preservation order that had already been delivered, and could have sent the parties to their respective corners for a protracted fight about executive privilege. It was immediately obvious to Aaron that this was not going to be Bob's opening investigative action. Subpoenas are effective and necessary investigative tools, but there can be other (often faster) ways to get documents that don't invoke the power of a court—and the lengthy fight that would likely go along with it. At this early juncture, a subpoena to the White House was premature. (And sure enough, we would soon secure voluntary production of documents from the White House without prompting a fight about executive privilege.)

As Aaron went back and forth with the agent, Jim grew concerned. Jim couldn't hear what the agent was saying, nor did he know what Aaron was thinking. He didn't understand why Aaron was drawing this out. The answer clearly had to be no.

Jim scrawled a note on a legal pad and passed it to Aaron. It read, *Bob would die if we did this without talking it through.*

That note hangs in Aaron's office to this day.

Aaron smiled at Jim, put the agent on mute, and said, "We are definitely not doing this today." Aaron then unmuted and gave the agent the news.

"Very well, sir," the agent said. "It's your call. Thanks for your time." The conversation ended.

Aaron stood from his desk. "Let's go talk to Bob."

Aaron was unfazed, but Jim paused to contemplate this short but stunning phone call. *The FBI wants to subpoena the White House? We are in a whole new world.*

Three

EARLY DECISIONS

On Monday, May 22, we moved into the Patrick Henry Building at 601 D Street NW. A low, rectangular building like many others found throughout Washington, the Patrick Henry building was unremarkable in pretty much every way, with the exception that it was only a few blocks from both FBI headquarters and Main Justice, two places where we would be spending a lot of time.

That day was primarily dedicated to getting oriented in the office and organizing the investigation. Almost from the moment we stepped inside, we knew Patrick Henry would not work for the long term. It had a dearth of actual offices, a tiny conference room, and a SCIF in the basement that was far too small. Not to mention it had zero windows and no soul—but this was common for most government buildings.

That evening, we came together for our first end-of-day meeting. A typical evening meeting would cover the daily media roundup, updates from Capitol Hill, and mapping out what we could expect in the morning—which was often upended by unpredictable after-hours occurrences.

We were joined that Monday by Beth McGarry, Bob's former executive first assistant US attorney in the Northern District of California. Bob had done quick work to secure McGarry. She stood about five feet tall, had graying blond hair, and never hesitated to say things like "We need to hurry the eff up." McGarry would serve as the SCO's executive officer.

The subject that evening was what we wanted to achieve for the coming week. First and foremost: Who would we look to bring on board? The SCO was not a week old, and we had already been presented with an onslaught of résumés—hundreds would eventually come our way. McGarry was the first to read them and sort them into categories of "looks good," "possible," and "no way," and then pass them to us. The résumés arrived from US attorney's offices and white-shoe law firms and prestigious law schools from all across the country. That week, Jim fielded separate calls from Harvard Law professors telling him they knew the best young person for the job. A bit later, a Supreme Court justice called to recommend a clerk. It seemed as if half of the assistant US attorneys at the Southern District of New York (SDNY) wanted to relocate to DC, as well as a fair number of prosecutors at the Eastern District of New York (EDNY). This wasn't a surprise. Ambitious prosecutors want big, complicated cases, and our assignment had the potential to be one of the biggest and most complex.

Bob had already recruited Jeannie Rhee, another attorney from Bob's firm and a former prosecutor. She had worked on a major investigation at the firm with Bob, Jim, and Aaron; she was smart, quick, and dedicated, with a phenomenally loud and infectious laugh. She would arrive within the first few weeks.

Aaron also spoke to the Department of Justice about getting a press officer. But unlike a typical press officer, this person's principal job would not be to convey information. As a prosecutor, Bob staunchly believed in not talking to the press, but he knew it was critical to understand and get information from the press. Reporters and their lines of questioning often channel what is happening in the outside world. While Bob did not think a prosecutor should spend energy reacting to outside events, he believed he could make better decisions by knowing as much as he could about what was going on beyond our four walls.

The DOJ offered us Peter Carr, who had worked with Aaron in the US attorney's office for the Eastern District of Virginia. As soon he heard Carr's name, Aaron said, "Send him." Aaron was confident Carr would represent the SCO the way Bob wanted. (This would turn out to be 100 percent the case. For nearly all of his many, many press interactions, practically his only words were, "No comment." And yet he brought back a lot of valuable information and context.)

We finished for the evening and went home. That night, a story broke in the *Washington Post* with the headline "Trump Asked Intelligence Chiefs to Push Back against FBI Collusion Probe after Comey Revealed Its Existence." The article claimed that Trump had meetings in March with both the director of national intelligence (DNI), Dan Coats, and the National Security Agency's director, Mike Rogers, and had asked each of them to "push back against" the FBI's investigation into Russia and the Trump campaign. Depending on what was said at these meetings, this could have been an attempt to obstruct justice by using the intelligence chiefs to intervene with the FBI. To Jim especially, these allegations had a Nixonian hue—trying to use the intelligence community to get the FBI to back off its investigation.

The next morning, Tuesday, May 23, Bob arrived at the office at 7:30 on the nose, which he would continue to do for the next two years. Aaron and Jim were on his heels, arriving shortly before 8:00, along with McGarry. All assembled at 8:30 in Bob's office, as we would throughout the entire investigation. The morning meeting was for operations—to discuss that day's calendar, strategy, and any legal issues. It typically started with a larger group and ended small, as Bob excused people from the meeting after receiving their input, often ending up with only three people—Bob, Aaron, and Jim—for the most sensitive strategic decisions.

The main topic of discussion that morning was the *Post* report. The takeaway: it was important that we talk to both DNI Coats and Admiral Rogers soon, and ideally before anyone else. The reason prosecutors want to interview witnesses early is simple: you want to get a witness's recollection of events before it might be affected by time, news, other inquiries, or—and this is crucial—other witness statements. Hearing what a witness has to say can lead another witness to change their story when it comes time for them to make a statement. This is often not done out of any ill will, and can be unintended. Memory can be malleable. People may struggle to remember what they had for lunch last Wednesday. But if they hear a spouse or friend answer this question first, it may affect the way they answer.

Prosecutors also want to be the first to speak with a witness because they can ask questions in a setting and manner designed to elicit the truth (including a potential prosecution for false statements if a witness lies to federal investigators). If a witness starts telling their story to others in a different setting, there is a risk that a less-than-full account could become "locked in" and make it harder to get the complete truth later.

As we were figuring how to secure interviews with Coats and Rogers, we also had to organize the structure of the SCO. That evening, Aaron stood at the whiteboard in his office and sketched out our avenues of investigation. He and Jim pitched them to Bob the following morning, and Bob was immediately on board.

One box Aaron had drawn was labeled "Team R." This group would deal with any Russia-related threads involving the Trump campaign other than Paul Manafort and Michael Flynn, both of whom received their own dedicated teams. In time, Team R would concentrate on people like George Papadopoulos, a Trump foreign policy adviser; Michael Cohen, Trump's personal lawyer and fixer in New York; and Roger Stone, a colorful Trump campaign adviser who dressed like a Marvel supervillain. Team R would also eventually take on the "active measures" investigation, which would look into a Russian disinformation campaign that had been run out of Saint Petersburg, Russia, throughout the 2016 election; as well as the Russian government's "hack-and-dump" operation.

The second box on Aaron's whiteboard was labeled "Team F," which stood for Trump's former national security adviser Michael Flynn. We formed this team early because of the interactions Flynn had had with the Russian ambassador, Sergey Kislyak, as well as the evidence of potential FARA violations involving Flynn and Turkey.

A third box was labeled "Team M," which stood for Manafort, Trump's former campaign chairman. Manafort appeared to be the most senior Trump campaign official with numerous, direct, and enduring connections to various Russians—including a billionaire oligarch named Oleg Deripaska—and Russia-aligned Ukrainians. We formed this team because of Manafort's senior role on the campaign, his connections to Russia, and the fact that there already existed credible evidence of possible crimes.

A fourth box was designated "Team IV" but would eventually be renamed "Team 600." This referred to Part 600.4 (a) of Title 28 of the Code of Federal Regulations, which gives the special counsel "the authority to investigate and prosecute federal crimes committed in the course of, and with intent to interfere with, the Special Counsel's investigation, such as perjury, obstruction of justice, destruction of evidence, and intimidation of witnesses."

Team 600 would deal with any possible obstruction-of-justice matters that had already occurred or might yet occur. Its immediate focus was Comey's assertion that President Trump had asked him to "let go" of the FBI's investigation of Flynn; the firing of Comey; and, potentially, the president's meetings with Coats and Rogers. We knew Team 600 would deal with the most difficult constitutional issues. We were an executive branch office with broad, but not unlimited, prosecutorial powers. We had to report to the acting attorney general and follow the rules of the DOJ. What would we do if the evidence showed the president had obstructed justice?

This was the most sensitive line of investigation. We already had a couple of lawyers in mind to lead Team 600, but Jim Quarles was an obvious choice. He had Bob's complete trust, and he had lived through Watergate.

The whiteboard had one final box titled "Legal Team." It was not lost on any of us that we were about to swim into uncharted waters. The investigation was likely to raise novel legal issues that might go all the way to the Supreme Court. There was only one name here, followed by three question marks: "Dreeben???"

Michael Dreeben was the longtime deputy solicitor general at the DOJ in charge of US criminal appeals in the Supreme Court. He was a highly respected expert on US criminal law and one of only a handful of people to have argued more than one hundred cases in front of the Supreme Court. For Bob, there was no other person for this role. We knew Dreeben would be invaluable for parsing any legal challenges, and that he would be fair and by the book. But could we get him given all the other work he had at the DOJ? (The answer would ultimately be yes.)

Team R, Team F, Team M, and Team 600, plus a legal team to ensure our analysis was airtight. That was how we would work. A prosecutor would be in charge of each of the investigative teams, and each would be paired with a lead FBI agent. In all matters, Bob would have the final say.

In addition to the morning and evening leadership meetings, Bob convened daily meetings of team leaders. These were intended to create a common operating picture while keeping details of the individual investigations within their respective teams. Bob was sensitive to oversharing in order to help prevent leaks and to keep people focused on their assignment.

In that first weekend, Bob emphasized again that we would not be chasing leads unrelated to Russia or the campaign. It was critical we adhere to the scope of our appointment order. We might have to make some decisions down the line about expanding scope, but we would not cast around for unrelated cases—not at the outset, not ever.

Bob made another early decision intended to safeguard our work: we would keep the DOJ informed, at a high level, of our actions. This was not an obvious choice, but it was one designed to build trust and minimize the potential for interference by the department. Under the special counsel regulations, Rosenstein, as the acting attorney general, had oversight of our investigation, and Bob had to comply with all DOJ rules and policies. But we were not subject to the day-to-day supervision of Rosenstein or any other DOJ official. We were required to provide updates only on the most significant matters—indictments, arrests, or other major developments that were sure to receive national attention. Rosenstein in turn had the power to request that we "provide an explanation for any investigative or prosecutorial step," and could reject an action if he concluded it was "so inappropriate or unwarranted under established Departmental practices that it should not be pursued." If he did this, he would have to notify Congress at the conclusion of the investigation.

A special counsel could try to maximize independence from the DOJ by going it alone and sharing information only when absolutely necessary. But for Bob, there was value in going beyond the bare notification requirements. As he saw it, you can't build trust if you don't communicate. We knew we would run a buttoned-up, focused investigation. Making that clear to Rosenstein as we went about our work could be helpful in countering any argument by Congress or the White House that we were "off mission." And by giving Rosenstein a window (although a very high-level one) into our work, it would be less likely that he would see a need to exercise his authority to overrule us. The decision to share information was made easier with Rosenstein in charge. He had appointed Bob as special counsel. He had an interest in protecting the office he had created, and like Bob, he was an institutionalist who cared about the DOJ.

Of course, there was some tension between keeping the DOJ informed and also maintaining our independence from the executive branch. After all, we were investigating Rosenstein's ultimate boss—the president. To help each side maintain separation while still fostering trust, Bob assigned

Aaron to stay in touch with Scott Schools, the most senior career official at the DOJ. Aaron talked to Schools as needed—they had the equivalent of a military hotline. They often called each other to address immediate and pressing issues.

Bob also had Aaron and Jim meet once every two weeks with Schools to provide more formal updates on the investigation. These were carefully planned out. We would never share any information that would compromise the integrity of what we were doing. Aaron wrote a precise outline for every meeting—reviewed and approved by Bob—that Aaron and Jim would walk through in the meeting with Schools.

Bob made one other decision in those early days to help protect the integrity of our work. We would not chase any unfounded leads in the infamous Steele dossier, a collection of documents produced by a former British intelligence officer, Christopher Steele. The dossier alleged that for years Trump had been a target of "cultivation" efforts by Russian intelligence; that Trump had various undisclosed business dealings with Russia; that the Russians were behind the hack-and-dump operation that had stolen emails belonging to various members of the Democratic Party (this was accurate, but the FBI already possessed evidence of this that was completely independent of the dossier); that Russia favored Trump over Clinton in the election (factually true and also not in dispute, even in May 2017); and, most salaciously, that Trump had hired Russian sex workers to urinate on a bed at the Moscow Ritz-Carlton, which the Russians allegedly held as *kompromat* if they ever wished to blackmail Trump.

There were many reasons for not dedicating energy to the dossier. In addition to having questions about its origins, we saw that it was mostly comprised of third- and fourth-hand accounts, not actual evidence. We had plenty of better leads all over the world that we wanted to pursue, including for the Russian hack-and-dump investigation. At that point, the dossier's validity or invalidity was irrelevant to us. We had evidence from other sources that the Russians had interfered with the election, that they did so to favor Trump over Clinton, and that there were numerous contacts between certain Russians, Russian intermediaries, and the Trump campaign. The FBI would pursue efforts to validate or invalidate information in the dossier, but it would not be part of the SCO's criminal investigation. We would expend our energy elsewhere.

But first we needed people—and fast.

Four

THE NEED FOR SPEED

A thorough and careful investigation was essential, but Bob knew that every day the SCO remained open was a burden on the country. He was sensitive to what an investigation like ours might do to the office of the president, regardless of who occupied that office. Having been FBI director for twelve years, Bob understood that an ongoing investigation involving the president could distract the White House, distort decision-making, and have an impact on foreign policy and national security. This did not mean we would shy away from investigating the president or his associates for any potential wrongdoing—we would go wherever the evidence led us. But it explained Bob's need for speed. "No lollygagging," he reminded us more than once.

Early on, Bob privately told Aaron he hoped to have the SCO's work wrapped up by Thanksgiving—six short months away. Aaron knew this was unlikely, but he understood Bob's reasoning. (Aaron did not share this target, such as it was, with the office.)

One week after Bob's appointment, on Wednesday, May 24, two prosecutors from the Southern District of New York (SDNY) took an Amtrak train from New York to Washington to give a presentation on a case they were running involving Paul Manafort. Manafort had been Trump's campaign chairman and also had maintained numerous business and personal ties to various Russians and pro-Kremlin Ukrainians. Although this was a case update and not a job interview, one of these two men would end up joining the SCO: Andrew Goldstein.

Andrew, who headed the public corruption unit at the SDNY, was joined by Assistant US Attorney Paul Monteleoni. They presented evidence about a pay-to-play scheme carried out by Manafort and a banker named Stephen Calk, the founder and CEO of the Chicago-based Federal Savings Bank. Their arrangement was straightforward yet audacious. Calk had gotten his bank to grant Manafort two loans, one for $9.5 million and another for $6.5 million, that appeared to be in exchange for Manafort helping Calk secure a senior position in the Trump administration. Calk gave Manafort a list of his preferred posts, including treasury secretary, commerce secretary, and defense secretary. That each of these would require Senate approval did not seem to faze either Calk or Manafort. (Calk interviewed to be the undersecretary of the army in January 2017; he did not receive that or any other post in the eventual Trump administration.)

Andrew and Monteleoni highlighted some interesting details of this arrangement. For starters, Calk had pushed the loans through despite Manafort defaulting on some prior bank loans. Additionally, some of the properties against which the loans were issued were in foreclosure, and, once executed, the loans represented Federal Savings Bank's largest single lending relationship. A few days after Calk's bank approved the larger of the loans, Manafort appointed Calk to a prestigious economic advisory committee affiliated with Trump's campaign. (Four years later, on July 23, 2021, Calk would be convicted in the SDNY for financial institution bribery and sentenced to a year and a day in prison. His conviction was upheld on appeal on November 28, 2023.)

The SDNY investigation was impressive and, considering the team had been at it for only three months, notable for its speed. We thought the information about Manafort could be useful in our investigation because it had the potential to help us unravel Manafort's financial arrangements—and if the conduct was criminal, it might give him an incentive to cooperate with us.

When the meeting ended, Aaron and Andrew had coffee at the Au Bon Pain across the street from the Patrick Henry building. They had never met before that day, but they knew many people in common across the Department of Justice. It was casual, but when Aaron left he knew he was going to ask Bob what he thought about bringing Andrew on to the team.

Aaron suggested it to Bob that afternoon. Bob replied, "Let's check with SDNY." Bob knew the SDNY as an elite office with many of the most talented prosecutors in the country, and Andrew had led some of its most sophisticated cases as head of the public corruption unit. But Bob and Aaron didn't know Andrew, so the office did its due diligence: Andrew submitted his résumé and a list of cases he had worked on (he'd prosecuted Sheldon Silver, the Democratic Speaker of the New York State Assembly; and he'd supervised the prosecution of Dean Skelos, the Republican majority leader in New York's state senate, among other cases); we interviewed him twice; we spoke with several of his SDNY colleagues; and we talked to the judge who had overseen the Silver case. The positive reviews gave Bob confidence that not only could Andrew jump in immediately and help drive the investigation forward, but also that he had the judgment and temperament necessary for this assignment. Andrew was offered a position in late June and would join the office in July.

The day after Andrew and Monteleoni gave their presentation, another Andrew came to our office: Andrew Weissmann.

Bob and Aaron had both worked with Weissmann at the FBI when he served as the bureau's general counsel from 2011 to 2013. He was intelligent and aggressive—before serving at the FBI, he had long experience prosecuting mobsters in New York and had also been a lead prosecutor in the Enron case, which involved accounting fraud at Enron, a Texas-based energy company, in the early 2000s.

Weissmann, who had requested to meet with us, headed the fraud section of the Criminal Division at the DOJ, so it was only a short trip for him to the Patrick Henry building. He sat on the uncomfortable blue couch in Bob's office and passed along information he thought was important for Bob to know. He outlined evidence of Manafort's conduct in business dealings in Ukraine—conduct entirely separate from the SDNY investigation. Weissmann was not in charge of this case. It was being run out of a separate unit at Main Justice, and Weissmann indicated that he was concerned it had been languishing for months if not years. He wanted to help move it along and thought Bob should take it over—or at least be aware of it.

We were learning a lot about Manafort. We already knew that going back to 2006, Manafort and his associate Rick Gates had received tens of millions of dollars for consulting work from pro-Russian Ukrainian politicians and organizations. The consulting that Manafort and Gates performed also occasionally may have qualified as lobbying work, and neither had ever registered under the Foreign Agents Registration Act.

Weissmann's presentation of the facts he possessed and his vision for how to proceed were striking. As he wrapped up that day, Bob and Aaron shared a look: *Should we hire him?*

This was not an easy question. Yes, Bob and Aaron knew Weissmann. He was dogged, organized, driven, and could move cases quickly. But he had a reputation for being unduly harsh with some defendants. And the fact that he had pulled this Manafort information together on his own volition, almost as though it had been a hobby, perhaps should have caused us to consider whether he was too interested in the investigation. But the upside—to be able to move Team M at lightning speed—was difficult to pass up.

We thanked him and Aaron closed the door. "I think we should ask him on." Bob raised an eyebrow. Aaron continued, "He'll help us move forward quickly."

"True," Bob said. He paused, then added, "But just for Manafort."

"Just for Manafort."

Bob nodded.

Aaron opened the door and jogged down the long hallway outside the SCO leading to the lobby. When he caught up with Weissmann, he asked, "Would you be interested in joining the office?"

Weissmann didn't miss a beat. "Yes."

"We'll be in touch." Aaron shook his hand. There was still some vetting and bureaucratic hoop-jumping to go through, but within two weeks, Weissmann would be the lead on Team M.

The other principal hire we were close to securing that week was Michael Dreeben from the solicitor general's office. The department had given him the green light to join the SCO. Dreeben insisted on bringing aboard his own team, and because Bob trusted him completely, that wasn't an issue. Dreeben's first hire was Elizabeth Prelogar, a fluent Russian speaker from Idaho who had clerked for two Supreme Court justices (and who would later become the solicitor general of the United States, representing the DOJ in all matters before the Supreme Court). We also reached out to Brandon Van Grack, who had been running the Flynn investigation at the DOJ. We wanted him to lead Team F. He would join within the month, and would work with Zainab Ahmad, a talented prosecutor who came from the Eastern District of New York, where she focused on terrorism cases.

As our team came together, we had on blinders in one particular respect: we did not know anything about the political affiliations of the people we interviewed or hired, which candidates they had donated to, or whom they had voted for. This was on purpose. To us, and to Bob especially, considering a potential hire's political leanings was totally anathema—indeed, Department of Justice rules prohibited us from considering such things. But as we would soon learn, not paying attention to the personal politics of some of our team opened an avenue of attack that would be exploited by the president. Several people in the office had made donations to Democratic candidates over the years, which was enough fodder for Trump to label us "13 Angry Democrats." This criticism was inaccurate and a complete sideshow. Bob was a Republican and he was the one calling the shots. Aaron, Bob's deputy, was a registered independent who had never donated to any politician. The largest donation ever made by Jim, Bob's senior counselor, happened to be to a Republican. Whichever politicians or parties anyone inside our office had supported in the past was completely immaterial to our ability to get the job done.

And yet there could have been some self-selection at work here. In 1988, Supreme Court Justice Antonin Scalia penned a lone dissent in the famous (in legal circles, at any rate) case of *Morrison v. Olson*, which revolved around the constitutionality of the statute establishing the independent counsel, the precursor to the special counsel. The other justices voted to uphold the statute, while Scalia warned that independent counsels might fall victim to a form of "self-selection," among other problems. When lawyers apply to work as prosecutors at the federal (or state or local) level, they have no idea whom they will bring cases against. They simply want good cases. One year it could be a bribery case against a Democrat, the next year a pay-to-play scheme against a Republican, and the year after that a corporate embezzlement case. The prosecutor's politics should play no role in these investigations.

But when a prosecutor joins a special or independent counsel, they have a pretty good idea who is being investigated and why. In our case, if a lawyer was skeptical of the possibility of a connection between members of the Trump campaign and Russian interference in the 2016 election, they might be unlikely to apply to our office. Conversely, if a lawyer thought they might be able to help uncover such a connection, they could be likely to submit their résumé.

This is not to say that everyone (or indeed anyone) who came to work for us was motivated by politics. We simply didn't know and we didn't ask.

We evaluated applicants based on their knowledge, experience, and ability to move our investigation forward quickly and thoroughly with all regard for the law and established rules. Yet there was a chance some applicants were attracted to the possibility that our office's work could result in criminal charges around, and perhaps even against, President Trump.

Maybe we should have been more sensitive to that possibility, including when considering Weissmann's interest in the Manafort case. But Bob never applied any political test to anyone who walked through our doors. He was committed to the ideal that in a rule-of-law democratic system there can be no political tests for prosecutors of any stripe. If you start evaluating prosecutors based on their politics, even a little bit, you will inevitably be making political judgments precisely when you should not be.

However, we did not foresee how easily people in politics and the media—including the president—would use the political histories of some of our team to impugn our office and our work. In May 2017, we felt that our team, as public servants at the Department of Justice who were led by Bob, would be trusted regardless of which politicians or parties any of us happened to support. We were wrong.

*   *   *

There was one more critical component to being able to move quickly: getting agents from the FBI to work in the same space as the prosecutors in the SCO. For Bob, this was essential. Having everyone under one roof would minimize the potential for leaks and keep the entire team of agents and prosecutors focused on our mission. But this setup was unusual. At first, Acting FBI Director McCabe was reluctant—the FBI wanted its people working under its direction, which is easier to do when agents do not sit with prosecutors. But Bob ultimately prevailed and we reached a compromise. Agents would be assigned to sit in the office, accompanied by an FBI "on-scene leader" who would work with us day in and day out.* In effect, the bureau would run a mini field office out of the SCO.

Which brings us to FBI Special Agent Peter Strzok (pronounced "struck"), then serving as a deputy assistant director in the FBI's Counterintelligence Division and the lead on Crossfire Hurricane. Aaron had known Strzok for more than a decade and had prosecuted espionage cases with him years earlier. Strzok was a bright and committed agent who was steeped in the facts of the FBI's Russia investigation. Aaron lobbied hard to bring him on, but the bureau was resistant. The FBI wanted to give him the opportunity to run a field office to develop him as a leader. The FBI also suggested that it might be better for our office to have a clean break from the FBI's original leadership on the Russia investigation.

But if speed were paramount, then of course we needed Strzok. As Aaron pointed out, "How can we *not* bring over the guy running Crossfire Hurricane?"

Strzok wouldn't come on until June, but then, within only a matter of weeks, he would be gone.

---

* An FBI counsel would also accompany the agents to assure they complied with FBI's rules. That counsel was not part of our office and would report to the FBI's Office of General Counsel throughout our existence.

Five

LIFT THE CLOUD

The most prominent witnesses Jim and Aaron interviewed early in the investigation were the nation's top intelligence officials: the director of national intelligence, Dan Coats, and the director of the National Security Agency, Mike Rogers. The *Washington Post* article on May 22 had reported that they'd been asked to "push back against the FBI's investigation into Russia and the Trump campaign." We wanted to ask them directly whether Trump had tried to pressure them to get Comey to back off the Russia investigation.

But because these were top administration officials, we had to come to an agreement with the White House about executive privilege before we interviewed them. In general, executive privilege protects communications between the president and his top aides from disclosure. We needed to know whether there would be any roadblock in what we could ask Coats, Rogers, and other senior officials about their interactions with the president.

On June 7, while we were still negotiating these issues with the White House, Coats and Rogers testified before the Senate Intelligence Committee. Unfortunately, we would not be the first to interview them. During their testimony, more than one senator asked about the *Washington Post's* May 22 article. They declined to provide details about their conversations with President Trump. When asked to elaborate, Coats responded, "I have never been pressured, I've never felt pressure to intervene or interfere in any way with shaping intelligence in a political way, or in relationship to an ongoing investigation." Rogers said, "In the three-plus years that I have been the director of the National Security Agency, to the best of my recollection I have never been directed to do anything I believe to be illegal, immoral, unethical, or inappropriate. And to the best of my recollection, during that same period of service I do not recall ever feeling pressured to do so." Rogers was asked again about this, and repeated, "I'm not going to discuss the specifics of conversations with the president of the United States, but I stand by the comment I just made to you, sir."

Two days later, on June 9, Michael Dreeben spoke with an official in the White House Counsel's Office and finalized an agreement about our ability to obtain executive branch documents and witness statements. We would gain access to White House documents and witness statements *provided* that they stayed within the executive branch, meaning such evidence wouldn't go to Congress or the courts. This meant that perhaps we would get better details from Coats and Rogers when we interviewed them.

The following Monday, June 12, we interviewed Rogers. Typically, prosecutors work up to top interviews like these, gathering documents and interviewing subordinates and other people who have knowledge of the events in question. Bob was less patient. His preference was to conduct high-impact interviews early and get to the heart of the matter.

Aaron interviewed Rogers with an FBI agent at the NSA complex, which also houses US Cyber Command, well outside the Beltway in Fort Meade, Maryland. This complex is colloquially known as "the Fort." Aaron, who'd been there before, was not a fan of the main building. The space inside was devoid of any natural light. It sucked the energy from you.

Aaron and the agent made their way to Rogers's office, which was located in the center of the main building among a nearly windowless arrangement of rooms. Once inside, they were greeted by Rogers and the NSA general counsel, Glenn Gerstell. Rogers was a four-star admiral in the US Navy, with brown hair, intense eyes, and a square jaw. Gerstell was tall and looked like a Wall Street lawyer. (Aaron would talk to Gerstell many times in the course of the investigation and came to trust his judgment and care.)

Rogers, perhaps because he had been in the military his entire professional life, weighed his words carefully as he answered Aaron's questions. Rogers went beyond his congressional testimony, but was still cautious. When discussing his interactions with the commander in chief, he seemed to want to get everything exactly right. Yet it didn't take long for Aaron and the FBI agent to discern that Rogers had been disturbed by what had transpired between him and the president.

The main topic was a call that President Trump had made to Rogers on March 26, 2017. This was six days after Comey had testified to Congress that the FBI was investigating the Russians' efforts to interfere in the 2016 election and the nature of any links or coordination between the Russians and the Trump campaign. The president told Rogers on their call that he was very frustrated with the FBI's Russia investigation, saying it made relations with the Russians difficult. "The thing with the Russians [was] messing up" his ability to get anything done with them, the president said, referring to the FBI's investigation. He insisted that news stories linking him to Russia weren't true and asked Rogers if he could publicly refute them. Rogers said that at no point had the president asked him to *do* anything toward the FBI investigation, and that he hadn't perceived the request to refute any media stories as an order. But the president's words nevertheless caught Rogers off guard.

Immediately after the president's call, Rogers and his deputy, Rick Ledgett, who had joined Rogers on the call, drafted a memo detailing what had been said. Then both men signed the memo and took the extraordinary step of placing it within a safe inside the NSA—possibly one of the safest safes anywhere in the world. The NSA gave us a copy of this memo, which we stored in our SCIF, but they insisted on holding on to the original.

Rogers said that President Trump raised the investigation on at least one other occasion, insisting he'd done nothing wrong and complaining that this "Russia thing has got to go away." This was also highly unusual, but Rogers perceived it primarily to be the president venting, and not an order or suggestion that he approach Comey or anyone else at the FBI. We learned from Comey's memos that on March 30 (four days after Trump's call to Rogers), Trump called Comey with a similar request. According to Comey's notes, Trump said that he "was trying to run the country and the cloud of this Russia business was making that difficult." He then asked what could be done to "lift the cloud."

Aaron thought the interview with Rogers was remarkable. But, at least on their face, the president's words could be taken as genuine expressions of frustration, and nothing more. Within a matter of weeks, Aaron interviewed Rogers's deputy, Rick Ledgett, who had been on Rogers's call with the president. Ledgett described the content of the call in the very same way, but added that the conversation had been one of the most unusual in his forty years of government service.

Two days after the Rogers interview, on June 14, 2017, Jim met with DNI Coats at his office at the Liberty Crossing Intelligence Campus, or simply "LX 1," just inside the western edge of the Beltway in McLean, Virginia. Before serving at the Office of the Director of National Intelligence (ODNI), Coats had been a senator from Indiana for a total of sixteen years. Coats's office was impressively large, with a desk on one side, a sitting area, and a massive round table in the corner. Jim conducted the interview at this table, accompanied by two FBI agents.

What struck Jim as he questioned Coats was how his demeanor changed whenever he recalled his interactions with Trump. Coats was tall and lanky, an affable midwesterner, but his quick smile disappeared when he spoke about his encounters with the president.

On March 22, 2017, Trump had asked Coats and the director of the CIA, Mike Pompeo, to stay in the Oval Office following the president's daily brief.

(Pompeo would later tell us he had no recollection of being asked to stay behind on this date.) The president asked both men whether they could state publicly that there were no links between him and Russia. Coats said he told the president that his job was to provide intelligence and not get involved in investigations.

Coats left the Oval Office on edge but maintained that he hadn't been asked to do anything improper.

Three days later, on March 25, Trump called Coats. The president again complained about the Russia investigation and how it had impeded his ability to get things done with the Russians. Coats told him that the investigations were happening and that the best thing to do was let them run their course.

More than once in the interview, Coats shook his head and said, regarding the president's fixation on Russia, "It's just the way he is. . . . It's just the way he is."

After about an hour of questioning, Jim wrapped up and said thank you. As the meeting ended, Coats rose from his seat at the table and went across the room to his desk and sunk into his chair. He leaned over his desk and hung his head. To Jim, it was almost as if Coats were saying, *Why are these people in my office interviewing me . . . about the president of the United States?*

As with Rogers before him, Coats had answered all our questions. Neither official contradicted what he had told Congress, but we now had a more nuanced understanding of their encounters with Trump.

Later that month, we interviewed Pompeo as well. The CIA director was dismissive of the interactions he'd had with Trump regarding the Russia investigation. Pompeo, who was the only one of the three intelligence chiefs to take his interview with a personal counsel at his side, maintained that Trump was "just being Trump." His basic message was, "You gotta understand—this guy is just different."

Possibly, but this tranche of interviews left us with questions. Why was

Trump so upset with the FBI's Russia investigation? Why was Trump asking his intelligence chiefs to vouch for his distance from Russia?

The interviews contributed to our view that an investigation into potential obstruction of justice was warranted. Before Bob's appointment, in the days immediately after Comey's termination, the FBI had already reached this same conclusion and opened a full investigation into whether the president had tried to obstruct justice, based largely on Comey's interactions with Trump and his memos recording them.* In the weeks following Bob's appointment, he independently reviewed the evidence—including this series of encounters—and determined that there was a sufficient factual and legal basis to investigate the president for obstruction of justice.

Not long after our visit to the DNI campus in Virginia, Jim put it pretty succinctly: "Either Trump knew he had done something improper and was trying to cover it up"—meaning, this could be obstruction—"or he knew he'd done nothing wrong and thought these guys, through their intelligence resources, would *also* know and therefore could back him up. Poof! His problems disappear."

This was our first glimpse behind the curtain. One takeaway from these interviews was that what you saw publicly with Trump really was what you got. Before then, we thought there might be two Trumps—the public version that appeared to say whatever he wanted, and a private version that was more measured. If nothing else, the president's daily brief, which cataloged the most serious threats facing the United States, might have produced different private conversations with his senior intelligence officials.

But apparently there was only one Trump.

---

* To put it mildly, opening a full investigation of the president of the United States for obstruction of justice was a momentous decision for the FBI. The FBI's Domestic Investigations and Operations Guide (DIOG) is a massive tome describing the rules governing FBI investigations. A "full investigation" may be opened if there is an "articulable factual basis" of possible criminal activity or a threat to national security. The FBI has two lesser options available to it, an "assessment" and a "preliminary investigation." A full investigation permits the FBI to use its complete panoply of investigative authorities.

Six

CONGRESS

The month of June 2017 would set the terms of our relationship with Congress. At that time, the Senate and the House were controlled by the president's party, and both bodies were investigating Russian election interference.

Getting this relationship right was critical. Parallel congressional investigations had undermined special and independent counsel investigations in the past. One high-profile example: Oliver North and John Poindexter were convicted by juries for their roles in the Iran-Contra scandal under President Ronald Reagan, but those convictions were thrown out on appeal because Congress had previously granted them immunity in exchange for their testimony.

We were particularly concerned about Congress obtaining information before we did (through documents or interviews) and then making it public in a way that could affect witness testimony or our ability to obtain additional evidence.

It was a given that we would be doing (and, in some cases, not doing) things that upset Congress. We knew the committees on the Hill had the power to make our jobs harder if they wanted to do so.

On May 31, we learned Comey would testify before the Senate Intelligence Committee. The next day, Vladimir Putin publicly denied his government's involvement in the hacking operation targeting the 2016 election, instead saying that "patriotically minded" hackers might have been behind it. In time, we would put the lie to Putin's denial and show that Russian military intelligence had carried out the whole thing.

On June 7, Coats and Rogers publicly testified before the Senate Intelligence Committee, followed by Comey on June 8.

We briefly considered trying to delay Comey's testimony. But Bob did not think it was worth the fight with Congress. "We're not going to throw our bodies in front of this one," Bob said. "We'd lose and just piss them off." We already had Comey's memos detailing conversations he had had with Trump—and we believed we were the only people who possessed them. It was the factual details in the memos that we cared most about not becoming public—and we expected that Comey would be careful in his testimony. We didn't want any other potential witness, including Trump, to be privy to Comey's recitation of the details of their interactions while we were still gathering evidence. Seeing or hearing Comey's account could affect their testimony.

As it turned out, Comey's testimony did not reveal anything about his interactions with the president that we didn't already know, and he didn't testify about many of the details documented in his memos. And while members of Congress mostly focused on Comey's own conduct and that of the president, Comey delivered a particularly dire and prescient message about Russia, which is worth quoting:

> We have this big, messy, wonderful country where we fight with each other all the time. But nobody tells us what to think, what to fight about, what to vote for—except other Americans. And that's wonderful and often painful. But we're talking about a foreign government, [Russia,] that, using technical intrusion [and] lots of other methods, tried to shape the way we think, we vote, we act. That is a big deal. And people need to recognize it. It's not about Republicans

or Democrats. They're coming after America, which I hope we all love equally. They want to undermine our credibility in the face of the world. They think that this great experiment of ours is a threat to them. And so they're going to try to run it down and dirty it up as much as possible. That's what this is about. And they will be back because we remain, as difficult as we can be with each other, we remain that shining city on the hill. And they don't like it.

Comey was right. We needed (and still need) to keep our eye on Russia. Time and again we would marvel at the audacity and cleverness of what Russia had done (and is still doing) as it set about its plan to divide the American people. Yet Comey's message about Russia was buried underneath all the talk of his memos and his meetings with Trump. Something similar would happen in the aftermath of our own investigation. Bob's message about Russia's attack on our country during the 2016 campaign could not have been any clearer, but if press coverage is any measure, it has gotten lost in the swirl around the close of our investigation and the way Attorney General William Barr handled our findings (which we will discuss later in this book).

We did learn one new thing at Comey's hearing, and it was significant: Comey had given a copy of some of his memos to a friend. We recognized the description of the friend as Daniel Richman, a Columbia Law School professor in New York City. As soon as Comey uttered the description on live television, Aaron was on the phone to the FBI, asking that they visit Richman immediately and obtain his copies of the memos. While the FBI was getting ready to visit Richman, Aaron called him personally to make sure he knew that everything would be held by us and no one else. Richman understood. Before Comey's hearing was over, agents in New York had Richman's copies in their hands.

The day after Comey testified, Trump turned to Twitter to call Comey a liar and accuse him of being a leaker. The leaker part was accurate: Comey made clear in his testimony that he had instructed Richman to share part of at least one memo with the media (the one about Trump asking him to "let[] Flynn go") in the hope that it would trigger a special counsel.

Later that same day, June 9, Trump told reporters he would be happy to provide his version of events under oath. He refused to say whether he had any tapes of his interactions with Comey (leading many to assume that he *did* have tapes, which he did not).

On June 12, a Trump ally, Chris Ruddy, the CEO of Newsmax Media, appeared on *PBS NewsHour* and stated that Trump was "considering, perhaps, terminating the special counsel." This was the first time that a Trump ally floated this idea publicly. It would not be the last.

The next day, we met inside the office to figure out how to position ourselves with respect to Congress. A key topic was Comey's memos. We knew the committees on the Hill wanted them, and we knew we weren't going to turn them over. The memos were in our SCIF right outside Bob's office in a locked filing cabinet that weighed 550 pounds and was bolted to the floor—so they weren't going anywhere. A primary question was: How were we going to message our decision to Congress?

The larger question was whether our office would have *any* regular interaction with Congress during our investigation. We understood that Comey had briefed congressional leaders—the so-called Gang of Eight—about Crossfire Hurricane. This arrangement was not unusual for intelligence matters,* but with Bob's appointment, the inquiry had principally become a criminal matter. The Department of Justice does not, as a matter of policy, share this kind of information with Congress or anyone else. The main reason for this is to safeguard ongoing criminal investigations. Congressional access to any criminal investigation could create the potential

---

* We knew from the inception of the office that our work was likely to turn up foreign intelligence and counterintelligence information relevant to the government's broader national security interests. We therefore established procedures that would identify and convey foreign intelligence and counterintelligence information to the FBI, which, in turn, would convey this information to the intelligence community as it ordinarily would.

for Congress to influence—or simply *appear* to influence—the prosecution of those criminal cases.

And so we knew that part of our message to Congress would be clear: "We're doing a criminal case now, and you're not going to hear from us again."

That same day, June 13, Rosenstein testified before the Senate Appropriations Committee. One topic was Bob and his position as special counsel. We were barely a month into our investigation, and already some people claimed that our office was pursuing phantom leads or was conflicted.

These supposed conflicts came directly from Trump. He asserted that there were three: First, that Bob's former firm had counted certain people in Trump's orbit as clients. The DOJ had already determined that this did not present a conflict. Second, that Bob, many years earlier, had been upset about some fees at one of Trump's golf courses at which Bob had been a member. In fact, Bob had left the club six years earlier on good terms and inquired at the time whether part of his initiation fee, which he had paid in 1994 before Trump owned the club, would be returned. He had had no contact with the club since then. Third, that Bob had purportedly asked Trump to be FBI director and was rejected. This too was false. When the president's personal counsel had raised these "conflicts" directly with us weeks earlier, we referred them to the DOJ. The DOJ determined that Bob had no conflicts. The president's own senior staff also told him that none of these "conflicts" were real. Yet he continued to repeat them.

During Rosenstein's hearing, he told the senators he would need "good cause" to fire Bob and he didn't have that. "Director Mueller is going to have the full degree of independence that he needs to conduct that investigation appropriately." We viewed Rosenstein's words as a validation of Bob's early decision to keep Rosenstein informed of the basic contours of our investigation to both build trust and gain independence.

The next day, June 14, 2017, Bob, Aaron, Jim, and Stephen Kelly, Bob's longtime head of congressional affairs at the FBI, visited the Hart Senate

Office Building to meet with the Senate Intelligence Committee, chaired by Senator Richard Burr of North Carolina. This was the first of four meetings with four separate committees to deliver the same message. Bob was firm. We were now conducting a criminal case and did not anticipate talking to them again. Bob was familiar with congressional oversight and the risk in staking out this position. But we could take risks like these because we had no interest in a long-term relationship with Congress for the simple reason that we were not long term. We had one broad but clearly delineated investigation to complete, and once we finished, our office would cease to exist.

As expected, there was intense interest in Comey's memos, but Bob was unwilling to part with them—even copies. Instead, he set up a reading room at Main Justice where lawmakers could review them. But that was as far as he'd go.

(Weeks later, Senator Burr revisited this topic with Bob by phone, angrily demanding that congressional staffers be permitted to take notes from Comey's memos and then return to the Hill to show them to lawmakers, but Bob didn't budge.)

On the evening of June 14, the *Washington Post* published an article titled "Special Counsel Is Investigating Trump for Possible Obstruction of Justice, Officials Say." The article mentioned our June 12 interview of Rogers and our June 14 interview of Coats (that same day), and called this "a major turning point" in the investigation.

We have no idea who the "officials" were who told this to the *Post*. Washington is a notoriously leaky place, but our office was not. We are not aware of anyone in the office who ever leaked anything to the press during our entire appointment. Not once. This was a priority for Bob, and something he made explicit to all of us. It was clear that if someone spoke to the press, they would not be permitted to remain in the SCO.

The next day, June 15, Trump launched a fusillade of tweets, including, "They made up a phony collusion with the Russians story, found zero proof, so now they go for obstruction of justice on the phony story. Nice" and "You are witnessing the single greatest WITCH HUNT in American political history—led by some very bad and conflicted people!" The DOJ, as well as Trump's own legal team, had moved on from Bob's supposed conflicts, but the president had not.

That same day, we toured our new office space at Patriots Plaza on Fourth Street SW, right around the corner from the DC offices of NASA. It was much farther from both FBI headquarters and Main Justice, but Patriots Plaza had more conference rooms, and the entire office space for prosecutors and agents was a SCIF, enabling us to handle classified material throughout. One of the FBI agents would nickname the central bullpen, containing a long table, the "viking ship."

Two days later, on Saturday, June 17, Trump took the extraordinary step of directing White House Counsel Don McGahn to tell Rosenstein to dismiss Bob. McGahn, to his credit, refused and resolved to quit his job rather than carry out the order. And thus, McGahn may have quietly averted Trump's own Saturday Night Massacre.

We would not learn of this until we interviewed McGahn a few months later, and the public would not become aware of it until January 2018, but rumors of our imminent dismissal continued to percolate throughout the media.

There was so much concern about this possibility that senior FBI leaders, still reeling from Comey's firing, reached out in mid-June to ask if we had done anything to ensure the survival of our work in the event Bob were fired. They wanted to know: Where would we go? How would we protect our evidence and our files? How would we prevent this material from potentially being destroyed?

Destruction of evidence by the administration was an almost unimaginable scenario, but anything seemed possible to the FBI in that moment. The bureau wanted to know if we were making regular backups of our network and if we'd be willing to move these to FBI headquarters.

After a series of discussions, we decided to use our office's disaster recovery plan—which was in place for events like a bombing or a tornado or some other act of God—to address the survival of our work. Among other things, the FBI began making regular copies of our network for safe-keeping at FBI Headquarters.

But beyond those few days of disaster planning in June, we didn't give much thought to being fired. Jim injected some levity into this situation: "Getting fired would be the ultimate obstruction," he said, "and it didn't work out so well for Nixon."

A few days later, on June 20, we returned to the Hill to meet with the House Intelligence Committee. The chairman, Devin Nunes, had delegated the meeting to a subcommittee, and we convened in a small SCIF on Capitol Hill. From the outset, the meeting was cordial, and Bob conveyed the same message: that we wouldn't be back anytime soon.

The next day, June 21, Bob, Aaron, and Jim returned to the Hill, this time to meet with the Senate Judiciary Committee at the Dirksen Senate Office Building, just northeast of the Capitol. Most of the committee showed up: the chair, Senator Chuck Grassley; the ranking member, Senator Dianne Feinstein; Senator Lindsey Graham; and many others.

The Senate Judiciary Committee wields significant oversight power with respect to the Department of Justice, and the members of this committee were among the most influential politicians in Washington. The room was small considering how many people were present, including many staffers. It was so cramped that we practically sat shoulder to shoulder with the senators.

The overall mood was slightly more adversarial than it had been at our other two Hill meetings. But for the most part everyone here knew Bob, some quite well, and appreciated the magnitude, complexity, and sensitivity of our assignment. Senator Feinstein especially held Bob in high regard—she had helped recruit him to be the US attorney for the Northern District of California nineteen years earlier. Bob delivered the same message: this was a criminal matter, and we would not be engaging with them. (We repeated this to the fourth committee, House Judiciary, later in the year.)

Senator Graham had the day's most memorable line. Speaking of the ultimate outcome of our work, he leaned forward and intoned in his unmistakable South Carolina drawl, "I know you have a hard job to do—I just don't want this to end up with a blue dress."

Senator Graham, who is gifted with a wry sense of humor and the timing of a stand-up comic, was of course referring to Ken Starr's Whitewater investigation, which had morphed into a detailed look at President Clinton's relationship with Monica Lewinsky. Part admonition, part subtle jab, we took Senator Graham's comment to mean that our inquiry should not drag on interminably or become a lurid sideshow. He wanted us to stay laser focused on Russia.

He was preaching to the choir as far as Bob was concerned.

As we made our way back to the Patrick Henry building that day, Aaron took note of the peculiar position we occupied. Some on the Hill wanted to protect us; others wanted to take us down. Normally, the executive branch would protect prosecutors from having to hand over evidence to Congress, but because we weren't normal prosecutors, and because we were investigating the president, we couldn't count on that protection.

In those early days we expected that most Americans would want us to complete our investigation. After all, it was underpinned by an established Russian counterintelligence investigation. Russia had tried to sway the election to Trump, and whether its contribution pushed American voters by a margin of 0.01 percent or 10 percent, the fact was the Kremlin's chosen candidate had won. From Moscow's perspective, they had achieved their objective. Our job was to determine how that had happened. Shouldn't everyone in America have wanted that?

As Comey said, the Russians had tried to dirty our democracy, and they weren't going to stop. It was imperative we learn as much as we could so that, hopefully, the United States could better guard against future Russian attempts to divide Americans, weaken our system of government, and tilt elections toward their favored candidates.

Seven

RUSSIA AND ITS GOVERNMENT'S SUPPORT FOR MR. TRUMP

Memories fade. But documents, such as emails and text messages, are forever—unless, of course, they are deleted or destroyed. This is why one of the earliest steps a prosecutor takes in an investigation is to seek to preserve all documents that may prove relevant later. Sometimes prosecutors send a formal preservation request—such as the one Bob had authorized on May 18 for the White House. But when it's obvious the subject already knows what an investigation is about, a preservation request is unnecessary; it can be a crime to delete or destroy documents knowing they might be relevant to a grand jury investigation.

On July 8, 2017, news broke of what became known as the Trump Tower meeting. "Trump Team Met with Lawyer Linked to Kremlin During Campaign," read the *New York Times* headline. We immediately wanted to know: Did any emails or other documents exist that could tell us more about this meeting? And if so, would Trump's team provide them to us voluntarily? From the moment the story dropped, not two months into the SCO's tenure, we knew this would be an early test of the Trump team's assurance of cooperation.

We were already in communication with Trump's lawyers related to other requests, and when the story came out, we asked if they had any documents concerning the meeting. It took two days, but the answer was yes. On July 10, the Trump Organization sent us a batch of emails. The following day, Donald Trump Jr., the president's eldest son, tweeted them publicly.

A few of us convened in the main conference room, which we'd nicknamed Sequoia, in our new space at Patriots Plaza to read what team Trump had sent over. (Our other conference rooms were named Elm, Oak, and Maple.) Joining the group was Andrew from the SDNY, who had officially started at the SCO five days earlier, on July 5. Andrew had been assigned to both Team 600 and Team R, and, as it turned out, the Trump Tower meeting would prove relevant to both.

We passed out copies of the emails and read them in chronological order. They showed an exchange between Donald Trump Jr. and his friend and business associate Rob Goldstone, a British publicist whose client list included a Russian pop musician named Emin Agalarov. Emin was the son of Aras Agalarov, a Russian real-estate developer friendly with both Putin and Yuri Chaika, the Russian equivalent to the US attorney general.

The email exchange had been initiated on June 3, 2016, by Goldstone, who as a Brit mislabeled Russia's prosecutor general as the "Crown prosecutor." He wrote:

Emin just called and asked me to contact you with something very interesting. The Crown prosecutor of Russia met with his father Aras this morning and in their meeting offered to provide the Trump campaign with some official documents and information that would incriminate Hillary [Clinton] and her dealings with Russia and would be very useful to your father.

Goldstone emphasized: "This is obviously very high level and sensitive information but is part of Russia and its government's support for Mr. Trump."

Trump Jr. responded, "If it's what you say I love it especially later in the summer." Later in the summer would be closer to Election Day. Trump

Jr. agreed to meet on June 9, 2016, at Trump Tower with Goldstone and a Russian government lawyer named Natalia Veselnitskaya.

In only a handful of messages, we had what looked to be an offer of assistance from the Russian government to the Trump campaign; an acknowledgment that the Russian government supported Trump in the election; and confirmation that Trump Jr. was enthusiastic about this support, so much so that he wanted to meet a Russian lawyer to discuss it. At one point while reading through the emails, Jim looked up and deadpanned, "Man, they say we are on a witch hunt. Anybody think there might be a witch here?"

As we continued to scrutinize the emails, Andrew had a personal decision to make. Five days earlier, he had left his home in New York where he lived with his wife and two young children. He had signed up for the SCO knowing he would be working around the clock and on weekends for many months, if not years. Amid all the rumors of Bob's possible firing, Andrew was debating whether it would be worth uprooting his family if there was a risk they would soon have to turn around and head back to New York.

But the Trump Jr.–Goldstone emails made Andrew's decision easier. Russia's interference in the election to benefit Trump sat at the heart of our investigation, and here was evidence *in writing* that assistance had been offered, and that the Trump campaign had been eager to receive it. Regardless of whether this conduct amounted to a federal crime, firing Bob now would be much more costly for Trump. On the heels of Comey's firing, it would be perceived as clear obstruction. Andrew decided not long after the revelation of the Trump Tower meeting to encourage his family to join him in DC. His wife agreed, and in the end they decided to stay in DC long term.

As with documents in many other cases, the emails provided an initial road map for an investigation and teed up many questions: What was the substance of this meeting? What information did the Russians offer, if any? What did the Russians want in return, if anything? Was there any follow-up? Did Trump know about the meeting, either before or after?

We learned that the meeting took place as scheduled on the afternoon of June 9, 2016. Veselnitskaya was joined by a man named Rinat Akhmetshin, a Russian émigré to the United States who had once served in the Soviet military.

Veselnitskaya and Akhmetshin ran a US-registered nonprofit whose purpose was to advocate against a US human rights statute called the Magnitsky Act. In its simplest terms, the Magnitsky Act authorized the US State and Treasury Departments to sanction Russian human rights abusers for actions they had taken inside Russia. Putin hated the Magnitsky Act. After the law passed in 2012, Russia announced its own anti–Magnitsky Act, which enabled the Kremlin to sanction American officials. Included in the first batch of sanctions was Preet Bharara, the US attorney for the Southern District of New York. Bharara had previously been Andrew's boss, and his office had prosecuted the Russian arms dealer Viktor Bout (nicknamed "the Merchant of Death"), in addition to other cases involving Russia.

The Kremlin also retaliated in another way: it suspended all adoptions of Russian children by American families, thereby permanently linking the unrelated issue of adoption to the Magnitsky Act.

The Trump Tower meeting lasted about twenty minutes. Trump Jr., Jared Kushner, and Paul Manafort attended on behalf of the campaign. They asked about the derogatory information on Clinton that Goldstone had promised in his emails. But the only information provided by Veselnitskaya was that certain funds allegedly derived from illegal activities in Russia had allegedly been provided to Clinton and other Democrats. Trump Jr. requested evidence to support those claims, but Veselnitskaya did not provide any.

It quickly became evident that what Veselnitskaya really wanted to talk about was the Magnitsky Act. This topic did not interest Trump Jr., Kushner, or Manafort. Trump Jr. suggested the issue could be revisited when and if candidate Trump was elected. During the meeting, Manafort and Kushner texted each other that the meeting was a "waste of time," and Kushner went so far as to ask his assistant to message him that he was needed elsewhere as a pretext for leaving early. After the meeting ended, Goldstone apologized to Trump Jr., and there was no follow-up throughout the rest of the campaign. Following the election, Veselnitskaya made efforts to contact the incoming administration, but we uncovered no evidence showing that the Trump transition team engaged with her.

In some ways, the Trump Tower meeting illustrated the limits of criminal law. Meeting with a Russian lawyer offering derogatory information as part of "Russia and its government's support" for a candidate is in the realm of what Congress intended to prohibit by banning foreign contributions to US political campaigns. US elections are meant to be fought between and among American interests, not foreign ones. However, not all bad conduct rises to the level of criminality.

After investigating the facts thoroughly, including interviewing six of the eight people who had attended the meeting (everyone except Trump Jr., who declined, and Veselnitskaya, who did not return to the United States), we concluded that neither the offer of assistance nor the desire of Trump Jr. to receive it was sufficient to bring criminal charges under the foreign contribution ban or any other statute. We did not have evidence that Trump Jr. or the others present willfully violated the law, or that the limited and vague information offered by the Russians in this meeting had sufficient monetary value to be subject to foreign-donation restrictions.

∗ ∗ ∗

As we investigated, we learned that Trump, his legal team, and several White House advisers had been aware of the emails offering Russian assistance going back at least a month before the July 8, 2017, *New York Times* story about the Trump Tower meeting. The Trump campaign had received a document request from the Senate Intelligence Committee on May 17, 2017, that clearly covered the June 9 meeting and the underlying emails. This raised the question of whether President Trump was trying to prevent Congress from obtaining the emails. If he had, this could have been an obstruction offense.

When the *Times* story originally broke, President Trump was en route to the United States from the G20 summit in Hamburg, Germany, where he'd had his first face-to-face meetings with Vladimir Putin. When White House Communications Director Hope Hicks told Trump that the *Times* was working on a story about the Trump Tower meeting, he directed her not to comment.

When it became clear that the *Times* was going to run its story, with or without comment from the president, Trump Jr. worked on a statement saying the meeting had been with "an individual who I was told might have information helpful to the campaign." The president rejected Trump Jr.'s version and dictated his own statement from Air Force One, saying that the meeting was about Russian adoption; he made no mention of the offer of derogatory information about Clinton.

Our job was to evaluate this conduct under the criminal law. In the end, the evidence did not establish that anyone had been trying to prevent us or Congress from receiving the emails, and the president's actions—including the statement about "adoption" that Trump dictated for his son—were explainable as part of a press strategy, and not as an effort to impede any investigations, particularly since nothing was deleted and we ultimately received the emails once we pressed for them.

While the Trump Tower meeting occupied the attention of the press throughout much of July and beyond, and while we devoted resources to investigating it, the main focus of Team R at this time was elsewhere: on a young Trump campaign adviser, George Papadopoulos, who had been told about another Russian plan to assist the Trump campaign.

Eight

DIRT IN THE FORM OF THOUSANDS OF EMAILS

Bob wrote "core" alongside the name "George Papadopoulos" on May 19, 2017, two days after Bob's appointment. The name Papadopoulos was also featured on the left side of a whiteboard that took up nearly a whole wall of Team R leader Jeannie Rhee's office. On the whiteboard was an outline of the major known touchpoints between the Trump campaign and any Russians or Russian intermediaries.

Papadopoulos, a foreign policy adviser to the campaign, was tied to an academic named Josef Mifsud, whose name was also scrawled on Rhee's whiteboard. In April 2016, Mifsud told Papadopoulos about a Russian government offer to assist the Trump campaign through the anonymous release of information damaging to Clinton—"dirt" in the form of "thousands of emails." It was this interaction that had originally prompted the FBI to open Crossfire Hurricane in July 2016.

Questions about Papadopoulos were, as Bob noted, at the core of our investigation: Why had Papadopoulos been given this information? What did he do with it? Had anyone else in the Trump campaign been involved?

Throughout the month of July 2017, FBI agents and analysts working with Team R pored through Papadopoulos's communications, internet search history, and other materials to assemble a day-by-day (and sometimes minute-by-minute) timeline of all communications and activity that might interest us. Then, in the last week of July, we received a travel alert: Papado-poulos, who had been spending the summer in Greece, was scheduled to fly on July 27 from Athens to Munich, Germany, and then to Washington Dulles International Airport. At Dulles he would pass through customs before catching a third flight to Chicago, where his family lived.

The evidence we had pulled together showed that Papadopoulos had lied to the FBI during a voluntary interview six months earlier, in January 2017, before the SCO existed. The travel alert meant we had a decision to make: Should we approach Papadopoulos when he landed at Dulles and seek another interview? Or should we arrest him for false statements as soon as he touched down in the United States?

* * *

In March 2016, George Papadopoulos was a twenty-nine-year-old American expat living in London. He had been a paid adviser on the presidential cam-paign of Ben Carson, and had previously worked at the Hudson Institute, a foreign policy think tank based in Washington, DC. In the first week of March, after a short back-and-forth that Papadopoulos had initiated, Sam Clovis Jr., the Trump campaign's national cochair and chief policy adviser, brought Papadopoulos on board as an unpaid foreign policy adviser for candidate Trump.

Papadopoulos joined Trump's campaign at a moment when it was scram-bling to bring on a number of "foreign policy experts." Trump had handily won the Super Tuesday primaries on March 1, making him the clear favorite to head the Republican ticket that November. He was now a serious candi-date and was facing public criticism for not having a foreign policy team.

On March 21, Trump met with the *Washington Post* editorial board and announced the names of Papadopoulos and four others as part of a team that would be headed by then-senator Jeff Sessions. (Sessions would later become Trump's first attorney general. It was this and other campaign activities that would later cause Attorney General Sessions to recuse himself in any matters related to the Russia investigation.) In announcing the names, Trump said, "George Papadopoulos, he's an energy and oil consultant, excellent guy."

In this same meeting with the *Washington Post*, Trump also made comments that were perceived as friendly to Russia, particularly coming from a Republican. He criticized NATO and the United States' support for Ukraine in its struggle against Russia in Crimea and contested regions along Ukraine's eastern border. Trump said, "Ukraine is a country that affects us far less than it affects other countries in NATO, and yet we are doing all of the lifting, they're not doing anything. And I say: 'Why is it that Germany is not dealing with NATO on Ukraine?'" He added: "Why are we always the one that's leading, potentially the third world war, okay, with Russia." Papadopoulos would later tell us that when he first joined the campaign, he was told one of Trump's main foreign policy objectives would be to improve relations with Russia.

Three days after Papadopoulos's role on the campaign was announced, he had a meeting in London with Josef Mifsud. Mifsud, a Maltese national who had worked as a professor at the London Academy of Diplomacy, maintained several Russian contacts. He became interested in Papadopoulos only after learning he had been named as one of Trump's advisers.

The meeting took place on March 24, 2016, over lunch at a London café. Mifsud was accompanied by a woman named Olga Polonskaya, whom Mifsud said was Vladimir Putin's niece. (Papadopoulos would later learn she was not.) They discussed a wide range of topics, including arranging a potential meeting between Trump and Putin. At some point, Polonskaya offered to put Papadopoulos in contact with other Russians, adding that she was friends with the Russian ambassador to the United Kingdom.

Not long after the meeting ended, Papadopoulos wrote an email to the Trump campaign's foreign policy team with the subject "Meeting with Russian leadership—including Putin":

I just finished a very productive lunch with a good friend of mine, Joseph Mifsud, the director of the London Academy of Diplomacy—who introduced me to both Putin's niece and the Russian Ambassador in London—who also acts as the Deputy Foreign Minister. The topic of the lunch was to arrange a meeting between us and the Russian leadership to discuss U.S.-Russia ties under President Trump. They are keen to host us in a "neutral" city, or directly in Moscow. They said the leadership, including Putin, is ready to meet with us and Mr. Trump should there be interest. Waiting for everyone's thoughts on moving forward with this very important issue.

The description was a bit inflated. Papadopoulos had not met the Russian ambassador, and Mifsud was not a good friend—but Papadopoulos had recently joined the campaign and presumably was trying to sound more impressive. Clovis, the campaign's chief policy adviser, responded, "This is most informative. Let me work it through the campaign. No commitments until we see how this plays out." Clovis said that any meeting with Russia should wait until after meetings with "our NATO allies," and then added, "More thoughts later today. Great work."

About a week later, on March 31, Papadopoulos met Trump in person for the first time at the Trump International Hotel in Washington, DC, at a gathering of Trump's foreign policy team. After the meeting, Trump's Instagram account posted a picture showing Trump, Sessions, Papadopoulos, and others huddled around an oval table somewhere inside the hotel. Papadopoulos would later tell us that he informed the group of the idea of a meeting between Trump and Putin during the campaign, and that Trump had been receptive.

Mifsud soon put Papadopoulos in touch with another Russian, Ivan

Timofeev. Timofeev, who lived in Moscow, worked at a Kremlin-friendly think tank called the Russian International Affairs Council. He also had connections to the Russian Ministry of Foreign Affairs. Starting in April and continuing through much of the campaign, Papadopoulos spoke over Skype and exchanged numerous messages with Timofeev in an attempt to arrange a Moscow visit for representatives of the Trump campaign, or for Trump himself.

In late April, Mifsud traveled to Russia—flying from London to Moscow on April 18 and returning on April 25. During that exact time period, as only the Russian government knew, units within Russian military intelligence had hacked into the email account of the Clinton campaign chair, the servers of the Democratic Congressional Campaign Committee (DCCC), and the servers of the Democratic National Committee (DNC), and were siphoning off tens of thousands of communications and documents. On April 19, Mifsud's first day in Moscow, those same Russian military intelligence units registered a website called DCLeaks.com, which would soon be used to release these emails and other data the Russians had stolen.

On April 26, Mifsud's first full day back in London, he met with Papadopoulos, this time at the stylish Andaz hotel near the Liverpool Street station, a short distance north of the City of London. Mifsud told Papadopoulos that he had just returned from Moscow, where he had met with high-level Russian government officials. He said that during this trip he had learned that the Russians had obtained "dirt" on Clinton in the form of "thousands of emails."

Ten days later, on or about May 6, at an informal setting over drinks, Papadopoulos suggested to a "representative of a foreign government"* that he had received indications from the Russian government that it could

---

* We used this wording, "representative of a foreign government," in the Mueller report to protect classified information; the actual names of the people Papadopoulos met with and the country they worked for were later declassified by the Trump administration, but we treat them anonymously here, as we did in our report.

assist the Trump campaign through the anonymous release of information damaging to Clinton. (It would be two more months—after Russian military intelligence started releasing thousands of stolen emails damaging to Clinton—until Papadopoulos's statement would be reported to the FBI by the foreign government.)

At the time of the meeting between Papadopoulos and the representative of the foreign government, the US cybersecurity firm CrowdStrike was beginning to learn that Russian hacking teams code-named Cozy Bear and Fancy Bear had illegally accessed servers belonging to the DNC. But this was not yet widely known, even inside the FBI or at other agencies, and none of the hacked emails had been publicly released.

In mid-June 2016, CrowdStrike joined the DNC in announcing the Russian hack—making clear it was the work of Russian intelligence. The media covered the announcement extensively. The Russian intelligence units in charge of the hack began releasing emails and other documents, including by way of DCLeaks.com and then, a few weeks later, by way of WikiLeaks, the online publisher of stolen documents. It was at that moment that the "representative of a foreign government" recognized that Papadopoulos had described something very similar on May 6—anonymous Russian releases of information damaging to Clinton. The foreign government contacted the FBI and described the conversation with Papadopoulos.

These were the central events that triggered the opening of Crossfire Hurricane.*

Over the years, there has been much criticism of the FBI and its decision to initiate Crossfire Hurricane. There have been two major investigations

---

* There were other contributing factors. As with Papadopoulos, the Trump campaign announced Carter Page as a foreign policy adviser in March 2016. Page had lived in Moscow from 2004 to 2007, and after returning to the United States, he had developed personal relationships with some Russian intelligence officers. In 2015, the DOJ charged one of those Russian intelligence officers with being an unregistered foreign agent; the charging papers described the intelligence officer's efforts to recruit Page. Page was never charged with a crime.

into its origins, one by the Department of Justice inspector general, the other by US Attorney John Durham. Durham began his investigation in May 2019, right as our office was closing, at the direction of Attorney General William Barr. Just before the 2020 election, Barr appointed Durham as a special counsel so that Durham could complete his work "without regard to the outcome of the election."

The DOJ inspector general would eventually conclude that Crossfire Hurricane had been opened for an authorized investigative purpose and with sufficient factual predication. Durham ultimately agreed there had been enough predication to open a preliminary investigation (his report said there was "no question that the F.B.I. had an affirmative obligation to closely examine" the Papadopoulos information), but he criticized the FBI for opening a "full" counterintelligence investigation at the time.

To us the issue was moot—Crossfire Hurricane had been opened before Bob had been appointed. But it was also not difficult to support the FBI's decision. There existed clear evidence that the Russian government (Russian military intelligence, no less) had engaged in a criminal hacking operation to obtain and release Democratic Party emails, and before almost anyone outside Russia knew about that operation, Papadopoulos had suggested *he* knew about it—and, in particular, he knew that a foreign power (Russia) had offered to assist an American political candidate in a US election in relation to that intelligence operation. Of course this was something the FBI should have investigated. It would have been a dereliction of duty for the FBI not to investigate.

*   *   *

The FBI had interviewed Papadopoulos in early 2017 as part of Crossfire Hurricane—and he had lied about nearly all his interactions with Mifsud and others that took place in the winter and spring of 2016. Papadopoulos admitted he had met with Mifsud and that Mifsud had told him about the Russians possessing "dirt" on Clinton, but Papadopoulos insisted that conversation took place *before* he had joined the Trump campaign, and that it had had nothing to do with his work for Trump, when the opposite was true. Papadopoulos also downplayed his interactions with Mifsud and Polonskaya and said nothing about his efforts with Timofeev to arrange any potential meetings with the Kremlin.

By lying to the FBI—which can be charged as a felony—Papadopoulos had materially hindered the way the bureau dealt with Mifsud. In February 2017, Mifsud happened to make a brief visit to the United States. The FBI approached him on February 10 in a Washington, DC, hotel lobby, but the agents didn't have all the information they needed to do an effective interview—precisely because Papadopoulos had lied to them. When the agents talked to Mifsud, he denied having had any advance notice of Russia possessing emails damaging to Clinton. Shortly thereafter, Mifsud left the United States and did not return during the course of our investigation.

Fast-forward to July 27, 2017. Papadopoulos's imminent arrival at Dulles meant we had a decsion to make.

We considered approaching him quietly for an interview. But Papadopoulos had already lied to the FBI, and we had little confidence he would tell the truth now just because the SCO was leading the investigation. An arrest for false statements was appropriate, and it might give him an incentive to cooperate and tell us what had really happened with Mifsud and the Russian offer.

There were countervailing considerations, however. If Papadopoulos didn't cooperate, our charges would become public within hours—and that could have an unpredictable impact on the overall investigation. To some potential witnesses, public charges for lying to the FBI might show how serious we were. But to others, it would reveal that Papadopoulos wasn't cooperating, potentially giving them an incentive to lie or shade the truth or, if arrested, to refuse to cooperate as well. Our charges could also potentially reveal details about the investigation before we had the opportunity to interview other witnesses, particularly other advisers to the campaign who had communicated with Papadopoulos.

Our lead prosecutor on Papadopoulos was Aaron Zelinsky, a young attorney with a quick wit and a booming voice. Zelinsky came from the US attorney's office in Baltimore and had joined the SCO in June. (With two Aaron Zs in the office, Zelinsky became AZ2 to Zebley's AZ1.) AZ2 was now pushing hard for an arrest of Papadopoulos. Aaron (AZ1) instantly agreed it was the right move, but first we needed to confirm with Bob—this would be our office's first arrest.

On the evening of July 25, Aaron went into Bob's office to talk it through. Bob sat behind his desk, the front edge of which had a line of small metal elephants—a decoration that he'd also had as FBI director. As the story went, the elephants were "drug weights" that had been seized in a case decades earlier.

When Bob and Aaron discussed an important decision, which they had done many times during their years at the FBI, their conversations often ended with Bob asking a simple question. "Should we do this?" It was no different with Papadopoulos.

Aaron said yes. As was typical for whenever Bob decided in the affirmative, all he said was, "Do it."

Once committed, we moved quickly. Since the FBI would make a "probable cause" arrest, we didn't need to get a judge to sign off on an arrest warrant in advance so long as we filed a complaint with the court outlining our evidence for the charges soon after the arrest. We were determined to keep the entire operation under seal as long as possible, but we knew that if Papadopoulos didn't cooperate, the charges would become public.

While the FBI worked out a tactical plan, Andrew and Rhee drafted the complaint we would file after the arrest. Throughout the day and evening of July 26, the two huddled in Rhee's windowless office in front of her computer, scouring the FBI's two-hundred-plus-page transcript of Papa-dopoulos's January 2017 FBI interview, as well the entire set of emails, text messages, and other evidence the bureau possessed pertaining to Papa-dopoulos.

Later that evening, Bob found Andrew outside Rhee's office and asked to speak with him. When it came to major decisions, Bob would often reach out to the people closest to an issue to make sure he had considered their views on the pros and cons.

Bob led Andrew to a quiet cubicle and asked, "You're good with this? How does this compare to other false-statements cases you've been involved in?"

Andrew, who had recently tried (and won) a false-statements case, said, "Is there a risk? Definitely." But Andrew told Bob he thought it was the right call. "This guy lied to the FBI and he's not going to be able to dispute it. Hopefully that will be enough to get him to cooperate."

Bob took a moment, and then said, "Good." He patted Andrew on the shoulder and headed back to his office. Bob had a similar conversation with Rhee that same night.

Once the draft complaint was complete, Andrew and Rhee sent it to Jim and Aaron for review. There are times when prosecutors draft complaints expansively to show the defendant (and the public or other potential defendants) exactly how much evidence investigators possess. But here, we wanted the complaint to reveal less in case it became public prematurely. There was another consideration as well: to maintain public trust in our investigation, it was important to avoid any allegations that might be construed as gratuitous, and not to infer too much from the facts we already possessed. "Probable cause" and all evidentiary standards involve some number of inferences, but there's a range, and ours would be very narrow—a practice that would extend all the way to the end of our office, including in our report. We wanted to leave no room for a court, the DOJ, Congress, the White House, or the public to question the accuracy or the precision of our investigation.

With these considerations in mind, Aaron and Jim used red and blue pens to edit the complaint. They narrowed it down to the allegations that would be essential to having the judge approve the arrest after the fact— while also making it crystal clear to Papadopoulos that he was facing serious charges. Their edits were aimed at ensuring that none of the allegations implied stronger connections between the Trump campaign and Russia than we could then prove.

On the afternoon of July 27, a team of FBI agents went to Dulles Airport. They waited for Papadopoulos in the international arrivals area. It didn't take long to spot him, a young man with thick eyebrows and a high forehead. At a moment when few if any people were paying attention, they approached him and told him he was being placed under arrest. He complied, turned over his phone, and the agents ferried him through border control. He was fingerprinted at a nearby FBI office, and then delivered to the jail in Alexandria, Virginia, where he spent the night in a general holding cell.

When agents picked him up the next morning, they brought him snacks and water. Papadopoulos was grateful—a fellow cellmate had stolen his breakfast that morning. He was presented in court in Virginia that afternoon. Before the proceeding, Andrew spoke by phone with Papadopoulos's lawyer, Thomas Breen, who was in Chicago and would not be able to attend the bail proceeding. Breen said he had spoken to his client, and Papadopoulos wanted to cooperate. That was a relief. We could keep the arrest and the complaint, which had been signed that morning by Chief Judge Beryl Howell in the District of Columbia, under seal. We agreed on a bail package and, after signing a bond and surrendering his passport, Papadopoulos went back to the airport and flew to Chicago, where he would live with family pending his efforts to cooperate with us.

Over the next two months, Andrew and Zelinsky (AZ2), made two trips to Chicago for multiday interviews with Papadopoulos. Sometimes they met at the FBI field office outside the city, and other times at Breen's offices in the historic Monadnock Building on West Jackson Boulevard.

Breen, who was in his late sixties and had a shock of white hair, a guttural voice, and a steely jaw, did his best to keep Papadopoulos focused. (Breen had a bum knee and sometimes used an electric scooter to move through the long hallways in the office. On one break after a particularly intense session, AZ2 tried out the scooter at Breen's invitation; Andrew declined.) We did what we could to get a detailed and accurate step-by-step account from Papadopoulos, but it proved to be more difficult than we hoped.

Papadopoulos shared some helpful information, including about what Mifsud had said about his own contacts with Russian officials just before he shared the information about the Clinton "dirt." But Papadopoulos's story shifted throughout our sessions, and we were never confident he had provided a complete account of what had happened. In the end, he agreed to plead guilty to one charge of lying to the FBI, but we did not offer him a full cooperation agreement.

Ultimately, Papadopoulos would be sentenced to fourteen days of prison time. After serving his sentence, he got a new lawyer and began claiming he had been set up as part of an international effort by US and allied intelligence agencies to go after Trump. He did a series of media interviews and wrote a book called *Deep State Target: How I Got Caught in the Crosshairs of the Plot to Bring Down President Trump*. On December 22, 2020, with less than a month left in office, President Trump granted Papadopoulos a full pardon.

* * *

Papadopoulos's arrest was not the only notable event for our office on July 27, 2017.

Within hours of the arrest, Scott Schools at the Department of Justice called Aaron and said that Rosenstein needed to see Bob and Aaron at the DOJ Command Center at 5:00 p.m. sharp. Aaron said we'd be there and that Jim would join us. When we arrived, Rosenstein already sat at a large table. Also at the table were Schools, another deputy, and Michael Horowitz, the DOJ inspector general. A thick stack of paper sat in front of Horowitz.

Bob, Aaron, and Jim took their seats. "We have become aware of text messages sent by Pete Strzok," Rosenstein said. "You need to see them." Strzok was the senior FBI leader who had been assigned to our office— at our request—and who had led the FBI's original Crossfire Hurricane investigation. Horowitz pushed the stack of paper toward Bob, who quickly flipped through the pages. After less than a minute, he looked up, made eye contact with Rosenstein, and said, "He's got to go." Rosenstein nodded, obviously relieved by Bob's quick and unequivocal decision.

The papers contained several months' worth of text messages between Strzok and a career FBI lawyer who in 2016 worked in the office of then–FBI deputy director Andy McCabe. The texts revealed that Strzok and the lawyer had expressed anti-Trump views during the campaign and the Crossfire Hurricane investigation. In one message from March 2016, Strzok said, "I cannot believe Donald Trump is likely to be an actual, serious candidate for president." In another message the lawyer told Strzok during the Republican primaries, "God[,] Trump is a loathsome human," to which Strzok replied, "Yet he may win." Strzok added, "Good for Hillary," and later texted, "Hillary should win 100,000,000–0."

The texts had come completely out of the blue. We had no idea they existed. We sat mostly in silence for the ride back to Patriots Plaza.

The next morning in Bob's office, with Aaron present, Bob delivered the news to Strzok: he would immediately be separated from all of our work. The news hit Strzok hard and he asked a few questions to understand why, but the DOJ had instructed us to say nothing, which is exactly what we did.

We were soon fortunate to land Dave Archey as our next senior FBI lead. Archey was a stellar agent who spoke multiple languages and had worked in several countries on counterintelligence and counterterrorism matters. (He would eventually retire from the FBI and take a job in Africa that required him to use French as his daily business language.) Archey ably managed the FBI team in the SCO through the end of the investigation.

Horowitz's investigation, which uncovered the text messages, would continue. In early December 2017, Rosenstein provided to Congress and the news media hundreds of messages between Strzok and the FBI lawyer. The public outcry was immediate and significant.

At a congressional hearing on December 13, 2017, Congressman Jim Jordan, Republican of Ohio, said to Rosenstein, "The public trust in this whole thing is gone. So it seems to me you get two things you can do. . . . You can disband the Mueller special prosecutor, and you can do what we've all called for and appoint a second special counsel to look into this."

Rosenstein defended Bob and our team. "Based upon what I know, I believe Director Mueller is appropriately remaining in his scope and conducting himself appropriately," he said. "And in the event there is any credible allegation of misconduct by anybody on his staff, that he is taking appropriate action."

The Strzok episode was particularly painful for Aaron, who considered Strzok to be an exceptional agent. We knew that Strzok had made no decisions in the short time he was with us that had affected our investigation. We had the processes in place to guard against exactly this kind of unforeseen circumstance. Every investigative action had been approved by a prosecutor, every warrant was approved by a court, and every arrest or charge was reviewed by Aaron and, ultimately and most important, by Bob.

Nevertheless, from the moment Bob dismissed Strzok, we had to operate under the perception held by many that we were out to get the president. That wasn't true, but the damage was done.

Nine

PAUL MANAFORT, RUSSIAN FRIENDS, AND BLACK CAVIAR

On the morning of July 26, 2017—two months after Bob's appointment and one day before we quietly arrested George Papadopoulos—FBI agents from the SCO executed a search warrant on the Northern Virginia condo of Paul Manafort, Trump's former campaign chairman.

The search team was overseen by Omer Meisel, a highly capable FBI special agent whom Bob trusted and knew from Meisel's service as an FBI assistant legal attaché in Tel Aviv years earlier. The agents arrived quietly at the Virginia condo before 6:00 a.m. As the sun rose over the DC-area sprawl, they approached Manafort's door and knocked, announcing themselves loudly enough that anyone inside could hear. No answer came. The agents used a key they had obtained in advance of the search to open the door and simply walked inside. As they passed the entryway, they found Manafort standing there in his pajamas. It was unclear whether he'd been in that spot the whole time, hoping the agents would go away if he didn't answer, but regardless, he could see they were the FBI and he didn't put up a fight.

In the days leading up to the search, we discussed whether to seek court approval for a "no knock" warrant, which would give FBI agents the authority to enter Manafort's condo without knocking and announcing themselves. No-knocks are typically used for dangerous suspects who might have a weapon, or when there's reason to believe a suspect will destroy evidence when agents arrive at the door. We lacked any real indication that the sixty-eight-year-old Manafort had guns in the condo, and although our early evidence indicated criminal violations with respect to his finances, taxes, and lobbying work, we didn't think he was dangerous or likely to destroy evidence. Before the search, Aaron had talked to the FBI about the suggestion of a no-knock, and later to Bob. As a former FBI agent himself, Aaron was familiar with the bureau's procedures for use of force in these scenarios and the calculations agents made. The ultimate question was obvious: Why take such a move against Manafort if it weren't necessary? Bob felt similarly. This was not going to be a no-knock search. "No battering ram," Bob said.*

Manafort's warrant covered a range of topics, so the agents had leeway to search for and seize many items, including phones, computers, files, and documents. The search lasted several hours, and when it was over, the agents left with multiple boxes of materials. (Before we reviewed any of it, we used a separate team of DOJ lawyers and FBI employees not associated with the SCO—known as a "taint" team—to sift out any material that could be subject to a claim of legal privilege.)

Manafort was important to our investigation for two main reasons. First, he had been Trump's campaign chairman between May and August 2016. Second, starting in 2005 and lasting for roughly the next decade, Manafort, along with his associate Rick Gates, had earned tens of millions of dollars from business deals involving certain Ukrainian and Russian individuals. Manafort's clients from this time had included a Russian oligarch named Oleg Deripaska, a man known as "Putin's favorite industrialist"; and a pro-Russian Ukrainian politician named Viktor Yanukovych. There had been dozens of contacts between people in Trump's orbit and Russians

---

* According to some in the media, we had conducted a no-knock entry. This was false.

or their proxies, but for us there was no single person inside the Trump campaign who had been more closely tied to Russia than Paul Manafort.

* * *

Manafort had been a political consultant for more than four decades. In the 1970s, he actively supported President Nixon, and during this time he crossed paths with a young Nixon acolyte named Roger Stone. Stone had worked for the Committee to Re-Elect the President, famously known as CREEP, and he was so committed to Nixon that he had Nixon's smiling face tattooed onto his back. Manafort and Stone became friends, and in 1980 they teamed up, along with a lobbyist named Charles Black, to form the political consulting firm Black, Manafort and Stone. One of their early clients was the real-estate developer Donald Trump.

Years later, in the mid-2000s, after Black, Manafort and Stone had shuttered operations, Manafort set up a lucrative consulting company that serviced clients in Ukraine and Russia. An important client of Manafort's was a pro-Russian political party in Ukraine called the Party of Regions (later renamed the Opposition Bloc). In 2010, Manafort and his firm, DMP International LLC, helped a prominent Party of Regions politician, the aforementioned Viktor Yanukovych, win the presidency in Ukraine. Once Yanukovych was in office, Manafort lobbied on behalf of Ukraine and the Party of Regions in the United States. Manafort was aided in these efforts by another American, his deputy, Rick Gates. Over the years, both men, but Manafort especially, had been handsomely rewarded for their work. Team M eventually charged that more than $75 million had flowed through offshore accounts belonging to either Manafort or Gates, money Manafort had used to pay for things in the United States, from homes to fine clothing to landscaping to expensive rugs and more. Team M also charged that Manafort did not disclose his ownership of foreign bank accounts to the relevant authorities; nor did he pay taxes on income he funneled through these accounts.

As to their lobbying work, neither Manafort nor Gates ever registered with the attorney general under the FARA statute for their work for Ukraine, Yanukovych, or the Party of Regions—and both had filed statements in 2016 with the Department of Justice that were rife with falsehoods explaining why they had not done so.

In 2014—the same year that Russia forcibly annexed Crimea from Ukraine—Yanukovych fled to Russia following a popular uprising in Kyiv known as the Maidan Revolution. Reports indicated that once safely in Moscow, he was welcomed by the Putin government as a sympathetic political exile. With Yanukovych gone, Manafort's ability to make money in Ukraine, which was now led by a pro-Western government, had been stunted. His heyday in Ukraine seemed to be over. Still, Manafort was owed $2 million for prior consulting work in Ukraine—and Manafort would take steps aimed at demonstrating his future value to his Ukrainian clients, so that he might be able collect some or all of that money.

Manafort and Gates started doing work for this set of Ukrainians in the 2000s, around the same time they had significant dealings with the Russian oligarch Oleg Deripaska, whose multibillion-dollar fortune came from aluminum and power companies.

Gates, who would eventually cooperate with our office, referred to the work he and Manafort had done for Deripaska as "political risk insurance." As Gates described it, Manafort would help elect or otherwise install officials in countries where Deripaska had business interests. In June 2005, perhaps in an act that was simultaneously ingratiating and self-aggrandizing, Manafort sent a memo to Deripaska describing work he had performed for him regarding the post-Soviet republics, referring to the need to brief the Kremlin and the benefits that his work could confer on "the Putin Government."

Later, in 2007, Manafort set up a fund called Pericles Emerging Markets, using offshore accounts in the Cayman Islands. Its sole investor was Deripaska. Once funded, Pericles pursued investment opportunities in eastern Europe, reportedly including Ukraine. The fund functioned for a time but ultimately failed. Deripaska claimed he had been defrauded and sued Manafort. This lawsuit, which was still pending in 2016, had the potential to be an expensive thorn in Manafort's side.

Despite this, Manafort's company had earned tens of millions of dollars from Deripaska, and during this period Deripaska had also loaned Manafort millions more.

We knew some of this prior to the search of Manafort's home in Northern Virginia, in part from email accounts belonging to Manafort and Gates.

A series of exchanges in these accounts stood out, as they chronicled Manafort's Russian and Ukrainian relationships, including those he maintained while serving as chairman of the Trump campaign.

One such exchange occurred in March 2016, shortly after Manafort joined the Trump campaign. (Not yet as chairman, but rather as an experienced but unpaid political consultant.) At Manafort's direction, Gates emailed a memo to Konstantin Kilimnik, a Russian national and an employee of Manafort's stationed in Kyiv. (The FBI ultimately assessed that Kilimnik had ties to Russian intelligence.) Kilimnik appeared to have access to Yanukovych and his inner circle, as well as Deripaska. The memo was a kind of heads-up, describing Manafort's involvement with the campaign and conveying his willingness to consult on Ukrainian politics in the future.

In a related series of emails from April 2016, Manafort followed up with Kilimnik to ensure that Deripaska and his people had received the news of Manafort's role in the Trump campaign. "How do we use to get whole[?]" Manafort had written. In answering, Kilimnik confirmed he'd sent the memo to Deripaska's deputy, who had been forwarding things "directly" to Deripaska. Gates would later tell our office that Manafort felt his position with the campaign would be "good for business," and that it had increased his chances of being paid the $2 million owed to him by the Ukrainians. By Gates's account, Manafort thought his role in the Trump campaign might also lead to Deripaska dropping the Pericles suit, which would have been a boon. But none of the emails answered the question of what Deripaska might ask of Manafort in return, or what he would do with any information Manafort provided him.

Later that spring, Manafort instructed Gates to send Kilimnik internal polling data from the Trump campaign. Gates did as he was told, making use of the encrypted messaging app WhatsApp, deleting each transmission after it was sent. For his part, Kilimnik was expected to share the information with Ukrainian oligarchs and, as Gates understood, Deripaska. As with earlier exchanges, Gates said these transmissions were intended to showcase Manafort's work and open paths to future business—that is, more money. Also in May, Manafort met with Kilimnik in New York, where they spoke about events in Ukraine and the Trump campaign.

In July 2016, when Manafort was ensconced as the campaign chairman, he emailed Kilimnik again. Manafort wanted to know if there had been any movement on "this issue with our friend"—that is, Deripaska and the Pericles suit. Kilimnik replied, "I am carefully optimistic on the question of our biggest interest. . . . I am more than sure that it will be resolved and we will get back to the original relationship with" Deripaska. Eight minutes after receiving this email, Manafort responded that "if he needs private briefings we can accommodate." We read this to mean that Manafort had been willing to give "private briefings" about the campaign to Deripaska. The emails did not explain what might come of these "private briefings."

Another exchange occurred at the end of July 2016. Kilimnik, who was in Moscow at the time, emailed Manafort, saying:

> I met today with the guy who gave you your biggest black caviar jar several years ago. We spent about 5 hours talking about his story, and I have several important messages from him to you. He asked me to go and brief you on our conversation. I said I have to run it by you first, but in principle I am prepared to do it. . . . It has to do about the future of his country, and is quite interesting.

"Tuesday [August 2] is best. . . . Tues or weds in NYC," Manafort replied.

We surmised that Yanukovych was the "guy" behind the "biggest black caviar jar," and we would eventually learn that these "important messages" concerned the then-low-simmering conflict between Russia and Ukraine being fought in Ukraine's east. Kilimnik would later propose to Manafort a "peace plan" that Manafort dubbed a "backdoor" for Russia to control eastern Ukraine, a region that Yanukovych would subsequently be allowed to rule.

On August 19, 2016, Manafort was forced to leave the Trump campaign following reports about his Ukraine- and Russia-related business activities.

In December 2016, after Trump had been elected, Kilimnik sent an email to Manafort. It read, "All that is required to start the process"—a reference to the "peace plan" for eastern Ukraine—"is a very minor 'wink' (or slight push) from" President-elect Trump. Kilimnik assured Manafort that Yanukovych "guarantees your reception at the very top level," and that Trump "could have peace in Ukraine basically within a few months after inauguration."

(A little over five years later, in February 2022, Russia would invade Ukraine and seize its eastern territory. Since this invasion, Putin has demanded this territory in exchange for "peace.")

These contacts raised questions for us. Was Manafort working directly with the Russians to influence both the election and US foreign policy in one of the most contested regions of the world? Or was he trying to demonstrate that he was a sophisticated and valuable political operative in order to collect past and future fees? If the latter, how far had he been willing to go?

Getting answers to these questions was precisely why his cooperation would be so important.

*　　*　　*

A main purpose of the search of Manafort's home was to find additional evidence of his connections with Russia—specifically, with Yanukovych,

Kilimnik, and Deripaska. We also believed we would find more evidence of financial crimes, which could help us bring cases against both Manafort and Gates. Any criminal charge should stand on its own and serve the interests of justice, but criminal charges also can incentivize a defendant to cooperate with the government.

Team M moved swiftly. Weissmann, working alongside a sterling former federal prosecutor named Greg Andres, subpoenaed bank and financial institution records, telephone and email records, tax records, and more. The agents and attorneys on Team M combed through it all—massive amounts of data—to trace Manafort's financial transactions and understand all that we could from his emails, text messages, and other communications.

At the same time, we were working with the DOJ to memorialize that our office was operating within the remit of Bob's appointment order. We had no doubt that Manafort was central to the SCO's investigation—a notion Manafort would ultimately test in court—but we did not want there to be any question.

We thought the best way to accomplish this was a memo from Rosenstein to Bob confirming Bob's authority to investigate and prosecute specific issues. The original one-page appointment order from May 2017 was worded categorically so that it could be publicly released—it did not refer to any specific area of investigation or specific individuals.

At the end of July 2017, Aaron went to each team leader, asking them to weigh in on what we would call the "scope memo." Team M noted several allegations about Manafort, one of which specifically named payments from the Ukrainian government during Yanukovych's tenure as president. Team R highlighted Papadopoulos. Team F relayed the broad strokes of its work on Michael Flynn, an investigation that by then was well underway. Team 600 had no reason to add anything, since any obstruction investigation resulting from our work was unequivocally covered by our original appointment order and the regulations governing a special counsel.

By August 2 we had a signed "scope memo" from Rosenstein.* It provided the specificity that the original appointment order did not. It also contained one provision that had not been in our draft. The memo clarified that Bob's authority to investigate matters that "arose or may arise directly from the investigation" was contingent on Bob consulting with Rosenstein before moving ahead. In other words, Bob could investigate a new matter under the "arose or may arise" provision only *after* he checked with Rosenstein. (The August 2 scope memo would ultimately be cited by a judge when denying Manafort's motion to dismiss the charges against him.)

On the morning of Friday, October 27, 2017, Weissmann and Andres presented the indictment of Manafort and Gates to the grand jury. This DC grand jury sat for our office and our office only for the entirety of our existence—in effect, it was the Mueller Russian election-interference grand jury. After reviewing the indictment, its members voted in favor and returned what's called a "true bill" to the court, which then issued arrest warrants for both Manafort and Gates.

On the morning of Monday, October 30, both men surrendered to the FBI Washington field office, as we had arranged with their lawyers. Both were then arraigned in DC district court. Their charges were: count one, conspiracy against the United States; count two, conspiracy to launder money; counts three through nine, failure to report foreign bank and financial accounts; count ten, unregistered agent of a foreign principal; and count eleven, false and misleading FARA statements. Manafort and Gates entered pleas of not guilty and, shortly thereafter, posted bond to cover bail—a $10 million bond for Manafort, a $5 million bond for Gates. If convicted on all counts, each faced maximum sentences of seventy years' imprisonment and significant financial penalties.

News of the indictment broke that same morning. At around 10:30 a.m., President Trump posted two tweets: "Sorry, but this is years ago, before

---

* We undertook a similar exercise in October 2017 to further clarify our scope on other matters.

Paul Manafort was part of the Trump campaign. But why aren't Crooked Hillary & the Dems the focus?????" and "Also, there is NO COLLUSION!"

Trump often used this phrase to deny a conspiracy with the Russians.

About an hour after the arraignment, the guilty plea by George Papadopoulos was unsealed. The timing was deliberate. By October 30, there was no longer any basis to keep his arrest and plea under seal. We had interviewed the people on the campaign he had interacted with, and we were done trying to get information out of Papadopoulos himself.

The existence of Papadopoulos's plea had the added benefit of showing the public that we were moving at a quick pace. We also thought that the unsealing, which included language about Papadopoulos's efforts to cooperate on Russia-related issues, could have provided additional incentive to Manafort and Gates to cooperate themselves. For Gates, this ended up being the case. But for Manafort, things would be much different.

Ten

INFORMATION WARFARE

It's well known that Russia—and the Soviet Union before it—has a long history of interfering with elections in other countries, going back to at least the 1920s. More recently, the world became aware of a Russian company called the Internet Research Agency (IRA), which had been running influence operations around the world for years before the 2016 election. (Indeed, as of this writing, the IRA remains active.) But the scale, sophistication, and audacity of the IRA's "active measures" targeting the 2016 US presidential election was on a new level.

The term "active measures" was first used in the 1950s by the Soviet KGB. According to the Marshall Center, active-measures tactics cover "a gamut of covert and deniable political influence and subversion operations, including (but not limited to) the establishment of front organizations, the backing of friendly political movements, the orchestration of domestic unrest and the spread of disinformation."[*] Key to active measures is the "deniable" component. It would defeat the purpose of an active measure if it was accompanied by an explicit or implicit statement: "The preceding was brought to you by an agent of the government of Russia," or, "We're the Kremlin, and we approve this message."

---

[*] Mark Galeotti, "Active Measures: Russia's Covert Geopolitical Operations," *Marshall Center Security Insight*, no. 31, June 2019.

The IRA, which was commonly referred to as a "troll farm,"* may not technically have been running Soviet-style active measures (its agents were not, for example, Russian intelligence operatives—they were employees of a private company), but the term captures the essence of the IRA's work on the 2016 election. The IRA itself called its work against the United States "information warfare."

What became known inside the SCO as our "active measures" investigation began in earnest in the summer of 2017, around the time of Papadopoulos's arrest and a few months before we would charge Manafort. The office was then quite busy. In addition to the Manafort and Papadopoulos investigations, we were interviewing senior administration figures about such issues as the firing of Comey and Trump's alleged requests for the FBI to "let[ ] go" of Flynn. Team F was working toward a guilty plea from Flynn for lying to the FBI; Team 600 had secured thousands of White House documents and was deep in its pursuit of a voluntary interview with the president; and Team R was already investigating the centerpiece of Russia's operations against the 2016 election: the Russian military intelligence operation to hack into the email accounts and servers of various Democratic organizations and then dump the stolen material at key moments of the presidential campaign to damage Clinton.

In late summer 2017, Facebook reached out to us and Congress to inform the US government that it had discovered fake accounts and ad buys running back at least two years—and that they had originated from Russia. The SCO, and the FBI before us, had been aware of Russian troll farm activity on social media—news reports about the IRA had been running for years before our office even existed. But tracking down and *attributing* those activities to specific people or organizations—with evidence that would hold up in a US court—seemed a herculean challenge. The information

---

* "Troll" refers to internet users who post inflammatory or otherwise disruptive content on social media or other websites. In this context, these trolls were paid operatives.

from Facebook, however, was a solid entry point and appeared to be one way we could begin to go about this.

Facebook's research had identified 470 fake user accounts that were associated with 3,000 social media ads purchased at a cost of $100,000. Facebook would release a public statement about this activity on September 6, 2017, explaining that most of the ads didn't "specifically reference" the election but instead concentrated on divisive issues roiling American society, from race to guns to immigration and more. All the fake accounts had been shut down for violating Facebook's terms of service, and now the company was revealing what had transpired on its networks.

In the course of our investigation, we would discover that within a week of Facebook's September 6, 2017, statement, an IRA employee named Irina Kaverzina sent an email to a colleague stating, "We had a slight crisis here at work: the FBI busted our activity (not a joke). So, I got preoccupied with covering tracks together with the colleagues. . . . I created all these pictures and posts, and the Americans believed it was written by their people." Facebook's public announcement had apparently alerted the IRA, prompting IRA employees to cover their tracks. This is sometimes the price of public disclosure.

We would ultimately attribute most, if not all, of this activity to the IRA. In short, Russians working from the IRA's headquarters in Saint Petersburg operated fake online US personas to carry out social media influence operations targeting US voters—first to stir up social strife, and later to favor Trump and denigrate Clinton. The IRA's operations fit the mold of active measures: Russian operatives masquerading as something they weren't in order to run a political influence operation.

It was also not the first time the IRA had been known to conduct operations on US soil.

On the morning of September 11, 2014, the thirteenth anniversary of the 9/11 attacks, residents of Saint Mary Parish, Louisiana, began receiving texts stating that a chemical fire was underway and that they should take shelter from toxic fumes. The original messages said to check the website "columbiachemical.com" for information. At around the same time, hundreds of Twitter accounts tweeted that a disaster was unfolding in real time. "A powerful explosion heard from miles away happened at a chemical plant in Centerville, Louisiana #ColumbianChemicals," someone using the name of Jon Merritt wrote. A search for that same hashtag revealed multiple eyewitness accounts of the explosion and fire. There were photos of flames and videos of surveillance footage from a nearby gas station showing the initial flash of the conflagration; there were images of plumes of black smoke rising skyward over what appeared to be the Louisiana bayou.

One Twitter account posted a screenshot of CNN's landing page, appearing to show that the explosion was now national news and that, to commemorate the 9/11 attacks, ISIS had taken responsibility. It was, according to a flurry of contemporaneous accounts, the latest terrorist attack on the US homeland.

But it was all fake. The IRA, in far-off Saint Petersburg, had made it all up—the alerts, the photographs, the eyewitness accounts.* Why did they do it? Perhaps it was just to prove they could and to sow whatever panic that followed. Or maybe they were practicing.

Now it was 2017, and we were investigating a much larger IRA operation. Facebook's outreach gave Team R a solid launch point. An early priority was to understand what the FBI already knew about the IRA's activities. In late summer, Aaron, Jim, and Rhee made the trip to FBI headquarters for a meeting in SIOC. It took place in "the AG's conference room," right off SIOC's lobby entrance, which was designed for use by the attorney general when he or she was in the building. It was an apt venue in which to discuss Russian operations against a US election. The room contained a long table and chairs; multiple screens, one of which displayed a constantly changing day-night map of the world; and a row of digital clocks across the top of

---

* The *New York Times Magazine* investigated and reported on this IRA operation in a 2015 article titled "The Agency." The story came complete with a photo of the IRA's office in Russia.

one wall, showing current times in places like London, Berlin, Moscow, and Beijing. This was Aaron's first time back in that room since his FBI days, when he accompanied Bob every morning to meet with the attorney general to go over that day's president's daily brief. Although it had been over three years, the room was completely unchanged.

When it came time to discuss the FBI's investigation into Russian social media operations, a lone data analyst with glasses almost as thick as Jim's spoke up. He walked us through the bureau's material and told us how he was conducting his investigation—seemingly all by himself and largely by hand. Aaron's initial thought was reminiscent of our first meeting with Brandon Van Grack at the Department of Justice regarding the Flynn investigation: this was too big and too complicated to be tackled with the resources currently allocated to it.

We thanked the analyst for his time and left the AG's conference room knowing we would take what the FBI had learned and greatly expand on it.

Next, we turned to Facebook, as well as other tech companies and various internet service providers. The Facebook ads and their associated expenditures were the tip of the iceberg and, standing alone, told us very little about who was behind the activity. We employed a prosecutor's most valuable tools—subpoenas, 2703d orders, and search warrants. (A 2703d order, or "d order," is a court order that requires the production of the details of an online account, such as date and time stamps of a message, and the details of who sent the message to whom. A d order does not ordinarily get you the content of communications—for that, a prosecutor needs a search warrant.)

The tech companies turned these process requests around with unusual speed, sometimes getting back to us within twenty-four hours. Even a jurisdiction like the SDNY, which was notoriously persistent in getting companies to comply in a timely manner, would often be forced to wait weeks or months for responses to these kinds of requests.

But this case was different. The companies understood that their platforms had been exploited by Russian trolls and, perhaps, that our work would contribute to their understanding of how the Russians had operated on their systems. Beyond that, there was public pressure to cooperate with the SCO's investigation, and to demonstrate that the companies themselves had not been (and weren't) asleep at the switch.

A special counsel's office is uniquely suited to conducting an investigation like this. It required significant resources and focus without distraction—both of which we had. And in our case, the tech companies' typical skepticism toward government investigations did not apply, at least not fully. This was for a number of reasons. First, the office was headed by Bob Mueller; second, we were unquestionably looking at malign activity by the Russian government; and third, in 2017 there still existed something of a political consensus around cooperating with efforts to uncover and respond to Russian interference.

Asking for this data was one thing, but processing it was quite another. We soon understood that we were facing terabytes of information. A single terabyte, which is 1,024 gigabytes, is the number of bytes necessary to hold about 310,000 images, or around 500 hours of high-definition video, or roughly 1 million books. At the start of the personal computer age, a terabyte would have required about 728,000 floppy disks. We had to find a place to store this data (which ended up being at the FBI), and more important, we had to develop the technical tools to sort and review it quickly to achieve Bob's requirement that we move at pace. Email correspondence, financial transactions, social media posts, subscriber information, and the like were all familiar terrain. Our challenge was parsing the data behind the social media activity, such as the originating internet address of a post. Doing so on a large scale would enable us to find and piece together related events and actions, and then make it understandable to a court. As with so many similar investigative challenges, the FBI figured out how to go about this.

The indictment charged that the IRA's operations were funded by Concord Management and Consulting LLC and Concord Catering. Both companies were controlled by Yevgeny Prigozhin, a longtime friend of Putin's who was commonly referred to as "Putin's Chef." In addition to catering (and information warfare), Prigozhin headed a private military company called the Wagner Group, which would be instrumental in the early stages of Putin's war against Ukraine.*

As the FBI agents and analysts delved deeper into the terabytes of information, they were able to look behind the curtain and discover a lot about the IRA. This company, founded in 2013 and headquartered in a nondescript low-rise building in Saint Petersburg, employed hundreds of people and was organized in ways that were recognizable to any person working at a media-related company of that size. It had designers, data analysts, IT professionals, search-engine-optimization engineers, and a finance section. In addition to crafting and posting social media content, its employees tracked metrics to determine what was and wasn't reaching their target audiences, and they made adjustments to meet their goals.

The division of the IRA that focused on the United States was referred to internally as the "Translator Department." By July 2016, at least eighty people worked in this group. Their original goal, according to the IRA's internal documents, was "spread[ing] distrust towards the candidates and the political system in general." By 2016, they were focused on the presidential election, and their instructions became more pointed: they were to "use any opportunity to criticize Hillary and the rest (except Sanders and Trump—we support them)."

The Translator Department had been laying the groundwork for an operation such as this since at least 2014, shortly before the Saint Mary Parish disinformation campaign. For most of June of that year, two IRA employees,

---

* Their friendship did not last. In June 2023, Prigozhin complained loudly about the course of Russia's war and ordered the Wagner Group to move against the Russian military, seizing the Russian city of Rostov-on-Don. His troops then began a march toward Moscow, ultimately backing down before reaching Red Square. Two months later, in August 2023, Prigozhin died in a suspicious plane crash. Afterward, Putin said in a televised meeting, "He made some serious mistakes in life, but he also achieved necessary results."

Aleksandra Krylova and Anna Bogacheva, took a tour of the United States. They visited Nevada, California, New Mexico, Colorado, Illinois, Michigan, Louisiana, Texas, and New York. Their visa application falsely listed "personal reasons" for the purpose of their trip, but their journey had one goal: to gather intelligence about the United States. For their trip they purchased cameras, SIM cards, and burner phones, and they had an "evacuation scenario" if things went sideways. When the trip was over and they were back in Saint Petersburg, they produced an intelligence report that was circulated within the IRA and among other members of the Translator Department.

Later that year, in November, another IRA employee traveled to Atlanta, Georgia, also to gather intelligence. Both teams had instructions to take photos, including of run-down buildings and people living on the street. These trips gave the IRA some fluency with American social issues and, along with their photos, the means to post original content.

In 2015, the IRA's Translator Department began posting material, including paid advertising, on social media platforms. They continued to do so throughout 2016 and into 2017. These ads were often linked to Facebook group pages the IRA had designed and that outwardly appeared to have been made by American citizens. The IRA's disinformation campaign cast a wide net, using page names like SecuredBorders, Blacktivist, United Muslims of America, Don't Shoot Us, Being Patriotic, Army of Jesus, Black Matters, and Heart of Texas. By 2016, the IRA's accounts across multiple platforms had garnered hundreds of thousands of followers. A single Translator Department Twitter account called "Tennessee GOP" (@TEN_GOP) had at least 100,000 followers at the height of its influence.

All these pages and accounts, as well as the ads linked to them, were managed using fictitious US personas the IRA had either made up or, in some instances, stolen by purchasing the identity information of real Americans, including their names, addresses, and social security numbers. In some instances, they used this data to open bank accounts; in others, they bought real bank account numbers. With real US bank account numbers in hand, the IRA was able to evade security measures at PayPal to set up accounts, which they then used to pay for items in the United States.

As Election Day drew nearer, the IRA's ads, posts, and messages—and the resulting online engagement with its content—intensified in frequency. Increasingly, this messaging took an anti-Clinton and pro-Trump stance, but it also sought to push Americans' buttons in an attempt to affect voter turnout. A sample from a handful of advertisements includes: "You know, a great number of black people support us saying that #HillaryClintonIsNot-MyPresident"; "JOIN our #HillaryClintonForPrison2016"; "Trump is our only hope for a better future!"; "Hillary Clinton Doesn't Deserve the Black Vote"; "BREAKING Thousands of names changed on voter rolls in Indiana. Police investigating #VoterFraud. #DrainTheSwamp"; and "Among all the candidates Donald Trump is the one and only who can defend the police from terrorists."

The IRA did not only spend money on ads and fake user accounts. It also spent money on campaign signs, a costume depicting a jailed Hillary Clinton, and a custom-built cage large enough to hold an American woman whom the IRA hired to dress up as Clinton at events in the United States.

Using more false personas with names like Josh Milton and Matt Skiber, IRA operatives organized real rallies, attended by real Americans, in places like New York, Pennsylvania, DC, and Florida, where these items and others were variously put to use. Taken together, multiple Russian-directed demonstrations occurred in the United States, some attended by only a few people, others attracting a few hundred. It was a remarkable feat. IRA operatives—sitting at their desks in Saint Petersburg, Russia—planned and advertised rallies at specific US locations, invited Americans to go there and wave banners the IRA had purchased, and then handed off logistical responsibilities for the event to real Americans.

(In one notable early action, an IRA persona convinced an American citizen to stand in front of the White House on Pennsylvania Avenue and hold up a sign that read, "Happy 55th Birthday Dear Boss." This American had their picture taken and unwittingly sent it back to the IRA. Three days later, Yevgeny Prigozhin celebrated his fifty-fifth birthday. We took from this and other communications inside the IRA that there was no question Prigozhin was their "boss.")

In all instances, the real Americans involved in these IRA-organized events seemed not to know that they were in fact receiving instructions from Russian trolls. The IRA agents went to great lengths to disguise their true identities. They pretended to be Americans and used hundreds of web-based email accounts hosted by US email providers. They also purchased space on US-based computer servers to set up virtual private networks (VPNs), which they used to access the fake US online accounts they had created.

Due in part to their successes, the IRA's operations crossed paths with individuals in the Trump campaign.

In Florida, at least three minor Trump campaign officials interacted by email with IRA operatives, accepting the IRA's help setting up and organizing various demonstrations. Similarly, people closely associated with candidate Trump either cited or retweeted posts from the IRA's @TEN_GOP account, including Donald Trump Jr., Eric Trump, Michael Flynn, Kellyanne Conway (Trump's final campaign manager), and Brad Parscale (the campaign's digital director).

In late August 2016, Trump's Facebook account posted images of a pro-Trump rally the IRA had organized in Miami. In the post, Trump said, "THANK YOU for your support Miami! My team just shared photos from your TRUMP SIGN WAVING DAY, yesterday! I love you—and there is no question—TOGETHER, WE WILL MAKE AMERICA GREAT AGAIN!" IRA employees monitored all these responses, and one of the employees responsible for operating the Matt Skiber account sent a message to a US Tea Party activist, saying, "Mr. Trump posted about our event in Miami! This is great!"

When we uncovered this evidence, it drove home just how deep the IRA's operation had burrowed into the election. The candidate they favored was commenting on and posting photos of an event in the United States that the IRA had organized from Russia.

Trump and his campaign officials had these interactions with the IRA unwittingly. No one on the Trump campaign would be charged with participating in this activity.

It is impossible to quantify the effect, if any, that the IRA's active measures had on the election outcome. But it is undeniable that they affected campaign activities. In addition to Trump's Facebook post, senior members of his team and prominent members of the US media who supported him (including Fox News host Sean Hannity) retweeted the IRA's content.

While it is impossible to measure their effect, it *is* possible to quantify the IRA's reach using metrics familiar to anyone who works in tech, advertising, or social media. In addition to the 470 Facebook accounts that purchased 3,000 ads costing $100,000, there were 120 Facebook pages that posted more than 80,000 pieces of content. This content reached at least 29 million US persons; Facebook itself estimated that IRA content on its platforms "may have reached an estimated 126 million people." Instagram accounts controlled by the IRA had hundreds of thousands of US participants. IRA-controlled Twitter accounts had tens of thousands of followers, including multiple US political figures on both sides of the aisle. In January 2018, Twitter announced that it had identified 3,814 IRA-controlled accounts responsible for over 175,000 tweets. At the same time, Twitter notified 1.4 million real people whom they believed had been in contact with an IRA-controlled account.

* * *

By late 2017, we were aware of most of these facts. Bob paused to ask whether we should take the time to charge a case when we had not found evidence that any member of the Trump campaign had knowingly participated in the IRA's activities. The importance of bringing the case seems obvious now—it cast a bright light on serious Russian interference, and it was important for the country to see that—but at the time, we thought about whether to charge the case for two related reasons. (Either way, the active-measures operation would have appeared in our office's final report to the attorney general.)

First, until this time, we had anchored all our criminal cases to the appointment order's primary investigative mandate: "links and/or coordination between the Russian government *and* individuals associated with the campaign of Donald Trump" (emphasis added). In other words, we considered charges when the evidence suggested a crime by a member of the Trump campaign involving Russian links or coordination. The IRA's efforts clearly linked to the campaign, but there wasn't evidence establishing a crime by any campaign member.

Second, bringing a case against the IRA would divert a portion of our limited resources. It would mean taking time away from the hack-and-dump case, where Bob wanted Team R to focus. Hack and dump was a Russian military operation that was directly related to Trump's campaign adviser George Papadopoulos as well as Trump's longtime associate and former adviser Roger Stone. It was at the core of the SCO's work. Bob wanted Team R sprinting on that investigation, not hitting pause to charge the IRA.

We considered whether the office could shift resources without making any appreciable sacrifices on the office's other work. Aaron sketched out a reorganization of Team R so that it could complete the work to charge the IRA case while not distracting itself from its work on hack and dump. The work streams would run in parallel under different leadership, not serially. Right around this time, Bob had shifted our target finish date to the spring of 2018 (we had blown past Thanksgiving 2017). We considered establishing Team AM (for "active measures"), an offshoot from Team R that would be headed by Rush Atkinson, a young prosecutor in our office who had distinguished himself as one of the driving forces behind Team R.

Bob decided against this proposal. Team R was functioning at a high level and should stay intact. We would charge active measures, and then push ahead on hack and dump. If that meant we were going to pass the spring target, then so be it.

The grand jury returned an indictment against the IRA on February 16, 2018. There were eight counts, but count one stood at the heart of the matter: conspiracy to defraud the United States. Members of the IRA had conspired to defeat US agencies from detecting and preventing foreign influence on our presidential election through fraud and deceit, and they had done it in myriad ways. They had evaded our ban on foreign contributions to political campaigns; they had evaded our ban on certain expenditures on elections; they had lied on their visa applications when traveling to the United States to gather intelligence; and they had—albeit from their desks in Russia using unwitting US persons—engaged in activity in the United States that required registration with the attorney general. (The grand jury also alleged that they had committed wire and bank fraud, as well as aggravated identity theft.)

Our indictment named the Internet Research Agency LLC; its main funders, Concord Management and Consulting LLC and Concord Catering; Prigozhin; and twelve IRA employees. It garnered the attention of the political establishment, the media, and the general public. Rosenstein, not Bob, announced the indictment publicly. This was by choice, because Bob, as a matter of habit and principle, eschewed press conferences. As always, he wanted the work to speak for itself.

A large group of us gathered around one of the SCO's televisions to watch Rosenstein. "The defendants allegedly conducted what they called 'information warfare against the United States,'" Rosenstein said, "with the stated goal of spreading distrust towards the candidates and the political system in general."

One thing we noticed about Rosenstein's remarks was that he never stated that the defendants' actions were designed to help Trump and disparage Clinton, even though that was one of the core allegations of the indictment. And at the end of his remarks, he added something that wasn't in the indictment: "There is no allegation," he said, "that the charged conduct altered the outcome of the 2016 election."

As we've written, that was accurate: we did not know whether the IRA's actions had altered the election. That was not relevant to the charges. The IRA broke the law in an attempt to affect the election, simple as that. But when prosecutors announce charges, they typically don't focus on what is not in an indictment. To some of us watching in the SCO, we understood why Rosenstein thought it was important to reassure the country that the special counsel hadn't determined that the IRA's actions had gotten Trump elected. But others found it curious that Rosenstein thought it was important to make that comment while also omitting that the IRA had tried to help Trump.

In the days that followed, President Trump himself commented on the indictment, picking up where Rosenstein left off. Two of his tweets from February read, "Russia started their anti-US campaign in 2014, long before I announced that I would run for President. The results of the election were not impacted. The Trump campaign did nothing wrong—no collusion!" and "Funny how the Fake News Media doesn't want to say that the Russian group was formed in 2014, long before my run for President. Maybe they knew I was going to run even though I didn't know!"

We believe that the IRA indictment was not only warranted but also a vital case for the office to bring. However, with the benefit of hindsight, we should not have charged the two Concord companies that funded the IRA. These companies faced a single charge—conspiracy to defraud the United States—which would result in a $500,000 fine if convicted. That wasn't worth the headache ultimately inflicted on the Department of Justice.

These two companies hired American lawyers and, because the rules of criminal procedure do not require corporations themselves to appear in court, the case moved ahead. Almost immediately, the government ran into the "graymail problem." This is when a defendant essentially forces the government to trim, if not abandon, its case by forcing the disclosure of sensitive and potentially classified information through the discovery process.

There are mechanisms to guard against this sort of maneuver, but they are not always effective. In this instance—with the risk of possible disclosures to the Russians of sensitive information—the DOJ made the decision in 2020 to dismiss the case against the Concord companies (the charges against the IRA and the Russian individuals named in the indictment remain in place). With no one at the defendant's table besides a US lawyer working for the Concord entities, the government rightly wanted no part in handing over material that would allow the IRA or its handlers to reverse-engineer how we had dissected their active-measures operation.

Some secrets had to be kept.

Eleven

THE CAMP DAVID INTERVIEW THAT NEVER HAPPENED

The more we learned during the investigation, the clearer it became that we would want to speak with the president directly, even if securing an interview would prove challenging. There was much we wanted to ask: What did Flynn tell Trump about his interactions with Russian ambassador Kislyak regarding US sanctions? What did Trump know about the Trump Tower meeting, which had been prompted by "Russia and its government's support" for his campaign? Did the offer of Russian assistance that had been delivered to Trump's campaign adviser George Papadopoulos ever reach candidate Trump? What, if anything, did Paul Manafort tell Trump about Manafort's interactions with Kilimnik or Deripaska? What, if anything, did Trump know about the Russian military intelligence hack-and-dump operation? What did Trump know about Roger Stone's potential advance knowledge of the dumping of those emails?

And we wanted to hear the president's account of his meetings with FBI Director Comey and why he had fired Comey.*

During the early part of our investigation, we mainly interacted with

---

* The Supreme Court's 2024 decision granting the president broad immunity for official actions would have complicated—if not eliminated—a prosecutor's ability to investigate whether Trump's termination of Comey had been intended to prevent the Russia investigation from implicating President Trump. This book describes multiple other lines of investigation that could have been similarly impacted by the Court's decision.

two lawyers on Trump's team: John Dowd, one of Trump's personal attorneys, and Ty Cobb, who worked in the White House. (And yes, Cobb, a man with a gray handlebar mustache that would not have been out of fashion in the 1910s, was a distant relation to his namesake, the Hall of Fame baseball player.)

Both men had been cooperative with our office. They told us they shared our commitment to speed in resolving these matters, if for different reasons than ours. They said they wanted to act quickly to exonerate President Trump. We heard them say more than once: "We just want to get this done so that you can clear the president. Do what you have to with Paul Manafort and everyone else, but just clear the president."

The two people in our office who most often interacted with Dowd and Cobb were Jim and Andrew. Sometimes Dowd and Cobb came to the SCO. They would be shuttled through the loading dock by our chief security officer, Ben Cohen, a former Marine. They did this to avoid being seen by the reporters who staked out the entrance to Patriots Plaza eighteen hours a day, sometimes on weekends. Other times Jim would avoid the reporters by meeting with Dowd in Dowd's car a couple of blocks from Patriots Plaza.

Cobb and Dowd played different roles. Cobb, representing the White House as an institution, promised full cooperation from day one. He was in charge of getting us documents from the White House (calendars, emails, paper notes, etc.) and introducing us to lawyers representing White House witnesses. Jim would sometimes run into Cobb at a Chinese restaurant that Jim frequented for takeout before heading home, where Cobb seemed to be a regular.

Dowd, on the other hand, was the president's personal attorney. He had a deep, gravelly voice, and his style was blunt. Dowd had been a lawyer since the late 1960s, first as a prosecutor and then in private practice. He was known for zealously representing his clients. He also had the odd habit of sending letters and emails in the Comic Sans typeface.

When Dowd met with Jim, he often would feed Jim tidbits of what he said the president was going through. "He's trying to deal with North Korea and this Kim Jong Un character," he might complain, or, "The president is in the middle of a border crisis. He can't be distracted by all of what you are doing." Jim recognized that Dowd was trying to be chummy in the hopes Jim might let something interesting slip that Dowd could then take back to the president. This was good lawyering on Dowd's part, but it never bore any fruit for him. Jim was pleasant, but he also stayed mum on anything substantive.

Regarding the president, Dowd and Cobb regularly told Jim and Andrew that there was "no there there." They claimed that neither the president nor his campaign had colluded with Russia, and that *if* Trump had told Comey to "let[] Flynn go," Trump had been exercising his powers under Article II of the Constitution, and also had been doing so when he fired Comey. Their strategy was to show that the White House was cooperating and was giving us all the evidence we needed, and in so doing, convince us that there was in fact no there there.

At first, both men accepted that unless we spoke with the president, it would be difficult for us to close our investigation quickly—how else could we say to the attorney general or the American public that we had conducted a full and thorough investigation? There was plenty of precedent for speaking with the president, too—every modern president involved in a major investigation had sat for an interview when asked. Reagan was interviewed about Iran-Contra; Clinton was interviewed during Whitewater; and George W. Bush was interviewed during the investigation into the public identification of CIA officer Valerie Plame (whose employment status was classified).

Throughout the summer and fall of 2017, the White House worked with our office more or less cooperatively to fulfill document requests and schedule interviews with White House personnel. Three weeks after Bob's appointment, we had reached an agreement with the White House that they would produce documents voluntarily. Whenever the White

House sent over materials, Cobb would show up with a manila envelope or a box and meet with Jim. The files were typically paper copies instead of digital, which Cobb said was to keep the number of people with access to the documents as low as possible.

Cobb said he was as interested in avoiding leaks as we were, and that paper copies would help with that. But while Bob ensured that the SCO was entirely buttoned up when it came to leaks, Cobb could not do the same for the White House. Early on it became apparent that whenever we conveyed requests to Cobb, those requests would hit the news soon after. On August 2, for example, we gave Cobb our first written list of documents that we needed from the White House, including items related to former national security adviser Michael Flynn. Two days later, on August 4, the *New York Times* reported: "Mueller Seeks White House Documents on Flynn." In September, almost our entire list of document requests was published in both the *Times* and the *Washington Post*.

We also provided Cobb with the names of people connected to the White House whom we wanted to interview, including Chief of Staff Reince Priebus, Press Secretary Sean Spicer, and Director of Communications Hope Hicks. Within weeks, the *Washington Post* reported, "Mueller Gives White House Names of 6 Aides He Expects to Question in Russia Probe." When that story came out, on September 8, 2017, Bob asked Jim to tell Cobb that the leak had not come from the SCO. Cobb told Jim he was sorry for the leaks, and that he believed this one had come from a former White House employee.

We accepted Cobb's explanation, but nevertheless became more guarded in our communications with him. We didn't want potential witnesses to know the details of our work, and we had no interest in churning the media swirl around our investigation. So we started conveying requests over the phone rather than in writing, and even then, we avoided providing details.

On October 23, Dowd came to the SCO to meet with Bob, Aaron, Jim, and Andrew. (This was not the first time Bob and Aaron had met with Dowd. He had first visited the SCO in June, shortly after Bob's appointment.) This visit was mainly pleasantries, but it gave Dowd the ability to tell his client he had had another meeting with Bob and that we were moving quickly and acting professionally. The day after our meeting, Dowd wrote an email to Bob: "We note that your inquiry of this President is being conducted in the midst of a very difficult, and toxic atmosphere against this President. That sad fact notwithstanding, we have advised the President that he can count on you and your team of agents and attorneys to conduct their work with unbiased integrity."

Within hours of this email, the *Washington Post* reported that the Clinton campaign had helped fund the research that produced the Steele dossier, the report on alleged Trump *kompromat* assembled by Christopher Steele. On October 25, 2017, the *Wall Street Journal* followed up with an editorial arguing the Steele dossier had tainted the FBI's Crossfire Hurricane investigation as well as ours, and that Bob "could best serve the country by resigning to prevent further political turmoil." Dowd forwarded the editorial to Jim by email, highlighted the line calling on Bob to resign, and wrote at the top of his email a single line: Jim, Tell Bob to stay on the job! It was an odd email to send, but we took Dowd at his word: that he didn't want Bob to resign, perhaps because he recognized our commitment to moving quickly.

Five days later, we unsealed Manafort and Gates's indictment, as well as Papadopoulos's guilty plea.

Throughout November 2017, we worked out the details for interviewing the president. A location was set: Camp David. We would do it on January 27, 2018. During this period, Jim would receive frequent assurances that it was still a go and that the president was eager to speak with us so that he could clear his name. In many criminal investigations, prosecutors interview the principal subject as a final or near-final step. In this instance, however, because it was the president and we were already far along in our investigation, we would take the interview whenever it was available.

As we negotiated the interview's ground rules, Dowd and Cobb pushed for it to be as short as possible, and they did not want it to be recorded or under oath. We wanted it recorded—there could be no dispute about what the president said—but it did not matter to us whether the president was placed under oath. Any interview would be subject to 18 USC § 1001, which makes it a felony to lie to federal investigators.

Andrew, with his public corruption experience, was tasked with drafting the questions. Andrew and Jim would lead the interview, and Bob and Aaron would be present, along with our lead FBI agent on Team 600, Michelle Taylor. Taylor, a former Army intelligence officer, was both meticulous and charismatic. For much of December, it looked as though the interview would actually happen.

In the meantime, we spent the fall of 2017 interviewing key players in the White House who had evidence relevant to our investigation: Reince Priebus; Hope Hicks; Sean Spicer; Stephen Miller, one of Trump's senior advisers; Jared Kushner, the president's son-in-law and another senior adviser; Don McGahn, the White House counsel; and several attorneys in McGahn's office.

It was during a weekend interview with McGahn that fall when Jim and Andrew learned that Trump, over Father's Day weekend in June 2017, had called McGahn. The president told McGahn that he should call Rosenstein, tell him that Bob had "conflicts," and that "Mueller has to go." The president said, "Call me back when you do it." Trump issued this directive three days after the press first reported that Bob was investigating not only the campaign but also Trump personally for obstruction of justice. McGahn didn't resist the president over the phone, but he refused to follow through with this directive and instead returned to the White House that weekend to clear out his desk. He was determined to resign instead of telling Rosenstein or anyone else at the DOJ to fire Bob. McGahn had only reluctantly revealed these events to us after conferring with his counsel in response to a final question that Andrew thought to ask as the interview was concluding—namely, had McGahn had ever considered resigning?

Naturally, we wanted to learn more about this episode directly from the president. Trump's recollection of this event was important to the obstruction side of the investigation, given how close in time this had happened to his learning that he was under investigation. At this juncture, we were the only ones outside of those involved who knew about this episode. The news had not leaked, at least not yet.

Also during this time, the leader of Team F, Brandon Van Grack, was negotiating a plea with Michael Flynn. On November 22, Flynn's counsel called Dowd and told him that Flynn was withdrawing from a joint defense agreement with the president. He also said that Flynn could no longer have confidential conversations with Trump or the White House.

About a week later, on December 1, 2017, Flynn accepted a cooperation agreement and pleaded guilty to making false statements to the FBI.

Flynn's statements revolved around calls he had with the Russian ambassador, Sergey Kislyak, in December 2016 in the waning days of the Obama administration. President Obama had recently announced sanctions in response to Russian interference in the 2016 election. Flynn called Kislyak and conveyed that Russia shouldn't escalate. Remarkably, the Russians didn't. Kislyak would later tell Flynn that the request had been received at the "highest levels" in Russia, and that the Kremlin had chosen not to escalate.

When news broke right before the inauguration about Flynn's interactions with Kislyak, Flynn lied and insisted that he had *not* talked about sanctions with the Russian ambassador. He lied to administration officials, and when he was interviewed by the FBI right after the inauguration, he lied to the agents questioning him.

Flynn's guilty plea was based on his lies to the FBI. That day, Cobb issued a statement: "[Flynn's] false statements . . . mirror [his] false statements to White House officials which resulted in his resignation in February of this year. Nothing about the guilty plea or the charge implicates anyone other than Mr. Flynn. The conclusion of this phase of the Special Counsel's work demonstrates again that the Special Counsel is moving with all deliberate speed and clears the way for a prompt and reasonable conclusion."

Cobb may have been trying to distance the White House from Flynn, but he wasn't wrong: we *were* moving with "all deliberate speed." Bob had been in his seat for a little over six months, and during that time Paul Manafort and Rick Gates, the president's former campaign manager and deputy campaign manager, had been indicted; one of the Trump campaign's foreign policy advisers, George Papadopoulos, had pleaded guilty; and now Trump's first national security adviser, Michael Flynn, had also pleaded guilty and was cooperating.

Soon after the announcement of Flynn's plea, Dowd began to strike a different tone regarding our prospective interview of the president. In the fall, he had told Jim more than once, "It's going to happen," but in December, Dowd started asking for conditions that weren't realistic, perhaps designed to give Dowd and the president a way out. On December 26, about a month before the scheduled date at Camp David, Dowd called Jim and said that they wanted a copy of Comey's memos *before* the interview, as well as a complete outline of our questions. Under no circumstances would we give them the Comey memos, and while we would provide a list of the topics we planned to address—we were not trying to surprise the president—we were not going to give them our questions.

By the New Year, an interview in late January looked increasingly unlikely. On January 18, Dowd had a conference call with Jim and Andrew. This time he had Jay Sekulow on the line with him. Sekulow, a polished lawyer with a PhD in religion in addition to a law degree, had argued multiple Supreme Court cases. He had been a part of Trump's legal team for several months, but we'd had little direct dealings with him. Going forward, we would interact with Sekulow more and more frequently.

Sekulow and Dowd told us they were doing a "full review" of their materials to be able to "decide what to do" about an interview. They said

January 27 was now impossible—they would not be prepared by then—and in any event the president would be at the World Economic Forum in Davos, Switzerland, that week. Andrew told them that we would be happy to find a quiet place at Davos to do the interview; Dowd repeated it was not happening that day. Sekulow added it had been difficult to get sufficient time with the president to prepare him. "Major policy issues keep coming up," he stated.

Then, on January 25, 2018, the *New York Times* ran an article describing the episode McGahn had revealed to us. It was titled "Trump Ordered Mueller Fired, but Backed Off When White House Counsel Threatened to Quit." The headline got it wrong: the reality was that McGahn had planned to quit, but he had not "threatened" this or told Trump about it in any way. The next day, the *Washington Post* ran a follow-up story stating that McGahn had not told the president directly.

The articles revealed what might have been evidence of an attempt by Trump to obstruct justice—he had tried to have Bob removed right as we had begun to investigate the president's own conduct. On January 26, Dowd wrote an email to Jim: "**Jim, the President never ordered or suggested to Don McGahn to fire Robert Mueller. He asked him to discuss the alleged conflicts with DAG/AAG Rosenstein. Don declined. End of story.**"

McGhan had told us that the encounter involved more than that. Dowd's narrative was inaccurate or at least incomplete. McGahn had found the president's request so problematic that he prepared to resign rather than go through with it. McGahn had been a credible witness in our dealings with him. He was still the White House counsel and had no agenda to be adverse to the president.

We would eventually learn from other witness interviews that the president, through his personal counsel and two aides, sought to have McGahn deny that he had been directed to remove the special counsel. Each time he was approached, McGahn responded that he would not refute the press accounts, because they were accurate in reporting on the president's efforts to have the special counsel removed. Around this time, Trump directed his staff secretary to tell McGahn to "create a record" and make clear that the president never directed McGahn to fire the special counsel. Trump also confronted McGahn directly in the Oval Office and again tried to get McGahn to say that Trump had never ordered him to fire the special counsel. McGahn refused.

The president's interactions with McGahn were high on our list of questions for the president. Dowd's email denying McGahn's account made us all the more interested in what the president might have to say.

On January 30, Dowd drove over to our neighborhood to meet with Jim. They met in Dowd's car on the other side of the Third Street intersection adjacent to the office. When Jim sat in the passenger seat, Dowd handed him a manila envelope containing what he called a "written submission" on behalf of the president. Then he said of Trump, "I can't let this guy testify. I will resign before he does." He also said that if we were thinking of issuing a grand jury subpoena requiring the president to testify, "I'm authorized to take it to the end if you guys pull the trigger." Jim knew this meant a legal battle all the way to the Supreme Court.

The "written submission" from Dowd was addressed to Bob and titled "Request for Testimony on Alleged Obstruction of Justice." It was twenty pages long (in Times New Roman, not Comic Sans), signed by both Dowd and Sekulow as "Counsel to the President." It contained a number of arguments as to why the president could not have obstructed justice and why an interview was inappropriate.

On February 1, Dowd and Sekulow came to the office to meet with Bob, Aaron, Jim, and Andrew. Their goal was clearly to get us to back down from insisting on an interview. Dowd noted all the evidence the White House had provided and said, "I submit to you that if you want to know what was on the president's mind, then you already have the best evidence."

Bob immediately responded: "I disagree. The heart of the case is his obstructive intent, or lack thereof, and the president has the best evidence on that issue."

Dowd and Sekulow argued that there was no basis for an obstruction case built around the president's interactions with Flynn and Comey. Bob jumped in again: "You asked us to reach a quick resolution on the president. In our plan, we would have had the ability to sit with him to do that." Bob continued: "This leaves a gap. We need evidence of what he was thinking; he's in the best position to address that."

In advance of this meeting, we had discussions within the SCO about the value of testimony by Trump. It was true that we were obtaining evidence about the president's intent from other sources. For example, when Trump first decided to fire Comey, he dictated to his aide Stephen Miller a letter he intended to send Comey announcing his termination. The letter was never sent; Trump's aides convinced him not to. The first draft of the letter began: "While I greatly appreciate you informing me that I am not under investigation concerning what I have often stated is a fabricated story on a Trump-Russia relationship—pertaining to the 2016 presidential election, please be informed that I, and I believe the American public . . . have lost faith in you as Director of the FBI." That initial letter may have been the best evidence of Trump's intent at the time—it indicated that he linked the Russia investigation and his decision to fire Comey. But because he gave multiple explanations for why he fired Comey, we were not then prepared to reach conclusions about his conduct and intent without hearing from him directly.

In the meeting, Dowd responded to Bob regarding our need for an interview, "You are better off with the record you have. I cannot in good conscience let him talk to you."

Bob refused to back off, though, and this had a clear impact. As the meeting ended, Dowd pivoted and asked us to winnow down the topics for an interview. Bob said, "Let us get back to you on that. I thought the door was shut."

"It's not shut," said Dowd. "The point of the letter was to engage with you. You all have been great. It's the best relationship I've had in fifty years."

"OK, that's something of a shift," said Bob. "Let's see what we can do."

On February 9, Dowd delivered another letter signed by him and Sekulow. This one argued that the president can't obstruct a counterintelligence investigation, because the purpose of such an investigation is to gather intelligence to inform the president. The letter concluded with a comment about the impact of our investigation on the president's ability to conduct foreign policy, particularly with respect to Russia. It then stated, "With all due respect, we have amply demonstrated there is no legal or factual basis with which to hold this President under inquiry any longer."

Over the next three weeks we had several follow-up conversations with Dowd and Sekulow. During the same period, our office brought four indictments, including superseding indictments against Paul Manafort and his deputy Rick Gates, as well as the indictment charging the IRA and others for the active-measures conspiracy. We also obtained two guilty pleas, including that of Gates, who had started cooperating with our office.

On March 1, Dowd and Sekulow called Jim, who was joined by Andrew. Dowd proposed what he called a "solution" to the interview in which we would provide questions to him as counsel, they would provide answers, and any follow-up interview would be based on a "script" created in advance.

Dowd repeated an argument he had made several times: "You already have an incredible record of detailed information, including intimate notes of White House staff and lawyers." We knew he was referring to the handwritten notes we had received from the White House Counsel's Office and other senior White House officials. But then he added, "If you want the truth, that's where it is. Having talked to the president, and putting aside the issue of integrity, I don't want you all to receive any information that is not completely accurate."

Jim responded that our objective was not to set a perjury trap for the president. "But," Jim added, "we need a traditional interview."

Andrew said that we were willing to give relatively detailed topics so Trump's team would be able to prepare. We agreed that we would all meet in person with Bob in the coming days to try to come to a resolution.

On March 5, Bob, Aaron, Jim, and Andrew met in the Elm conference room at Patriots Plaza with Dowd and Sekulow. Bob sat directly across from Dowd, who kicked it off: "We are on track for an interview, but we need to know what the questions are so we can make a judgment. I'm looking at an hour with two or three of you talking to him. No transcript, not under oath."

Bob said the interview needed to be recorded, and that one hour "is way too short." But he agreed to give them a detailed list of subjects in advance.

"I just don't see that working," said Dowd in response. "They'd have to commit me before I'd agree to that," he said, presumably meaning commit him to a mental institution.

Then, for the first time in all of our discussions with Dowd and Sekulow, Bob explicitly mentioned the possibility of a grand jury subpoena. "A critical issue in the investigation remains the president's intent with regard to certain activities. We have to get that from him. Our alternative to a voluntary interview is a subpoena, but neither you nor we want to go down that road." Dowd had asked for this meeting in order to reach a resolution, and it was clear that we were not making progress.

"If you issue a subpoena, he's not testifying, period," said Dowd, raising his voice. "It would be war. The president would take the Fifth," he said, referring to the Fifth Amendment. "This is really unfair. You're threatening me."

Bob said he understood Dowd's frustration, but repeated that it was important for us to get the president's side of the story. He said we had been careful to go out of our way not to put the president in a difficult spot. Bob then noted the recent indictment against the IRA, which charged thirteen Russians but which also made clear that people on the Trump campaign had acted "unwittingly" in their contacts with Russian trolls. Bob also said he didn't want any further delay. "No similar investigation has moved as fast as this one," Bob said. "The sooner we are able to accomplish this, the better we'll be."

Dowd backed off a bit and said we would have to whittle down what we were asking for; he needed to prepare a "solid script" that the president could stick to. But he added: "We would move to quash a subpoena. I have authority to take this all the way to the Supreme Court." He said he needed to speak with the president, and the meeting ended. As Dowd walked out of the conference room, he turned back to tell Bob, "Your treatment of people has been tremendous."

Three weeks later, Dowd resigned as the president's counsel. He never told us why, so we could only speculate. It could have been a change of strategy by the White House. It could have been a disagreement between Dowd and Trump about the wisdom of testifying. But our biggest concern was that, with Dowd on the way out, an already protracted process was going to be dragged out even longer.

On April 18, Sekulow came to our office by himself and met with Jim and Andrew. He said he wanted to get things back on track, and that the president was close to bringing on new lawyers.

After the meeting, Jim found himself in the vestibule outside the Elm conference room with Sekulow. He wore a dark suit and circular tortoise-shell glasses. Fox News played in the background on a wall-mounted TV. Sekulow was waiting for the all-clear from our security chief, Ben Cohen, that his car had arrived in the loading dock so he could leave without being filmed by the CNN crew outside.

"We are talking to people with high stature to take over the representation," Sekulow said. "Just finalizing everything now."

"Good," Jim said.

"You know them, actually. I think you've worked with them in the past. They are like-minded people who share our desire to get to the goal line."

Jim was keeping Sekulow company as a courtesy, and he didn't press him on who this might be.

Sekulow continued, "There's a third person too, but I'm hopeful he won't join." He did not divulge this person's identity. Just then, Cohen came in to say the car was downstairs. Sekulow said goodbye and left the room.

A few days later, Sekulow called Jim to talk about Trump's incoming team. "The two you know are Jane and Marty Raskin," he revealed.

Jim smiled. The Raskins were a husband-and-wife defense team who had a sterling reputation—and Jim knew and liked them. In fact, Jim and Jane Raskin had worked at the same firm for several years in the 1980s. He was a little surprised they would take this assignment, but he also knew that they were excellent lawyers whom we could deal with professionally. "That's great. It'll be nice to see them. It's been a while."

Sekulow then said, "And the third person is, well, America's Mayor."

Jim thought for a brief moment. "Rudy?"

"That's correct," Sekulow said. "Rudy Giuliani is coming on too."

Twelve

AMERICA'S MAYOR

Bob attended only one meeting with Rudy Giuliani, President Trump's newest personal lawyer.

The meeting took place on April 24, 2018, in the windowless Elm conference room at Patriots Plaza, with its drop-paneled ceiling, mismatched office chairs, and audibly buzzing fluorescent lights.

Sekulow had requested the meeting to introduce us to Giuliani and the Raskins. We came to the meeting with one goal in mind—for the president's new legal team to agree to an interview. We met with Bob in advance and confirmed that if the president's lawyers hedged on an interview or tried to throw up roadblocks, Bob would repeat that an interview was necessary for us to complete our investigation. If that didn't work, Bob would raise the issue of a subpoena.

At 4:00 p.m. sharp, we walked into Elm. Giuliani, Sekulow, and Jane and Marty Raskin were already there. Giuliani wore a black suit with pinstripes and flashed a large, diamond-encrusted New York Yankees World Series ring on his left ring finger. He chatted with Sekulow while the Raskins stood slightly off to the side.

Bob shook everyone's hand and then we sat, Bob in the middle of one side of the long table, Giuliani directly opposite him. Right before starting,

Bob looked at Giuliani, and then at the others, and said, "Our ability to work well together depends on having what we say in this room stay in this room."

Giuliani immediately agreed. "We have great respect for the work you've been doing," he said. "And you've been doing it in secrecy and in a professional way." He then said: "We want to resolve this and come to an agreement soon on an interview. We want to get this done."

Sekulow added, "World leaders raise the investigation with the president and even ask him if he's still going to *be* president. We have to get this behind him." We had heard a version of this comment in nearly every meeting with the president's lawyers—how our investigation was burdening the president and affecting his ability to conduct foreign affairs.

Bob responded: "We recognize how important it is for the president to be able to do his work, and we also understand the impact on others who get drawn into the ambit of an investigation. With that in mind, we have moved as swiftly as possible. And we've had no leaks."

Giuliani returned to the subject of an interview. He said that in a "normal case," they would give an "attorney proffer" before agreeing to an interview, in which they—as the president's lawyers—would tell us what the president would say if asked about certain topics.

Bob cut off Giuliani: "That would not be sufficient. We need to hear from him directly."

Marty Raskin interjected, "Can an interview be done in writing, like Reagan did?"

We knew what he meant: Reagan had answered written questions during the Iran-Contra investigation, which had been conducted by an independent counsel, Lawrence Walsh. But we also knew Reagan gave two in-person interviews to the Tower Commission, led by a former US senator, John Tower, as part of its investigation of the Iran-Contra affair. We had done research on every president over the previous fifty years who had been subject to an investigation similar to ours; each had agreed to an in-person interview at some point during his presidency.

Bob answered, "No. We need to be able to evaluate his testimony and ask follow-up questions."

Jane Raskin then spoke. Unlike Giuliani or Sekulow, Jane had spent the bulk of her career as a criminal defense lawyer. She had a reputation for being quick, direct, and no-nonsense. "If you can't make a decision about the president with all the evidence you already have, then why would we bring him in?" she asked. "How would that be in the president's interest?"

We understood what Jane meant: in a normal case, if a prosecutor doesn't have sufficient evidence to prove a client committed a crime, it can be dangerous for a defense attorney to agree to an interview in which the client could potentially incriminate himself. But this was not a normal case. Among other things, as we told the president's lawyers on multiple occasions, the president—who has a responsibility under Article II, Section 3 of the Constitution to "take Care that the Laws be faithfully executed"—has a special obligation to testify and complete the record of events.

Jane's question was enough for Bob. In a matter of minutes, they had gone from "we want to get this done" to sounding like they might not agree to an interview at all. "We feel strongly about the need for his testimony," Bob responded. "We'll take whatever route is necessary, including a subpoena, to finish up our work."

"We'd rather you not," Giuliani said. Bob's mention of a subpoena appeared to have a similar impact as it had with Dowd back in March. Giuliani backtracked a little, saying they were still open to an interview, but wanted it to be "the final interview of the investigation," and that a decision on the president's conduct should come soon afterward. He said, "It is not in our interest to delay. We want to figure it out, and to do it quietly."

Bob replied: "'Quietly' is our mantra."

Giuliani asked how long an interview would take, saying it should be limited to two and a half hours. Bob countered with six. Sekulow said, "Six is not reasonable. Bill Clinton's interview was four hours."

Andrew responded that that situation had been different. "The Bill

Clinton interview was essentially about a single topic; what we are looking at is considerably broader."

Giuliani ended the back-and-forth by saying that length should not be a sticking point, "But we'd need to take a lot of breaks."

Giuliani moved to a new topic, one we had also prepared for: whether we had the authority to indict the president, if such an extraordinary step were warranted. He asked, "Do you plan to follow the regulations? Because I don't think you can indict the president." He pulled a piece of paper from a folder he had brought with him and quoted from the DOJ's Office of Legal Counsel (OLC) opinion stating that a sitting president cannot be indicted.*

We had spent substantial time scrutinizing this same OLC opinion, and we'd assumed Trump's team would raise it at some point. The opinion had been written in 2000, at the end of the Clinton-Lewinsky-Whitewater scandal. It concluded that indicting a sitting president would impermissibly interfere with the president's ability to carry out his Article II duties as assigned by the Constitution. This opinion had been preceded by a similar one written by the OLC in 1973, during the Watergate scandal. This earlier version had reached the same conclusion.

However, while the OLC opinion made it clear that a sitting president could not be indicted while in office, it also stated that he could be investigated during his presidency and could be indicted when he is no longer president. In effect, the opinion concludes that a sitting president is granted a period of temporary immunity from prosecution, which lasts only as long as he remains in office. After he leaves office—whether by the natural expiration of a term, resignation, or impeachment—the OLC opinion states that the period of immunity ends.

We'd had two decisions to make regarding the OLC opinion: First, would we adhere to it? And second, if the answer was yes, would we tell the president's lawyers or keep it close to the vest?

---

* *A Sitting President's Amenability to Indictment and Criminal Prosecution*, Memorandum Opinion for the Attorney General, Office of Legal Counsel, October 16, 2000.

As to the first question, the special counsel regulations required us to "comply with the rules, regulations, procedures, practices and policies of the Department of Justice." Regardless of whether we agreed with the OLC opinion (some in the SCO thought its reasoning was flawed), it would have been difficult to argue that it was not a policy or practice of the DOJ. The department had twice taken the position, in writing, that a sitting president could not be indicted. Accordingly, we could not simply ignore the OLC opinion; under the regulations governing Bob's appointment, we had to follow it.

However, if extraordinary circumstances arose, then we could ask the department to revisit the opinion. If we did so, we would still be following the regulations. For example, if we had evidence proving Trump truly was a Manchurian candidate, a puppet who was being directed by Russia in a way that was an immediate and ongoing threat, then the public interest in an indictment might be so great as to warrant pushing the department to revisit the OLC opinion and authorize an indictment in order to safeguard the nation.

The second question was what to tell the president's legal team. If we told them that we planned to follow the opinion, that would take pressure off of Trump and likely would decrease our leverage. It might make him less likely to sit for an interview, and less likely to cooperate in other ways as well. Several of us in that room—Bob, Aaron, Andrew, Giuliani, and both Raskins—had been US attorneys or assistant US attorneys at one time or another. Prosecutors know how critical the prospect of a potential indictment is to getting subjects of an investigation to cooperate. It is indispensable in many of the most difficult and important cases. The fear of criminal charges often leads people to meet with prosecutors—either to admit to wrongdoing with the hope of obtaining leniency, or to give a firsthand account to persuade prosecutors of their innocence.

For all these reasons, we knew there could be a tactical advantage to keeping open the possibility of indictment when we spoke with the president's lawyers, despite our view that we needed to follow the OLC opinion. But if they asked the question squarely, there would be a cost to not being up-front about what we had already decided internally. We would not give the president or his legal team a legitimate reason to complain that we weren't following the department's policies and regulations. We also were trying to think ahead: if we ultimately decided to subpoena the president (we were confident that a president can be subpoenaed in a criminal matter even if he cannot be indicted), then we would need the department's support for any ensuing legal battle. Playing loose with DOJ regulations would not aid that effort.

As we considered the issues raised by the OLC opinion before our April 24 meeting, Bob raised an additional consideration: the harm to the presidency in having the potential of an indictment hanging over the president's head. Bob had served as FBI director for twelve years. No living person, including presidents, had been party to as many president's daily briefs as he had. He possessed a unique appreciation for what a president confronts day in and day out. Bob's position was that since we had decided to follow the OLC opinion—and we did not have evidence in hand that would compel us to ask the DOJ to revisit it—then we should not leave President Trump thinking we were *considering* indicting him. It was a matter of integrity for Bob, and also reflected his respect for the institution of the presidency itself.

So when Giuliani pointed to his copy of the OLC opinion, Bob answered, "We plan to follow the regulations."

Sekulow then asked a different question: "Do you believe you have the authority to indict the president?"

Bob kept that window slightly open. He responded, "We are well aware of the OLC opinion."

Giuliani leaned forward, placing both hands flat on the table, and asked the question again: "Do you actually think you have the authority to indict the president?"

Aaron said: "I think we can say the following: The OLC opinion states

DOJ's policy on this issue. The special counsel regulations require us to follow DOJ policy and procedure, and as Bob said, we are following the regulations." This answer made it clear that we were playing by the rules, but also left open the possibility of returning to the department to ask it to rethink the opinion if warranted.

Giuliani then asked how we viewed the president's status at that moment. Was Trump a witness, a subject, or a target of our investigation? These are terms of art for prosecutors. A witness is someone who knows something about events being investigated but whose own conduct is not under investigation. A subject is the broadest category—it covers anyone whose conduct is within the scope of the investigation. A target, under DOJ policy, is someone for whom there is "substantial evidence linking him or her to the commission of a crime and who, in the judgment of the prosecutor, is a putative defendant."

Bob answered that the president was a subject.

Giuliani asked, "Is he a subject regardless of the OLC opinion?" In other words, were we not labeling Trump a "target" simply because he couldn't be indicted? Or was he a subject because there was not enough evidence to make him a target?

Bob said that we had deliberately withheld making a judgment about the president's conduct, but we would get back to them if we could say more.

As the meeting ended, Bob repeated what he'd said at the opening: "I want to again stress the confidentiality of these discussions." Giuliani said he agreed and that they intended not to acknowledge that this meeting had taken place.

The next day, April 25, Jim and Andrew reached out to Sekulow and Jane Raskin. We clarified for them that we viewed the president as a subject regardless of the OLC opinion. Andrew then asked, "When will you get back to us about an interview?"

Sekulow said, "We are working twenty-hour days here. We're trying to have an answer for you in the next two weeks."

In the days that followed, there was another change in the legal team around the president that would affect our negotiations. Ty Cobb, who had emphasized the White House's cooperation with our investigation, was replaced by an established DC lawyer named Emmet Flood. Like Cobb, Flood represented the White House as an institution, not Trump personally. He was one of Washington's top defense lawyers and was known as a staunch defender of the powers and prerogatives of the presidency. He had represented Bill Clinton in his impeachment proceedings; George W. Bush in proceedings related to his firings of various US attorneys; and Vice President Dick Cheney in the DOJ's investigation into the leaking of the identity of a CIA officer.

On May 15, 2018, Flood came to the office to meet with us for the first time. We viewed Flood's involvement as an opportunity, believing he would not want us to subpoena the president under any circumstance. If he understood that a subpoena was a serious possibility, then he might use his leverage and experience within the White House to push the president and his counsel to agree to a voluntary interview.

The meeting started in Elm at 1:30 p.m. Flood sat in the same seat as Giuliani had on April 24, directly across from Bob. Aaron, Jim, and Andrew sat around the table. Flood began by saying he had been in his position for only a couple of weeks, but that it was a good time "to give you the flavor of my thinking on the matters at hand." Flood spoke in long, professorial soliloquies, often dropping in quotations from Supreme Court cases to make sure we knew he had done his homework. Two minutes into our meeting, the contrast between Flood's style and Cobb's—who was casual, informal, and direct—could not have been plainer.

Flood said that he was aware of our request to interview the president. He said that his view, on behalf of the White House and not Trump personally, was that "it would not be good for Article II to have the president be involved in any Article III proceedings." We understood what he meant: Article II of the Constitution lays out the powers of the presidency;

Article III lays out the powers of the federal courts. If we issued a grand jury subpoena to Trump and he challenged it, then the federal courts would have to resolve the matter—which meant the courts would be weighing in on critical aspects of executive power. Flood continued, "I'd expect an Article III judge to tread very gingerly here."

When Flood paused, Bob said, "We are toward the end of our investigation. We have been trying to have an ongoing and open dialogue with the White House and not to surprise you, just as we have had an open dialogue with the president's lawyers." Bob continued, saying, "The big issue at this juncture is an interview of the president. It is a critical last piece of the investigation and we have been in discussions about it for months. We have accommodated certain concerns of counsel, and it is now time for them to agree to an interview."

Flood responded in his deliberate style, saying he did not have a "settled view" on the issue, and that the decision to agree to an interview was principally a question for the president's personal counsel. He said his interest was in avoiding a subpoena, which should be an absolute "last resort." "If you did issue a subpoena," he intoned, "a court would ask: Has everything short of an interview been done?"

Bob said he appreciated the point, but the interest in avoiding a subpoena should go both ways: it would not be an issue if the president agreed to an interview, which was in the country's interest. Flood repeated that he was still getting up to speed and expected to share more of his thinking on these issues, likely in writing, in the coming weeks. With that, the meeting ended.

The next day, May 16, Giuliani spoke to multiple press outlets about our April 24 meeting—the same meeting that he had promised to keep confidential. He misstated several details.

The *New York Times* reported, "Mr. Trump's lead lawyer, Rudolph W. Giuliani, said the special counsel's office displayed uncertainty about whether Mr. Trump could be indicted." The *Times* then quoted Giuliani:

"'When I met with Mueller's team, they seemed to be in a little bit of confusion about whether they could indict,' Mr. Giuliani said. 'We said, "It's pretty clear that you have to follow DOJ policy."'" The article continued: "Mr. Giuliani said that one member of Mr. Mueller's office acknowledged that the president could not be indicted." Giuliani made similar comments to CBS News and CNN.

Bob decided he would never again meet or speak with Giuliani—and he never did. For Bob it was a matter of trust. Giuliani had promised that he would keep the meeting confidential. Then he broke this promise and broadcast inaccurate information.

Jim and Andrew called the Raskins and Sekulow to ask if they knew about or supported Giuliani's comments—we needed to know how far the breach of trust extended. They said they hadn't known in advance and apologized that it had happened. Jane asked that we give her the opportunity to show that she could be an "honest broker" in dealing with us. From that moment, Jim and Andrew endeavored to deal exclusively with the Raskins and Sekulow.

Aside from the breach of trust, we now knew that our decision to tell the president's lawyers that we viewed the OLC opinion as DOJ policy, and that the special counsel regulations required us to adhere to DOJ policy, would make it more difficult to secure a voluntary interview. Giuliani put it starkly when he told the *Times* that since we could not indict the president, we shouldn't have the power to subpoena him either. He told CNN, "Do you really need an interview? [. . .] You've got all the facts. You've got all the documents. You've got all the explanations. We're happy to tell you they're not going to change."

The April 24 meeting with Giuliani may have been a turning point in our negotiations over an interview. Some commentators criticized us for making a tactical error. The president's team now knew that an important piece of a prosecutor's leverage—the prospect of a criminal charge—had effectively been removed from the table. This may have been why Giuliani thought there would be little repercussion for his media appearances.

We believed Giuliani was wrong about our ability to issue a subpoena: while the OLC opinion prohibited an indictment of the president, it expressly authorized the ability to investigate the president while memories were fresh and documents were available. And we still hoped that the potential use of a subpoena could be an incentive for the president to agree to an interview.

Thirteen

THE RUSSIAN MILITARY INTELLIGENCE OPERATION

When Bob was first appointed, we knew that a core aspect of the SCO's work would be to investigate the Russian military intelligence operation to hack into the Democratic Party's computer networks, steal information, and then dump it publicly.

Some details of this hack-and-dump operation were already public. In June 2016, the Democratic National Committee (DNC) and the cybersecurity firm CrowdStrike publicly confirmed the Russian government's intrusion into networks at the DNC. Then, in October 2016, almost exactly a month before Election Day, the Office of the Director of National Intelligence and the Department of Homeland Security announced that the Russian government had been behind the whole thing.

Once Bob had been appointed, however, it became our job to figure out exactly what had transpired, who precisely had been involved, and whether criminal charges should be brought. As with active measures, *attribution* was central to our work.

Aspects of this operation appeared in our charges against George Papadopoulos, and other aspects would be used in the case we would eventually bring against Trump's longtime associate Roger Stone. While the cases against Papadopoulos, Stone, and the perpetrators of hack and dump were separate and charged as different offenses, we viewed them as essentially one case.

Hack and dump was a classic government intelligence operation run by Units 26165 and 74455 of the Main Intelligence Directorate of the General Staff (GRU) of Russia's military intelligence apparatus. Unit 26165 was responsible for hacking into Democratic networks, while Unit 74455, among other things, facilitated the dissemination of the hacked material. They used false-name online personas and the online organization WikiLeaks as conduits for dumping the data they had stolen.

The GRU amplified these data dumps with fake American personas, posting about them on social media and other outlets. One of Unit 74455's officers, the aptly named Aleksey Potemkin, managed computers the GRU used to access the accounts of these fake American personas. (The term "Potemkin village" originally referred to stories about fake villages erected in Crimea to impress the Russian empress Catherine the Great. It has come to mean an elaborate facade designed to hide an undesirable reality.)

When the SCO started, there were teams of FBI agents, as well as the US attorney's office for the Western District of Pennsylvania and the DOJ National Security Division, who were chiefly responsible for complementary aspects of hack and dump. One set of agents was looking into one of the GRU personas from Unit 74455 that was dumping stolen data, and another set of agents was investigating the hacking undertaken by Unit 26165.

The team investigating Unit 74455 visited us for a presentation in early 2018. It took place over a single morning and, by prosecutorial standards, was thin. The other team's work was further along—these agents had already uncovered a lot of evidence that told a clear story. We wanted to consolidate the entire case in our office and work it as a single conspiracy.

In February 2018, Aaron set up a series of meetings, one with the US attorney for the Western District of Pennsylvania, Scott Brady; another with the assistant attorney general at the Department of Justice's National

Security Division, John Demers; and the last with the head of the National Security Branch at the FBI, Carl Ghattas. Aaron made the same pitch to each of them: he summarized the hack-and-dump case and labeled it as one of the SCO's most important efforts, and he told them that all of the FBI's pertinent work ought to be brought together and charged as a single conspiracy undertaken by the GRU. He stated that the SCO could make the case in only two months. (Aaron shared Bob's commitment to speed but was being a bit aspirational—although not by much.)

These officials saw the logic of the argument and had no problem consolidating the work under Bob. Ghattas said he would make arrangements with the FBI, and some of its agents ended up working closely with us.* The DOJ seemed somewhat relieved that any matter concerning Russia and possible coordination with the Trump campaign was now in our hands—or, more precisely, out of theirs. As Bob had foreseen, it would be easier for him to take any possible flak for cases involving Russian election interference. With these steps, we now had the entire case in our office.

* * *

The GRU had started its operation in earnest on March 19, 2016, when it sent spearphishing emails to employees of the Clinton campaign, including its chairman, John Podesta. Spearphishing is a more targeted form of phishing, which is when hackers pretend to be something or someone they're not—a business, a government agency, a colleague—in order to dupe people into handing over sensitive information or downloading malware that allows the hackers to access accounts or networks remotely. In this case,

---

* The US Attorney's Office in the Western District of Pennsylvania (and Brady himself), kept moving on other GRU hacking cases. In October 2018, three months after our hack-and-dump indictment, a grand jury sitting in the Western District of Pennsylvania returned an indictment charging certain members of Unit 26165 with hacking the US Anti-Doping Agency, the World Anti-Doping Agency, and other international sports associations. See *United States v. Aleksei Sergeyevich Morenets*, no. 18-263 (W.D. Pa.).

the GRU sent an email with an embedded link to Podesta that appeared to be from Google security. Podesta clicked the link, which took him to a GRU-created website, where the Russians collected his password. They were subsequently able to steal around fifty thousand emails from his account.

The GRU continued sending spearphishing emails to other campaign and DNC employees throughout March and April. This enabled the GRU to gain access to dozens of computers across the DNC and another organization, the Democratic Congressional Campaign Committee (DCCC). Masking its agents' location in Russia by using virtual private networks (VPNs) it had leased in Malaysia and the United States, the GRU installed custom malware on the DNC and DCCC computers. (The GRU used Bitcoin, much of which we were able to trace, to pay for the VPNs and other expenses.) This malware, known as "X-Agent" and "X-Tunnel," enabled the hackers to record and view screens in real time, track keystrokes, and collect passwords and files, such as emails, internal communications, and opposition research, and then exfiltrate this data back to the GRU's network. Much of this stolen information would transit the VPNs and different servers the GRU had leased or compromised—intermediate stops generally known as "hop points"—before finally landing in the GRU's lap in Moscow.

While this hacking was underway, the GRU laid the groundwork for the dumping phase of the operation. On April 19, 2016, Unit 26165 registered DCLeaks.com through a service that anonymized the registrant. Once again, they paid using Bitcoin.

The timing was significant. One day earlier, on April 18, Josef Mifsud boarded a plane in England and flew to Moscow. He returned to London one week later and told George Papadopoulos that the Russians possessed "dirt" on Hillary Clinton in the form of "thousands of emails." Ten days later, Papadopoulos would say that he received indications of a Russian offer to help the Trump campaign via the anonymous release of information damaging to Hillary Clinton. At the time, hack and dump was still running as a secret Russian government operation, and it would be more than a full month before the GRU began dumping any of the stolen material.

The first dump occurred on June 8, 2016, on DCLeaks.com. This initial tranche of data didn't garner much attention.

On June 14, 2016, CrowdStrike, working under contract to investigate the hack for the DNC, publicly announced it had "identified two sophisticated adversaries on the network—COZY BEAR and FANCY BEAR." These were CrowdStrike's unofficial code names for Russian intelligence (or Russian intelligence–backed) hacking teams that had been active for years. CrowdStrike said that Cozy Bear began infiltrating Democratic servers in the summer of 2015, and that Fancy Bear had made their initial breach more recently in the early spring of 2016. Our work would eventually focus on Fancy Bear and confirm that they were part of the GRU.

The following day, starting at 4:19 p.m. Moscow time, members of Unit 74455 logged into a Moscow-based server to search for a unique set of phrases in English. Perhaps making use of online translation tools to look for terms that made more sense in Russian, the GRU looked up "some hundred sheets," "some hundreds of sheets," "worldwide known," and "company's competence," as well as "think twice about," "dcleaks" and a favorite of conspiracists the world over, "illuminati."

A little under three hours later, at 7:02 p.m. Moscow time, a supposed lone "Romanian" hacker calling themselves Guccifer 2.0 published their first blog post on a WordPress site they had just created. The post included the unusual phrases the GRU had searched for. It read (bold emphasis added):

> **Worldwide known** cyber security company CrowdStrike announced that the Democratic National Committee (DNC) servers had been hacked by "sophisticated" hacker groups. I'm very pleased the company appreciated my skills so

highly))) . . . Here are just a few docs from many thousands I extracted when hacking into DNC's network. . . . **Some hundred sheets!** This's a serious case, isn't it? . . . I guess CrowdStrike customers should think twice about **company's competence.** Fuck the **Illuminati** and their conspiracies!!!!!!!!! Fuck CrowdStrike!!!!!!!!!

It wasn't only the use of these phrases that we relied on, though. By matching material we knew had been stolen by the GRU to some of the documents Guccifer 2.0 released that day, we concluded that Guccifer 2.0 was, in fact, the GRU—not some nonexistent Romanian hacker.

Following this, the GRU intensified its attacks through the dumping of the stolen material.

On June 22, seven days after Guccifer 2.0 was introduced to the world, WikiLeaks used Twitter to direct message, or "DM," Guccifer 2.0, suggesting that the hacker "send any new material [stolen from the DNC] here for us to review and it will have a much higher impact than what you are doing."

On July 14, the GRU used Guccifer 2.0 to email WikiLeaks an approximately one-gigabyte archive. The GRU used the Guccifer 2.0 Twitter account to send WikiLeaks instructions for how to open the archive. Then, on July 22, three days before the start of the Democratic National Convention in Philadelphia, WikiLeaks released over twenty thousand emails and other documents stolen from the DNC. Some of these documents appeared to show that Democratic Party officials favored candidate Clinton over Bernie Sanders, another candidate vying for the Democratic nomination. (Days later, Debbie Wasserman Schultz, the chair of the DNC, resigned in the fallout.)

On July 27, 2016, during a wide-ranging press conference at the Trump National Doral Miami hotel, candidate Trump responded to a question about Putin and Russia: "I have nothing to do with Putin.

I've never spoken to him. I don't know anything about him other than he will respect me." Trump also addressed the DNC hacks: "And if it is Russia—which it's probably not, nobody knows who it is—but if it is Russia, it's really bad for a different reason, because it shows how little respect they have for our country, when they would hack into a major party and get everything."

He ended his comments with what sounded like a message: "But it would be interesting to see—I will tell you this—Russia, if you're listening, I hope you're able to find the thirty thousand emails that are missing. I think you will probably be rewarded mightily by our press. Let's see if that happens." The "thirty thousand emails" was an apparent reference to government emails that had been stored on Clinton's private server and which had been a part of an FBI investigation publicly described by Comey earlier that month (July 2016).

About five hours after Trump's message, and for the *first time*, GRU Unit 26165 sent spearphishing emails to addresses in Clinton's personal office. While the evidence available to us did not establish a knowing conspiracy between the Russian government and the Trump campaign, this was an example of a kind of "call-and-response," whereby a person—in this case, Trump himself—calls for an action from another party, and that party responds. This was a remarkable sequence of events, but our job was to determine whether these actions were criminal. We considered whether the call-and-response between Trump and the GRU constituted illegal coordination. We concluded that it did not. Bob determined (and our report would reflect) that we would use standard criminal law, which required an actual agreement, either tacit or explicit, between two parties to amount to a criminal conspiracy. In other words, a criminal charge would require more than the two parties taking actions that were informed by or responsive to the other's actions or interests.

We would also gather evidence that showed how the Trump campaign had built a strategy around using the stolen materials. After he started cooperating, Rick Gates, Manafort's deputy, told us that by the late summer of 2016 the campaign was planning press strategy and messaging around dumps by WikiLeaks of Democratic information stolen by the GRU. By then, it was already being publicly reported that WikiLeaks was peddling material that had been stolen by Russian intelligence.

During the campaign, Roger Stone bragged publicly that he knew ahead of time about WikiLeaks' dumps of stolen materials. He had left the Trump campaign in August 2015, but he remained close to the team and to Trump in particular. In June and July 2016, before the Democratic national convention, Stone told the campaign that he had information indicating WikiLeaks possessed documents that would hurt Clinton. In July and August, Stone claimed to have heard via an intermediary from Julian Assange, the founder of WikiLeaks, that his organization was planning to conduct a "very damaging" dump against Clinton on or about October 2, 2016.

In early August 2016, Stone stated publicly, "I actually have communicated with Assange. I believe the next tranche of his documents pertain to the Clinton Foundation, but there's no telling what the October surprise may be." WikiLeaks denied any communication, and Stone later revised his story, saying he had learned information about WikiLeaks' plans through an intermediary. Perhaps most notably, on August 21 (before any of Podesta's emails had been dumped), Stone tweeted, "Trust me, it will soon the [*sic*] Podesta's time in the barrel. #CrookedHillary."

Stone's tweet seemed to predict one event that happened on October 7, 2016. In fact, three "October surprises" occurred that day.

First, the *Access Hollywood* video became public. Recorded in 2005, this video featured audio of Trump saying that because he was famous, he could grab women by their genitalia and get away with it.

Second, less than one hour after the *Access Hollywood* video came out, WikiLeaks dropped a large batch of Podesta's emails—the first release of emails from his account. Until that time, the public didn't know that the

GRU possessed his messages. This is what Stone seemed to be referring to in his August 21 tweet.*

Third, the Office of the Director of National Security and the Department of Homeland Security issued a joint statement saying that US intelligence was confident the Russians were responsible for the hack-and-dump operation. They said that disclosures by DCLeaks, Guccifer 2.0, and WikiLeaks were "consistent [with] the methods and motivations of Russian-directed efforts."† (Our office was able to take this intelligence assessment several steps further and collect evidence that could be used in court to prove the GRU had been behind these activities.)

Less than a week later, on October 12, WikiLeaks used Twitter to DM Donald Trump Jr., saying that it was "great to see you and your dad talking about our publications. Strongly suggest your dad tweets this link if he mentions us" and then provided a weblink. WikiLeaks explained to Trump Jr. that the link would help the campaign in "digging through" Podesta's emails. Two days later, Trump Jr. tweeted out the link.

Team R pulled together the evidence about the GRU's hack-and-dump scheme to prepare an indictment. Team R relied on computer scientists, cyber agents, and analysts from the FBI, many of whom set up in our office at Patriots Plaza to spend hours upon hours poring over data. While we were aware of intelligence insights about these activities, we charged the case using standard law enforcement tools: subpoenas, d orders, and search warrants.

For example, we used old-school techniques to trace the Bitcoin payments and data dumps back to the GRU. Bitcoin payments are basically

---

* Between October 7 and running a full month to the eve of the election, the GRU used WikiLeaks and other means to release roughly thirty-three tranches of documents stolen from Podesta's email account.

† *Joint Statement from the Department of Homeland Security and Office of the Director of National Intelligence on Election Security*, DHS Press Office, October 7, 2016.

anonymous, hidden behind strings of characters and code. However, all Bitcoin activity is logged on a public ledger known as a blockchain. In essence, the payment itself is public, but neither the payer nor the payee is identified.

However, there are labor-intensive ways to figure out who paid whom, for what, and when. We knew the GRU made extensive use of burner email accounts for Bitcoin transactions. For example, an email account with the username "gfadel47" received hundreds of Bitcoin payment requests from around one hundred different email accounts. On or about February 1, 2016, gfadel47 received an email that read, "Please send exactly 0.026043 bitcoin to" a specific Bitcoin address—an amount that was equivalent to about ten dollars at the time. A short while later, a transaction matching these exact instructions was added to the blockchain in a way we could now attribute to the GRU.

We used similar techniques to match files dumped by WikiLeaks, DCLeaks, and Guccifer 2.0 to files stolen by the GRU. We were able to see evidence of some data transfers between Guccifer 2.0 and WikiLeaks, but not all. Some of the files had distinct features that we could look at after WikiLeaks dumped them. By looking at these files, we could confirm that the data dumped was a match for data that we could prove had been stolen by Unit 26165 at the GRU.

Team R's indictment charged members of GRU Units 74455 and 26165, twelve Russian citizens in all. The charging theory was straightforward. The GRU defendants had engaged in a hacking conspiracy that violated the Computer Fraud and Abuse Act. We also charged several counts of aggravated identity theft, because the GRU sometimes used stolen identities to facilitate its hacking conspiracy. And we charged a money-laundering conspiracy, because the GRU executed financial transactions—primarily using Bitcoin—to carry out its activities.

As we wrapped up our work on hack and dump, we looked closely at whether the evidence we possessed showed that Stone had joined the overall conspiracy or had been an "accessory after the fact." Ultimately, we concluded that the evidence was insufficient to establish either. (Stone would eventually be charged at the beginning of 2019—and subsequently tried and found guilty—for making false statements to Congress about his activities in and around the WikiLeaks dumps.)

In early July 2018, the week before Team R presented the indictment to the grand jury, Aaron quietly met with senior State Department officials to alert them to the coming charges. The State Department informed its ambassador in Moscow, Jon Huntsman, that Russian intelligence officers would soon be charged by the SCO. Huntsman and the embassy had to be prepared for the Russians to retaliate.

The indictment was announced on Friday, July 13, 2018. Three days later, on July 16, President Trump was in Helsinki, Finland, for his first official summit with Vladimir Putin. Following a two-hour private meeting, the two leaders took to a stage, each at his own podium, and answered questions from a large pool of reporters from all over the world.

We watched the press conference from inside the SCO. It covered many topics. Putin flatly denied Russian election interference in the 2016 campaign, and President Trump appeared to take Putin's word over the hard evidence marshalled by Trump's own Department of Justice. Putin didn't answer directly when asked about the indictment of the twelve GRU officers and whether the Russians would be willing to extradite them so they could face charges in a US court. Instead, he said he would be willing to allow the SCO, including "Mr. Mueller," to travel to Moscow in order to observe the Russian authorities "interrogate . . . these individuals who [the special counsel] believes are privy to some crimes."

It was a ridiculous offer that would have been dangerous to accept. Putin knew that none of us were about to travel to Russia for any reason, let alone to observe staged interviews.

Later in the press conference, Trump was asked whether he believed Putin's denial of Russia's role in the hacking operation. Trump responded,

"He just said it's not Russia. I will say this: I don't see any reason why it would be."

In two sentences, the president had gutted what we thought was a critical message for Americans to hear. Three days earlier, our indictment had laid out, with detailed, courtroom-ready evidence, that Russian military intelligence had executed the hack-and-dump operation to interfere in the 2016 election.

The facts no longer seemed to matter.

Fourteen

SUBPOENA THE PRESIDENT?

"We're not yet at an impasse on a voluntary interview of the president, but we are seriously considering a subpoena," Aaron said in a meeting at Main Justice on May 4, 2018. He was updating Scott Schools and Ed O'Callaghan, Rosenstein's new principal deputy who had only been on the job for about a month. O'Callaghan was an imposing figure, standing well over six feet tall with a thick black beard, but he spoke with a smile and a disarming Brooklyn accent. Aaron had known O'Callaghan for nearly two decades, going back to Aaron's FBI days in the New York Field Office and O'Callaghan's time as an assistant US attorney at the SDNY. He brought long and valuable experience to his new post.

The May 4 meeting was the opening to what would be a four-month-long back-and-forth with Main Justice about the extraordinary step of issuing a grand jury subpoena for President Trump's testimony. Over the course of the investigation, we issued more than 2,800 grand jury subpoenas. But a subpoena for the president's testimony would be different. The only other time a sitting president had been subpoenaed to appear before a grand jury was when Bill Clinton had been subpoenaed by Ken Starr. But that was under a different statute, where Starr, as an independent counsel, had full authority to exercise the powers of the

Department of Justice and the attorney general, including the authority to appeal.

As a special counsel, Bob did not have that authority. The independent counsel statute lapsed in 1999 after the Starr investigation and was not reinstated. The special counsel regulations replaced that regime with the intention of bringing the role of a special prosecutor under the attorney general. The rules governing a special counsel provided that the DOJ, not the special counsel, would determine which cases it would take to, and arguments it would make in, the US Courts of Appeals and ultimately the Supreme Court. As a result, we could not effectively enforce a subpoena for President Trump without Rosenstein agreeing that the department would authorize appeals to do so. The bottom line was that the attorney general—not Bob—would ultimately determine the positions we could take if there were a legal battle over the subpoena. (This was not the case for Starr. Starr could decide on his own what positions to take on appeal. The difference in appellate authority was so stark that the independent counsel statute specified that the attorney general could present briefs *in opposition* to the independent counsel's arguments.)

The main reason for our May 4 meeting with the DOJ was to place a marker that we may need their support for our legal positions. By this time, we had told the president's lawyers—Dowd, Sekulow, Giuliani, and the Raskins—that a subpoena might be necessary. We understood that both the president's lawyers and the White House lawyers were almost certainly reporting our conversations to the DOJ to try to persuade Rosenstein not to support our issuance of a subpoena.

The story of our back-and-forth with the DOJ over a subpoena has never been told. Each year in our UVA Law School class, the question that sparks the most interest is "Should we have subpoenaed the president?" When that question is the final exam, we get great papers, and they usually break down roughly 50 percent in favor and 50 percent opposed.

*   *   *

If we ever were able to interview the president, we had two buckets of questions we wanted to put to him.

The first concerned Russia-related issues before he had taken office in January 2017. These questions concerned, for example: Roger Stone's apparent foreknowledge of WikiLeaks' impending dumps of Democratic data stolen by Russian military intelligence; the details surrounding the Trump Tower meeting; and the nature of other contacts between members of the Trump campaign and various Russians or their proxies. Since these matters covered a time period *before* Trump was in office, we believed we were on firm footing. A subpoena would still be unprecedented, but these matters would not be subject to any claims of executive privilege for the simple reason that Trump was at that time a private citizen, albeit one running for the presidency.

The second bucket concerned events *during* Trump's presidency involving efforts to interfere with the Russia investigation—that is, questions about potential obstruction of justice. These questions concerned, for example, Trump's request to FBI Director Jim Comey that he let go of the Flynn investigation, Trump's decision to fire Comey, and Trump's meeting with senior Russian officials in the Oval Office the following day. It was in this meeting that Trump stated, "I faced great pressure because of Russia. That's taken off. . . . I'm not under investigation." Did he fire Comey to relieve the "great pressure" of the FBI's investigation? And did Trump later direct McGahn to have Bob removed, and then try to get McGahn to create a false record denying it had happened?

The questions in this second bucket raised two main legal issues: whether executive privilege would bar us from asking Trump about his actions while he was in the White House, and whether the obstruction-of-justice statutes could apply to the conduct we were investigating.

Broadly speaking, executive privilege protects the president's communications with his advisers, as well as those advisers' communications when they are gathering information to assist the president. If a president and his advisers had to worry that everything they said would be subject to outside scrutiny, then the president may not receive full and frank advice.

However, two prominent court cases had delineated certain limits on executive privilege.

The first, *United States v. Nixon*, established that executive privilege is not absolute. In 1974, the Supreme Court unanimously held that "neither the doctrine of the separation of powers nor the need for high-level communications . . . can sustain an absolute, unqualified Presidential privilege of immunity from judicial process under all circumstances."

The second, a 1998 opinion by the DC Court of Appeals (one step below the Supreme Court), was in a case that became known as *Espy*. It involved a grand jury subpoena for White House documents pertaining to the former secretary of agriculture Mike Espy. In short, the *Espy* case held that a grand jury subpoena can overcome a claim of executive privilege if it seeks important evidence that is not practically available from another source.*

Bob addressed this very issue in a May 16, 2018, letter to Jane and Marty Raskin, explaining once again why we wanted the president's testimony. Using language that tracked the *Espy* decision, Bob wrote: "Hearing the president's firsthand account is critical. His knowledge and intentions play a central role in resolving important issues, and his personal recollections and understandings are not available from another source." Bob also stated the clear public interest: "We also believe it is in the interest of the presidency and the public for an interview to take place. It would complete the record of events in ways that other investigation cannot."

---

* The *Espy* case was investigated by an independent counsel, Donald C. Smaltz. Smaltz issued a grand jury subpoena to the White House in October 1994. Espy was indicted on thirty criminal charges in August 1997; sixteen months later, in December 1998, a jury acquitted him on all charges. (Our arrangement with the White House avoided the issue of executive privilege for its production of documents to us. We agreed the documents would not leave the executive branch absent further discussion with the White House.)

We were confident in our position on the issue of executive privilege and *Espy*, and the department never seriously questioned this. However, the road through the courts on this issue likely would not have been easy. For example, the subpoena in the *Espy* case, which was for White House documents and not the president's testimony, took nearly three years to litigate—and never even reached the Supreme Court.

In addition to claims of executive privilege, our obstruction-of-justice inquiry raised both statutory and constitutional issues that were subject to much debate. Not just internally at the SCO, but also within the Department of Justice. The debate was over the scope of the statute that covers obstruction of justice.

The statute, 18 USC § 1512(c), states:

(c) Whoever corruptly—

(1) alters, destroys, mutilates, or conceals a record, document, or other object, or attempts to do so, with the intent to impair the object's integrity or availability for use in an official proceeding; or

(2) otherwise obstructs, influences, or impedes any official proceeding, or attempts to do so,

shall be fined under this title or imprisoned not more than 20 years, or both.

Paragraph 1 applies to obstruction involving a document or object, and paragraph 2 refers to acts that "otherwise" obstruct a proceeding. One of the most basic kinds of obstruction is destroying evidence—such as shredding files—but obstruction can also involve creating false documentary evidence. We believed one of the episodes of potential obstruction that we were investigating—Trump's attempt to get McGahn to create a record stating the president had *not* instructed him to ask Rosenstein to remove Bob—fell squarely within the statute because McGahn had been pressured to create a false document. This also could have constituted witness tampering, another form of obstruction.

But unlike that episode, most of the president's other potentially obstructive acts—such as firing Comey or pressing Comey to "let[] Flynn go"—did *not* involve documents or a witness changing his testimony. We concluded that those other actions by Trump could potentially fall under 1512(c)(2), which prohibits corrupt actions that "otherwise" obstruct, influence, or impede an official proceeding. The "official proceeding" in this case would be the grand jury's investigation of Russian election interference.

As we engaged with both the president's counsel and the department about a potential subpoena, there were two disputes about whether section 1512(c) applied to the president's conduct. The first was whether the president had been exercising his Article II presidential powers such that he should not be subject to legal examination or prosecution. For example, the president has the power to appoint and dismiss officials in the executive branch, including the director of the FBI. He also has the power to start, control, and end federal criminal prosecutions. The president's lawyers argued that it was improper for us to ask questions about why he fired Comey, or why he told Comey to have the FBI "let[] go" of its investigation of Michael Flynn, because taking these actions was within his official powers granted by the Constitution. In short, they argued he was immune from prosecution for these actions.

The second dispute was about the scope of the obstruction statute. The president's lawyers argued that section 1512(c) was limited to actions that impaired the availability of evidence in an official proceeding, such as destroying documents or influencing witnesses—and accordingly could not apply to actions like the firing of Comey or an attempt to remove the special counsel.

After extensive research and analysis into both of these issues by our legal team, we concluded that section 1512(c) could apply to certain of the president's official actions if they had been taken for what the statute calls a "corrupt" purpose. We reasoned that Congress has the authority to prohibit a president's *corrupt* use of his authority against an official proceeding. A rule against "corrupt" action would not, by our measure, impermissibly undermine the president's ability to carry out his duties. It would also protect the integrity of the administration of justice.

We also concluded that the statute was not limited solely to the impairment of evidence such as document destruction or witness tampering. For example, if the president acted with a corrupt purpose when telling Comey to let Flynn go—such as to protect himself from being implicated in a crime—that could amount to an obstruction offense, in our view, even though it did not involve a document or an attempt to influence a witness. We described this legal analysis in detail in our report.

We didn't know it at the time, but just as we were starting our subpoena discussion with the DOJ, another person weighed in with the department on these very issues.

On June 8, 2018, the once-and-future attorney general, William Barr,[*] submitted a nineteen-page memo to Rosenstein and Assistant Attorney General Steven Engel, who was then head of the DOJ's Office of Legal Counsel. In his memo, Barr argued that section 1512 did not apply to President Trump in the manner Barr imagined we might be seeking to apply it. We say "imagined" because Barr had no actual insight into our work, so far as we knew.

Given that Barr was a private citizen at that time, his memo was remarkably timely. It posited (fairly accurately) that we were then "demanding that the President submit to interrogation about [obstruction] incidents, using the threat of subpoenas to coerce his submission." Barr's bottom line was that a prosecutor, even a special counsel, should

---

[*] Barr served as attorney general from 1991 to 1993 under President George H. W. Bush and would serve again under President Trump starting in early 2019.

not be allowed to require an examination of the president regarding these incidents, end of story.

According to Barr, section 1512 prohibited only corrupt acts that impaired the integrity or availability of evidence, for instance, an act that destroyed a document or induced a witness to change his testimony. Barr's memo stated that a president's conduct can "obviously" be considered obstruction of justice in the "classic sense of sabotaging a proceeding's truth-finding function. Thus, for example, if a President knowingly . . . induces a witness to change testimony . . . then he, like anyone else, commits the act of obstruction."

But Barr maintained that the obstruction statute did *not* apply to what he termed the president's "facially-lawful" actions—such as firing an FBI director or ending a federal criminal prosecution—even if such an action were done with corrupt intent and impacted a grand jury proceeding. In other words, even if Trump fired Comey for a corrupt purpose, that could not be a crime, in Barr's view.

We wouldn't become aware of Barr's memo until December 2018, the day before his Senate confirmation hearing for attorney general. Nevertheless, his memo seemed to capture the fundamental issues Rosenstein and the department would raise throughout that summer when it came to subpoenaing the president. Barr may have previewed the department's position when he wrote: "It is inconceivable to me that the Department could accept Mueller's interpretation of 1512(c)(2). It is untenable as a matter of law and cannot provide a legitimate basis for interrogating the President."

As it turned out, five years after our office closed, the Supreme Court issued two rulings that agreed in large part with Barr's interpretation. In a case called *Fischer v. United States*, a defendant convicted for his role in the January 6, 2021, assault on Congress challenged the scope of the same obstruction-of-justice statute that was at issue in our investigation, section 1512(c)(2). In late June 2024, the Supreme Court ruled by a vote of 6–3 that section 1512(c)(2) prohibits only acts that impair the availability or integrity of documents, records, objects, or other things used in an official proceeding. A few days later, on July 1, 2024, the Supreme Court issued an opinion in *Trump v. United States*, which addressed Special Counsel Jack Smith's prosecution of Trump for his role in the January 6 assault on Congress. The Supreme Court held, also by a vote of 6–3, that presidents have complete immunity when they exercise their "core constitutional powers," and have "presumptive immunity" for all of their "official" acts.

The full meaning and implications of these cases may take years to develop. But both rulings illustrate the difficulties we would have faced had we pursued a subpoena for Trump's testimony on obstruction topics all the way to the Supreme Court. The rulings also show why the DOJ may not want a special counsel to press theories of criminal liability that could result in adverse decisions. Indeed, when the DOJ takes cases to the Supreme Court, there is a risk that the Court will restrict rather than enhance the options available to prosecutors.

*   *   *

Bob's May 16 letter about the importance of an interview did not get an immediate response from Trump's lawyers. Instead, after a series of emails, calls, and meetings during the ensuing weeks, the Raskins told us that they would agree to an interview on preelection Russia-related topics only. There could be no questions on obstruction. Bob rejected this proposal.

By the end of June, it was becoming clear that a subpoena might be the only way to secure the president's testimony on obstruction. Aaron called Schools at the DOJ and relayed the president's latest position. Aaron explained that "evidence from the president is likely to be of significant value to our evaluation of the issues."

Schools did not immediately respond, so Aaron continued: "If we can't negotiate a resolution, we'd like to point to a subpoena as our next step." Aaron told Schools we wanted the department to agree to enforce a subpoena in the courts, including the Supreme Court if it came to that. "We have written materials that go through the evidence and our analysis" as to why a subpoena was necessary and appropriate, Aaron said.

Schools responded in his muted southern drawl, "Think we'll want to see those."

Four days later, on July 3, we delivered to Schools and O'Callaghan a memo, "Preliminary Assessment of Obstruction Evidence," with a set of supporting documents. The takeaway was on page 1: the president had refused an interview; we had gathered significant evidence on obstruction and had determined that the law enabled us to compel the president's testimony; and, finally, "we have concluded that the issuance of a subpoena is justified." There was no immediate response from the department. (On July 6, 2018, after a decades-long career at the Department of Justice, Schools left to take a job in the private sector.)

During the rest of July and into August, the Raskins raised new arguments against our obstruction inquiry. For example, they maintained that the president could not have obstructed justice if there had been no underlying crime, claiming that questions about obstruction were inappropriate without proof that there had been "unlawful collusion between Russia and individuals associated with the 2016 campaign." As we told the Raskins, and as they must have been aware, this was wrong as a matter of law. Obstruction is its own crime and requires no underlying offense.

On August 8, the Raskins backtracked further: they would only consider a list of specific written questions on Russia-related topics—and no interview. Bob rejected this as well.

That same day, Emmet Flood from the White House joined the fray. He sent us a letter and cc'd O'Callaghan at the DOJ. Flood was adamant that we should not be permitted to ask any questions about the president's "mental processes or purposes for taking official action." He urged us to reach an agreement with the Raskins, and closed by saying that if we could not do so, then "I expect this office will have to obtain a definitive opinion of . . .

Acting Attorney General [Rosenstein] on some or all of the legal questions." In this single letter, Flood was aligning himself with the president's private lawyers and invoking the power of the Department of Justice (for which we worked) to overrule us. He also echoed the memo (that we had not yet seen) written by Barr, who would soon be nominated to be the attorney general overseeing our investigation.

On August 10, we returned to the DOJ. O'Callaghan asked how the president's obstructive conduct linked up with the Russia investigation. We responded that obstruction was its own offense; it did not require any linkage to an underlying crime. And in any event, links *did* exist, which we listed. Among them was Roger Stone's apparent advance knowledge of WikiLeaks' possession of the Clinton emails, and evidence that Stone had forecast to Trump when the first WikiLeaks release would occur. We told O'Callaghan that we were not saying these episodes demonstrated a Trump-Russia conspiracy, but that the evidence provided substantial motive for the president to interfere with our investigation.

Following this meeting, the department's position began to take shape. Their idea was to move in stages, starting with written questions. This did not track with any typical prosecutorial approach. Prosecutors always prefer in-person interviews so they can ask follow-up questions and evaluate credibility.

During a meeting with O'Callaghan on August 22, Aaron and Jim rejected the department's idea of starting with written questions. Aaron reiterated a core point—prosecutors do interviews. O'Callaghan again asked whether we could show a greater connection between Trump and Russian election interference. He ended the meeting by saying that Bob would need to meet with Rosenstein. This was the meeting between principals that was necessary to resolve the issue.

On August 28, Bob, Aaron, Jim, and Andrew went to Main Justice and met with Rosenstein, O'Callaghan, and Steven Engel (the head of OLC). The meeting took place in the DAG's conference room at 1:15 p.m.

That morning, we sent a memo to the department identifying links between our Russia investigation and the president's potentially obstructive acts; the memo also explained why a subpoena for the president's testimony on obstruction had support in the law and DOJ practice.

Bob opened the meeting: "We are at an impasse. We have decided a letter stating our intention to issue a subpoena is the way to go." The letter would tell the president's counsel that we would issue a subpoena absent a commitment to a voluntary interview. Bob then added, "We need his testimony on Russian interference, the core of our investigation, and on obstruction issues. His intent is a key obstruction question; we have no direct evidence on that."

Jim backed this up by summarizing the president's obstructive conduct that related to Russian contacts and interference. He mentioned a few specifics, among them Stone's forecasts to Trump about WikiLeaks dumping GRU-stolen emails. As he concluded, Jim said, "We are not saying any one of these is Russian collusion; we are saying the president has a Russia-related motive to obstruct our investigation."

We also raised the issue of timing, repeating our position that now was the moment to send the letter about a subpoena. If a subpoena were litigated to the Supreme Court, we knew it could take a year or more to be resolved. We wanted this clock to start as soon as possible, and written questions would only cause more delay.

Bob gave Rosenstein his bottom line: "We are pressing for a letter now that clearly states our intention to use a subpoena. This is the correct investigative step."

Rosenstein did not appear convinced. He asked again about going through stages, meaning written questions first. Bob shook his head. We should press for it all at once.

Engel questioned whether section 1512(c)(2) applied at all, and asked whether we needed an underlying offense or an inherently obstructive act (such as destroying a document). He also said that obstruction topics could trigger a subpoena fight, and it may be better to get at least some information through written questions.

Bob said he would consider this, but that any written responses would be over-lawyered and likely useless.

As we rode back to the SCO after the meeting, we were not optimistic that we had changed many minds.

We soon heard back from the DOJ. Their position was not a surprise given the tenor of the meeting. As a first step, they would support a subpoena for testimony about Russia and the campaign, but only after we first submitted written questions. At least for now, they would not support a subpoena or written questions about obstruction topics. We thought this was the wrong strategy for all of the reasons Bob had given Rosenstein. But we needed the DOJ to enforce a subpoena, and we saw no viable option but to go along.

The alternative was to move forward with a subpoena without the department's support. However, as things stood, the department would have ordered us not to proceed. Had we proceeded anyway, the department would have ordered us to withdraw it or prevented us from enforcing it in the courts.

So we drafted a letter for the president's team saying that we would pose written questions to the president, but only on the condition that they commit to a live follow-up interview. None of us as prosecutors had ever relied on written questions to obtain witness testimony, and we knew a follow-up interview would be necessary. Our letter specified that this was a package deal, and absent the president's agreement, "we will have no choice but to issue a grand jury subpoena." Because the department's support at this point was for Russia-related topics only, we said that we would forgo seeking answers about Trump's time in office until a later juncture.

We specified a timeline: if the president committed to a follow-up interview, we would send questions on September 7, and he needed to respond in writing by September 28. We sent the draft to the department to make sure they would be on board with a subpoena if the president's lawyers rejected the package deal. The timing was important: if a subpoena became necessary, we wanted to issue it well in advance of the midterm elections.

But the department struck the language requiring an up-front commitment to an interview in exchange for us starting with written questions. O'Callaghan called Aaron to discuss. Aaron immediately said: "There is no scenario under which we don't need an interview. The letter has to say that—that they are agreeing now to a package deal of written questions and an interview."

Aaron acknowledged that if by some miracle the written questions were answered fully, we could forgo an interview. He pointed to a section in the letter stating that our "current assessment" was that we needed to talk to the president in person. O'Callaghan paused, then agreed that the provision of written questions—with the language about our *current* assessment—gave the president's team some hope of avoiding an interview altogether.

With that, on August 31, O'Callaghan (and through him, the department) agreed to our letter. It closed with: "Unless we can reach agreement to proceed on this basis before September 7, *including agreeing on an in-person interview as described herein*, we will have no choice but to issue a grand jury subpoena in order to obtain your client's answers through testimony." (Emphasis added.) Later that day, the Friday of Labor Day weekend, we sent it to the Raskins.

We did not hear back until September 5. Early that afternoon, the Raskins emailed asking for our written questions, but without making any commitment to a follow-up interview. They stated: "Our differences with respect to future contingencies that may never come to pass ought not delay implementation of a reasonable written question and answer procedure."

Jim responded quickly: "You . . . describe[] an in-person interview of your client as a contingency that may not be necessary. . . . Accordingly, we intend to seek the information we have requested through a grand jury subpoena."

Jane Raskin then requested an immediate phone call. Jim and Andrew obliged. "Why are you so sure you'll need follow-up questions?" she asked.

Jim responded, "The flip answer is forty-six years of practicing law." Everyone on that call knew that no one ever answers interrogatories in such a way as to avoid having to give a subsequent deposition. For example, if someone says, "I don't remember," lawyers will want to probe that with follow-up questions. Jim added, "It's also clear that for many of our questions, there will be a need for follow-up regardless of the answer." We had drafted our questions to be as detailed as possible, but many of them would require an initial answer that inevitably would prompt one or more follow-up questions. Jim concluded: "You need to commit to an interview up front."

Jane answered, "We will speak to our client and get back to you expeditiously."

Two days later, in the late afternoon of Friday, September 7, Jane Raskin rejected our proposal, calling our demand for a follow-up interview "artificial" and "premature." We were particularly struck by her use of "premature"—we had been trying to secure an interview with President Trump for nearly a year. And she knew as well as we did that written answers would never be sufficient.

First thing Monday, we spoke with O'Callaghan. Our position had not changed. The president should commit to an interview, or we should serve a subpoena. If we did, we would still submit written questions in advance and, if they were answered to our satisfaction, then we would pull the subpoena.

The department rejected this. O'Callaghan said, "Get written answers and then we'll support a subpoena." This was not what we had agreed to. The DOJ had agreed that if the president did not commit to an interview now, it would support us serving a subpoena. But not anymore.

We walked into Bob's office to report the latest development. Sitting at his desk, he listened carefully and paused. We had lost the support of the Department of Justice on this issue. Bob had always questioned whether subpoenaing the president would have been worth a court fight that could last a year or more. While he still regarded talking to President Trump as an important investigative step, Bob thought that speaking with him would not get us evidence like the "smoking gun" Nixon tape, which Archibald Cox had subpoenaed and which contained the president's voice approving a plan to obstruct the FBI's Watergate investigation. And even if we did subpoena the president and the courts enforced it, President Trump could still assert his Fifth Amendment rights and refuse to answer our questions, as Dowd had suggested.

Bob decided: we would not subpoena the president now. We would wait at least until we received the president's written responses.

Seven days later, on September 17, we submitted seventy-eight questions to the president's lawyers. We would not receive answers for more than two months.

Fifteen

PARDONS ON THE TABLE

Much of a prosecutor's time is spent trying to get people to tell the truth. Sometimes prosecutors have to force the issue. Insiders who may be involved in a criminal conspiracy often hunker down and hope everyone else involved stays silent as well. As we've discussed, one way prosecutors can break through the silence is to bring criminal charges against an insider in a way that would encourage them to cooperate and tell the truth. The federal justice system grants benefits to cooperators for precisely this reason. A cooperator might get zero or little jail time, while others involved in a conspiracy can face years in prison. For these reasons, Bob would often refer to the criminal justice system as a generator of highly valuable intelligence.

In our investigation, we were trying to get the truth out of several people connected to the president who might have preferred to stay silent or beneath our radar. That's one reason we arrested George Papadopoulos when he flew into the United States from overseas. It's why Rick Gates's decision to cooperate was so important to our work. And by the spring of 2018, there were three other key insiders who we believed might possess significant information: Michael Cohen, Paul Manafort, and Roger Stone. We knew all three would need a strong incentive to cooperate, and we ultimately brought criminal charges against each. We did so first and foremost because they had engaged in criminal conduct. But we also wanted them to cooperate and tell the truth.

How the president responded to our investigations of these three individuals revealed an additional type of interference with which we had to contend, one involving the president's unique powers and public megaphone.

*　*　*

In the summer of 2017, not long after Bob had been appointed, we obtained bank records for an account in the name of "Essential Consultants LLC," a shell company created by Michael Cohen. Cohen had been a lawyer for the Trump Organization and someone the press had dubbed a loyal "fixer" for Trump before his presidency—someone who took care of problems for his boss.

The bank records revealed that the Essential Consultants account had been created late in the campaign, in October 2016, and that Cohen had used it to make a payment of $130,000 to the account of a lawyer who represented an adult film star and producer named Stephanie "Stormy Daniels" Clifford. The records also showed deposits from a Russian-backed entity—which was our basis for accessing the account in the first place. The bank records prompted all manner of questions: Why did Cohen create Essential Consultants at the end of the presidential campaign? What was behind the payment to Daniels's lawyer? Why was Cohen receiving money from an entity tied to Russia?

We soon determined that the $130,000 payment appeared to be so-called hush money, intended to prevent Daniels from telling anyone about a sexual encounter she allegedly had with Trump back in 2006. The timing of the payment from Cohen's Essential Consultants account was notable: it came mere days after the public airing of the *Access Hollywood* tape, in which Trump bragged about his ability to grab women's genitalia with impunity, and which, at least initially, had led some Republicans to call for Trump to withdraw from the presidential race.

The payment to Daniels, which had not been disclosed or reported as a donation to the Trump campaign, may have violated federal campaign finance laws if it had been intended to influence the campaign. We realized that this could be the basis for charges that might lead Cohen to cooperate. But the payment to Daniels was not what interested us; we wanted Cohen's cooperation regarding two Russia-related issues: the payments that had come from a Russian-backed entity, and Cohen's involvement in a defunct business deal known within the Trump Organization as Trump Tower Moscow. The Trump Organization had been trying to secure a deal to build in Moscow for several years, including into 2016.

We became aware of the payment to Stormy Daniels only a few months into our tenure—forcing us to face the kind of "blue dress" issue that Senator Lindsey Graham had warned about. We had come to an early crossroads. Should we fully investigate the hush-money payment—including whether Trump himself was involved? Doing so could lead to charges and to Cohen cooperating on the Russia topics we cared about, but it could also steer us into a salacious campaign-finance prosecution having nothing to do with Russia—and having to do with an adult film star. If we'd been an ordinary US attorney's office, the answer would have been straightforward: you go where the evidence takes you and you investigate. But the scope of Bob's appointment order did not include this conduct. We would not do a Whitewater-style investigation that expanded beyond Bob's mandate.

So we came up with a hybrid solution: we would refer the hush-money aspect of the case to the Southern District of New York, the jurisdiction where Cohen resided, while we would hold on to all Russian aspects of the case. If the SDNY were able to make a campaign-finance case against Cohen, that could help push him to cooperate with both of our offices. The decision was made easier because of Andrew's relationship with the SDNY; we referred the case to the public corruption unit that Andrew had been in charge of up until our investigation. We knew that we would be able to coordinate and share information where appropriate, but that the SDNY would be solely responsible for decisions related to the Stormy Daniels payment. Rosenstein spelled out this division of labor as part of a second "scope" memo to Bob in October 2017.

Roughly six months later, on April 9, 2018, FBI agents working with the SDNY executed search warrants on Cohen's home, hotel room, and office in New York City. Cohen would later tell us that in the immediate aftermath of the searches he was particularly concerned that the FBI would find out about two things: the payments to Daniels and the details of Trump Tower Moscow and how he had lied about them under oath when he testified before Congress in the fall of 2017. (It turned out that the payments from the Russian-backed entity to Essential Consultants LLC had nothing to do with Trump Tower Moscow or the campaign; they were tied to consulting work Cohen had done after the election.)

Trump Tower Moscow had been a potential $1 billion deal to develop a Trump-branded skyscraper in Moscow. Cohen led the effort for the Trump Organization, and a former colleague of Cohen's acted as the agent for the real-estate development company on the Russian end of the deal. On October 28, 2015, a few months before the first Republican primaries, Trump signed a letter of intent for the project. A few days later, the former colleague emailed Cohen, explicitly linking the deal to the election: "Buddy our boy can become President of the USA and we can engineer it. I will get all of Putin[']s team to buy in on this, I will manage this process. . . . Putin gets on stage with Donald for a ribbon cutting for Trump Moscow, and Donald owns the republican nomination."

Cohen worked on the project through the spring and early summer of 2016. In May of that year, Cohen and the former colleague discussed traveling to Moscow with Trump during the campaign to advance the deal. Cohen pursued the Russian government's approval as late as June 2016, about a month before the Republican National Convention, which would make Trump the official Republican nominee. Despite Cohen's effort, Trump did not travel to Russia in 2016, and negotiations over the project ultimately fizzled.

This timeline caused a problem for Cohen: in the wake of our investigation and Congress's parallel investigations into Russian election interference, he had lied about the project both publicly and while under oath in front of Congress in the fall of 2017. He insisted that the deal had become moribund in January 2016, well before Trump became the presumptive Republican nominee, and that Trump had barely been involved in the negotiations. Cohen told these lies to adhere to what he later described to us as the "script" and the "party line" developed to minimize Trump's connections to Russia (including Trump Tower Moscow). Throughout the campaign Trump repeatedly claimed to have had nothing to do with Russia. Trump Tower Moscow contradicted that.

After the SDNY searches in April 2018, Trump initially stood by Cohen. On the day they occurred, the president told reporters he had "just heard that they broke into the office of one of my personal attorneys—a good man." He went on to say that the searches were "a disgrace . . . [they're] an attack on our country, in a true sense. [They're] an attack on what we all stand for." We were not involved in the searches, but the president's comments were striking. Trump was the head of the executive branch of government; it was his own Justice Department that had carried out the searches pursuant to a court-approved warrant. To call them "an attack on what we all stand for" was notable. We had grown used to his criticisms of our investigation, but these comments were on a new level. They made us think he must have been concerned about what the FBI might find.

Trump called Cohen shortly thereafter. According to Cohen, the president told him to "hang in there" and "stay strong." Cohen received other messages from people close to Trump, who told him that "the boss loves you," and "everyone knows the boss has your back."

About a week later, the *New York Times* ran a story suggesting Cohen's relationship with Trump might be souring. The headline read: "Michael Cohen Has Said He Would Take a Bullet for Trump. Maybe Not Anymore." Trump responded in a series of tweets: "The New York Times and a third rate reporter [. . .] are going out of their way to destroy Michael Cohen and his relationship with me in the hope that he will 'flip.' [. . .] Michael [is] a fine person with a wonderful family. [. . .] Most people will flip if the Government lets them out of trouble, even if it means lying or making up stories. Sorry, I don't see Michael doing that despite the horrible Witch Hunt and the dishonest media!" To Trump, "flipping" was a bad thing; to prosecutors it meant telling the truth.

Cohen was communicating with a lawyer at the time who was close with Rudy Giuliani. The same day as the *Times* story and Trump's tweet stating, "I don't see Michael doing that," this lawyer reached out to Cohen. In an email, the lawyer said he had spoken to Giuliani, who by that time had joined Trump's legal team, and that the conversation was a good one. "Very Very Positive," the lawyer wrote to Cohen. "You are 'loved' . . . they are in our corner. . . . Sleep well tonight[], you have friends in high places."

Initially, Cohen did "stay strong." He didn't "flip." The Trump Organization was paying his legal fees, and he thought that the president would take care of him. He later told us about a series of conversations he'd had with the president's personal counsel that led him to believe that if he stayed loyal and "on message," Trump would either pardon him or have the investigation shut down.

These were powers unique to the president. Only the president can pardon people accused or convicted of federal crimes. Only the president can shut down federal investigations and not risk being fired by a superior—he might be impeached or voted out of office for doing this, but those are political remedies. Only the president can use his bully pulpit to tell tens of millions of Americans that a legitimate, well-predicated investigation run by his own Department of Justice is a "Witch Hunt" and an "attack on our country."

For several months, the campaign to dissuade Cohen from cooperating worked. He would not cooperate with the SDNY. He agreed to be interviewed by us about Trump Tower Moscow, but he repeated the same lies he'd told Congress: that all discussions about the deal ended in January 2016 and that Trump had barely been involved.

But in August 2018, everything changed for Cohen. He would later tell us that he had grown increasingly concerned that remaining loyal to Trump would require too much personal sacrifice, including a possible guilty verdict, fines, and significant prison time before any hoped-for-but-by-no-means-guaranteed presidential pardon. On August 21, he pleaded guilty in the Southern District of New York to eight felony charges, including two counts of making illegal campaign contributions in the form of hush-money payments. During the plea hearing, Cohen told the court he had worked "in coordination with, and at the direction of, a candidate for federal office"—that is, Trump—in making those payments.

That ended the president's support for Michael Cohen.

* * *

Just as the president appeared to be using his official powers to influence Cohen not to cooperate, he used similar tactics with Paul Manafort.

Manafort and his deputy Rick Gates had been indicted by our office in the Eastern District of Virginia (EDVA), where both men lived, and in Washington, DC, where Manafort and Gates carried out some of their work. The Virginia charges were based on bank fraud and tax evasion; the DC charges were based on violations of the Foreign Agents Registration Act (FARA).

Gates would later tell us that in January 2018, after the DC indictment, Manafort told him that Manafort had talked to the president's personal counsel and learned that they were "going to take care of us." Manafort told Gates it was "stupid" to plead guilty, that they should "sit tight" and "we'll be taken care of." Gates asked Manafort outright if anyone mentioned pardons, and Manafort said that no one had used that word.

Gates was not persuaded by these assurances and started cooperating with our office soon after the DC indictment. But Manafort decided to sit tight and exercise his right to trial.

In late March 2018, Manafort filed a motion to dismiss the Virginia charges on the grounds that Rosenstein's appointment of Bob violated the special counsel regulations, and even if it didn't, the Virginia indictment went beyond any authority outlined in the appointment order. Manafort claimed that the order appointing Bob had improperly given him an expansive and illegal "blank check" to pursue anything he wanted. Manafort's alleged financial crimes mostly preceded the election and did not involve Russia directly. Accordingly, Manafort claimed, Bob must have used this "blank check" to pursue him, rendering the whole EDVA indictment illegitimate. We had anticipated this exact argument months earlier when we obtained the August 2, 2017, scope memo from Rosenstein saying in plain language that investigating these crimes was related to our Russia mandate and well within our scope.

The judge who presided over Manafort's Virginia case, T. S. Ellis, III, quickly made it clear he was no fan of special counsels. During oral arguments on the motion to dismiss on May 4, Judge Ellis commented that he was concerned about a special prosecutor having "unlimited powers to do anything he or she wants." He added, incorrectly in our view: "When a [special counsel] is appointed, he's appointed to get an indictment. He's appointed to go after somebody." Judge Ellis suggested that the charges against Manafort had nothing to do with Russia and were simply a "means of exerting pressure" to get to Trump. In a comment that made headlines in every major media outlet the next day, Judge Ellis said: "You really care about getting information that Mr. Manafort can give you that would reflect on Mr. Trump and lead to his prosecution or impeachment or whatever."

Michael Dreeben argued for the SCO. He pointed out that Rosenstein's August 2 scope memo made it clear we had authority to prosecute Manafort. The memo stated explicitly that allegations related to Manafort's receipt of money from the Ukrainian government under President Viktor

Yanukovych—which was a source of money at the heart of Manafort's fraud and tax crimes—were within the scope of our appointment. The memo contained a one-sentence grant of authority to do the precise case that Manafort claimed Rosenstein had not authorized. The August 2 memo had never been seen outside a small circle of people in the executive branch—and even here, when we submitted it to Judge Ellis and Manafort's lawyers, we filed it under seal with heavy redactions removing anything unrelated to Manafort. Dreeben also explained how Manafort's dealings with Russians and Russian-aligned Ukrainians were at the core of our mandate, and that those dealings had continued throughout the campaign.

Following this hearing, Trump proclaimed that Judge Ellis's comments showed that our entire investigation was a "witch hunt." The reality was that Manafort had committed serious crimes, and we wanted him to cooperate because we wanted to know more about a series of interactions he'd had with Russians during the campaign: Why had he discussed a Ukrainian "peace plan" during the campaign with his associate Konstantin Kilimnik? Why had he used Kilimnik to pass internal campaign polling data to a Russian oligarch, Oleg Deripaska? Why had he offered Deripaska "private briefings" about the campaign? It was (and would remain) difficult to determine the motivations behind these actions. Manafort could have been using his position in the campaign for business only—to "get whole" with the Russians, as he had put it in an email to Kilimnik, and to recoup some of the money his Ukrainian clients owed him. Alternatively, the Russians could have been enlisting Manafort in an election-interference conspiracy. Or it could have been both. No Russian witness was going to clarify any of this for us; nor did we have visibility into what had ultimately been done with the data that had been passed to Kilimnik. We were hoping that Manafort's indictments, and convictions, if they came to pass, would convince him to cooperate and tell us the truth.

While we awaited Judge Ellis's decision on Manafort's motion to dismiss, we learned that Manafort and Kilimnik had tried to tamper with two of the witnesses in the DC case alleging FARA violations. Team M responded by bringing a superseding indictment against Manafort and Kilimnik in DC that included charges of obstruction of justice. The judge overseeing the DC case promptly revoked Manafort's bail and remanded him to jail to await trial. Hours after Manafort was placed into custody, Trump called it "Very unfair!" and Giuliani gave a series of interviews, saying the quiet part out loud: "When the whole thing is over, things might get cleaned up with some presidential pardons."

At the end of June, Judge Ellis issued his ruling, denying Manafort's motion to dismiss. Having reviewed our scope memo, Judge Ellis found that the charges were "squarely" within Bob's core mandate to investigate links or coordination between the Russian government and individuals associated with the Trump campaign. He stated it even more clearly than we had: Manafort had been the chairman of the Trump campaign, and the charges were about his work for Russian-backed politicians. Judge Ellis found that Bob had been properly appointed, that he did not have a "blank check," and that he was subject to Rosenstein's supervision as specified in the August 2 scope memo. The ruling, particularly coming from a judge who had expressed general skepticism about special counsels, gave us measures of both relief and vindication.

Manafort's trial began on July 31, 2018. The next morning, as testimony was about to begin, President Trump issued the first in a series of tweets slamming the prosecution.

"This is a terrible situation and Attorney General Jeff Sessions should stop this Rigged Witch Hunt right now, before it continues to stain our country any further. Bob Mueller is totally conflicted, and his 17 Angry Democrats that are doing his dirty work are a disgrace to USA!" The second tweet came minutes later: "Paul Manafort worked for Ronald Reagan, Bob Dole and many other highly prominent and respected political leaders. He worked for me for a very short time. Why didn't government tell me that he was under investigation. These old charges have nothing to do with Collusion—a Hoax!" And toward the end of the day, Trump tweeted, "Looking back on history, who was treated worse, Alfonse Capone, legendary mob boss, killer and 'Public Enemy Number One,' or Paul Manafort, political operative & Reagan/Dole darling, now serving solitary confinement—although convicted of nothing? Where is the Russian Collusion?"

We paid attention to these tweets for two reasons. First, they had the potential to affect the trial. The jury was not sequestered. Trump's tweets were amplified across most major media outlets. There was a risk one or more jurors would see and be influenced by the president's comments, particularly the ones about Manafort being a "Reagan/Dole darling" and that he was "serving solitary confinement," which seemed designed to engender sympathy. (A federal judge, not our office, made the decision to put Manafort in pretrial detention due to his obstructive conduct directed at witnesses after he had been charged, and he was not in solitary confinement.)

Second, the tweets raised questions about what the president was attempting to achieve. Why was he weighing in so strongly on behalf of Manafort? We knew from speaking to other witnesses that Trump had complained about Manafort. Trump had told his staff secretary that he never liked Manafort and that Manafort did not know what he was doing on the campaign. We also knew Trump discussed with aides whether and in what manner Manafort might be cooperating with our investigation, and whether he possessed any information that could be harmful to the president. We saw the tweets as an out-in-the-open form of potential obstruction. Was Trump using his megaphone to influence the jury and help Manafort get acquitted? That could keep Manafort from cooperating and could also undermine confidence in our entire investigation.

Two weeks later, on August 16, the testimony in Manafort's Virginia trial had concluded (including from Gates, who took the stand against his former boss and mentor), and the jury began deliberations. The next day, while the jury was still out, Trump had an impromptu exchange with reporters in front of the president's helicopter, Marine One, on the White House's South Lawn. When asked if he would pardon Manafort if convicted, Trump spoke loudly over the rotor noise: "I don't talk about that now. I don't talk about that." He then added, "I think the whole Manafort trial is very sad when you look at what's going on there. I think it's a very sad day for our country. He worked for me for a very short period of time. But you know what, he happens to be a very good person. And I think it's very sad what they've done to Paul Manafort." Watching from inside the SCO, we discussed how extraodinary these comments were. While the jury was deliberating Manafort's fate on eighteen criminal charges, the president—the chief executive responsible for federal prosecutions, including this one—was telling the world (and the jury) that Manafort was a "very good person" and that it was "very sad" what "they"—meaning us—had "done" to him.

Four days later, on August 21, Manafort was convicted on eight counts of bank fraud and tax evasion; the jury hung on the remaining and related counts, with eleven jurors in favor of conviction and one opposed. This was the same day that Michael Cohen pleaded guilty in New York to crimes related to the hush-money payments to Stormy Daniels.

The following morning, Trump made an early call-in appearance on the television program *Fox & Friends*. During the exchange with the show's hosts, Trump said, "[Cohen] makes a better deal when he uses me, like everybody else. And one of the reasons I respect Paul Manafort so much is he went through that trial—you know they make up stories. People make up stories. This whole thing about flipping, they call it, I know all about flipping. . . . Almost ought to be outlawed." One of the hosts asked about a pardon for Manafort; Trump didn't answer directly, but said, "I have great respect for what he's done, in terms of what he's gone through."

As for Cohen, not long after the call-in, the president tweeted, "If anyone is looking for a good lawyer, I would strongly suggest that you don't retain the services of Michael Cohen!" followed by, "I feel very badly for Paul Manafort and his wonderful family. 'Justice' took a 12 year old tax case, among other things, applied tremendous pressure on him and, unlike Michael Cohen, he refused to 'break' - make up stories in order to get a 'deal.' Such respect for a brave man!"

As we watched all of this from inside the SCO, it was difficult to view the president's comments on Manafort as anything other than advice not to "flip" in an effort to reduce his sentence, while also suggesting that a pardon was on the table. Jim tried to make light of the situation. When he walked around the office during this period, he would quip as he passed colleagues, "Pardon me. . . . No, seriously—pardon me." Yet we still hoped Manafort would cooperate. In an ordinary case, convictions on eight felony counts would be a strong incentive for a defendant to cooperate in hope of getting a lower sentence. But there was nothing ordinary about what the president was doing.

It so happened that the president's tweets about Manafort's convictions coincided—almost to the day—with the peak of our discussions with the department about issuing a subpoena for the president's testimony, including on matters of obstruction of justice.

A few weeks later, on September 14, Manafort pleaded guilty to conspiracy and FARA violations in the parallel DC case; following this, he signed an agreement to cooperate with our office. But within months, it became clear that Manafort was not cooperating. The judge overseeing Manafort's DC case determined Manafort had lied to us and to the grand jury concerning his interactions and communications with Kilimnik, including their discussions regarding a "peace plan" for Ukraine (something Manafort referred to as a "backdoor" way for Russia to control eastern Ukraine).

Two days after Team M notified the court that Manafort had breached his cooperation agreement, on November 28, 2018, Trump gave a press interview in the Oval Office. He said that it was "actually very brave" that

Manafort did not "flip." When asked again about a possible pardon for Manafort, Trump replied, "It was never discussed, but I wouldn't take it off the table. Why would I take it off the table?"

We were never able to get fully truthful information from Manafort, who was ultimately sentenced to a total of 7.5 years in prison. A pardon appeared to be around the corner and significant questions would likely remain unanswered. We asked ourselves throughout this chain of events what we could do in response to the kind of interference we were seeing from this president.

Andrew Weissmann, who led Team M, tried to address the president's expected pardon. In the fall of 2018, following Manafort's trial convictions in Virginia and his guilty pleas in Washington, DC, Weissmann started to provide some of our nonpublic evidence to the Manhattan District Attorney's Office (led at the time by Cyrus Vance). Why? If the Manhattan District Attorney brought its own charges against Manafort and secured convictions under New York state law, Manafort would be beyond the reach of a presidential pardon.

When Aaron learned of this, he immediately intervened. He understood why Weissmann had taken this step: Manafort appeared to be acting in ways that were best explained by an expectation of a presidential pardon. But providing nonpublic federal evidence to a state prosecutor in these circumstances was inconsistent with the Principles of Federal Prosecution. There was no federal interest in partnering with a district attorney to pursue a third prosecution of the same person for the same conduct. Under the principles of federal prosecution, government attorneys are supposed to *decline* to prosecute someone if the person is subject to effective prosecution in another jurisdiction. Weissmann's approach turned this standard on its head: our office would be seen as seeking another prosecution of someone we had already prosecuted—twice. It was too close to what Attorney General Robert H. Jackson had warned against in his famous address back in 1940: a prosecutor should not pick someone they think they "should get"; rather, they should "pick cases that need to be prosecuted."

Aaron conferred with Bob, who saw the harm this end run could do to our office's work and reputation. Bob immediately halted Weissmann's effort. Aaron called the Manhattan District Attorney's office and explained our need to change course. It was fine for them to have all the evidence that had been admitted at Manafort's trial—those records were available to anyone—but we would not provide any nonpublic information. (As it turned out, in March 2019, the Manhattan District Attorney's office brought a sixteen-count indictment against Manafort alleging mortgage fraud, falsification of business records, and other crimes. The New York trial judge dismissed all charges on the ground that they violated New York's double-jeopardy rules because they stemmed from the same conduct that had been the subject of Manafort's federal trial in Virginia. The dismissal of the indictment was unanimously upheld on appeal.)

*　*　*

Roger Stone perhaps had the good fortune of going last when it came to his legal fight with our office. He'd seen how the president had treated Cohen, and he'd seen how the president had treated Manafort, and he could draw his own conclusions: better not to cooperate.

We were interested in Stone because he had communicated during the 2016 campaign with Guccifer 2.0—the Russian military intelligence (GRU) persona who had dumped emails that had been stolen by other members of the GRU from DNC and DCCC computer networks. Stone later boasted that he had advance knowledge of WikiLeaks' release of some of these stolen emails. Based on interviews with Michael Cohen, Rick Gates, and others, we learned that Stone was the apparent connection between the campaign and WikiLeaks, and that he had spoken about WikiLeaks with senior campaign officials and, allegedly, with Trump himself. Gates remembered a lengthy telephone conversation between Stone and Trump that had taken place while Trump and Gates were in a car to New York's LaGuardia Airport.

Although Gates could not hear Stone's words, shortly after the call Trump told Gates that more releases of damaging information would be coming.

By the fall of 2018, we had also developed evidence that Stone had repeatedly lied to Congress about his outreach to WikiLeaks regarding the stolen emails and his communications with the Trump campaign around the stolen emails; and that he had intimidated a witness into supporting his false story. We began to prepare an indictment in November 2018.

At the end of that month, we finally received the president's answers to questions we had posed in writing about Russia-related topics. In response to questions about the president's communications with Stone regarding WikiLeaks, the president's written answer stated: "I have no recollection of the specifics of any conversations I had with Mr. Stone between June 1, 2016, and November 8, 2016. I do not recall discussing WikiLeaks with him, nor do I recall being aware of Mr. Stone having discussed WikiLeaks with individuals associated with my campaign." (This overly lawyered response is representative of nearly all of Trump's written answers and stands as a good example of why Bob had been so skeptical of receiving written answers in the first place.)

While we prepared Stone's indictment, on November 29, 2018, Michael Cohen pleaded guilty to lying to Congress about the Trump Tower Moscow project, pursuant to an agreement with our office that recognized Cohen's cooperation. Andrew traveled to New York for the plea. We told the judge that Cohen had been cooperating with us and that we expected to write a letter at Cohen's sentencing that would detail his assistance in our investigation. In pleading guilty, Cohen said that he had lied to Congress to be consistent with Trump's "political messaging" and "out of loyalty" to Trump.

Three days later, on December 2, Stone appeared on ABC's *This Week* and said there was "no circumstance" under which he would "testify against the president."

The next day, Trump posted a long tweet about Stone: "'I will never testify against Trump.' This statement was recently made by Roger Stone, essentially stating that he will not be forced by a rogue and out of control prosecutor to make up lies and stories about 'President Trump.' Nice to know that some people still have 'guts!'"

In contrast, after Cohen's lawyers filed their sentencing memorandum later that week, the president tweeted, "'Michael Cohen asks judge for no Prison Time.' You mean he can do all of the TERRIBLE, unrelated to Trump, things having to do with fraud, big loans, [...], etc., and not serve a long prison term?"

Stone was indicted on January 24, 2019, on charges of obstruction, witness tampering, and making false statements. The following day, Stone appeared in court, after which he told reporters, "There is no circumstance whatsoever under which I will bear false witness against the president, nor will I make up lies to ease the pressure on myself. . . . I will not testify against the president, because I would have to bear false witness."

Several days later, on February 3, the president told CBS News, "Roger is somebody that I've always liked." He was then asked whether he would pardon Stone, to which he replied, "I have not thought about it. It looks like he's defending himself very well. But you have to get rid of the Russia witch hunt."

Roger Stone would be found guilty of all counts on November 15, 2019, roughly six months after our office closed. On the day of Stone's conviction, President Trump posted two tweets: "So they now convict Roger Stone of lying and want to jail him for many years to come. Well, what about Crooked Hillary, Comey, Strzok, Page, McCabe, Brennan, Clapper, Shifty Schiff, Ohr & Nellie, Steele & all of the others, including even Mueller himself? Didn't they lie?" followed by, "A double standard like never seen before in the history of our Country?"

Stone's prosecution team was headed by Aaron Zelinsky (AZ2). Working with him were two accomplished lawyers from the DC US attorney's office, Jonathan Kravis and Michael Marando, and a former SCO attorney named Adam Jed, another lawyer handpicked by Dreeben to serve on the office's legal team. Following Stone's conviction, Zelinsky and his colleagues requested Stone be given a prison term of seven to nine years, which was precisely what the federal sentencing guidelines called for. But Attorney General William Barr took the extraordinary step of overruling them. He had the US attorney in DC withdraw the sentencing recommendation the team had sent to the court and instead requested that the judge be more lenient on Stone. In our decades of collective experience as prosecutors, we had never seen this happen. In protest, Zelinsky and the three other prosecutors involved resigned from the Stone case—and one of them resigned from the department altogether. Ultimately, Stone was sentenced to a little over three years in prison.

In July 2020, right before Stone was to report to the Federal Correction Institution in Jessup, Georgia, President Trump commuted his sentence. Then, in late 2020, after the election and before the end of Trump's term, he granted full pardons to Stone, Manafort, Michael Flynn, and George Papadopoulos, among others.

The president did not grant pardons to either Rick Gates or Michael Cohen, both of whom had cooperated with our office. Gates did not spend time in prison. Cohen spent more than a year in prison before being released by the court for a term of home confinement.

With these final actions—the pardons and the nonpardons—Giuliani's prediction from June 2018 seemingly had come true: "things . . . [got] cleaned up with some presidential pardons."

Sixteen

GIULIANI RETURNS

At 10:45 p.m. on November 14, 2018, Jim received an urgent call from the president's team—including Rudy Giuliani. It was the first time any of us had heard Giuliani's voice since our April 24 meeting, not counting whenever we happened to catch him on the news. By this time, it had been nearly two months since we had submitted written questions to the president, and we still had not received any answers. The president and his team had blown several deadlines. The latest deadline was the next day, November 15.

Jim figured the phone call was to report yet another delay, but that wasn't the issue. "We just received some papers," Sekulow said. The papers involved an individual who was never charged with a crime, someone we'll call Person-A. "We want to talk to Bob right away," Sekulow demanded.

Before Jim could respond, Giuliani jumped in: "We're getting ready to give you the president's answers, but now we feel like we're being set up in some way."

Jim frowned. He wasn't sure what Giuliani meant—we weren't trying to set up anyone. At the time, we were investigating WikiLeaks' release of documents during the summer of 2016; that trail intersected with Person-A.

Team R had drafted some papers regarding Person-A, which had been sent to Person-A's lawyers, and now Trump's team somehow had a copy. This appeared to be what had set off alarms.

Jim asked Giuliani what he was talking about. The implication was that we were trying to get the president's written answers only so we could turn around and somehow show that they were false—either by securing possible testimony from Person-A or pointing at other evidence.

Jim assured Giuliani and Sekulow he would communicate their concerns to Bob and told them we would be in touch. Jim didn't see why this was a big deal.

The following morning, at 10:30 a.m., the president's team called Jim again. This time Andrew joined. Giuliani repeated what he'd said the day before: "We feel like we are being set up." We assured him this was not the case. Giuliani then insisted on a "face-to-face" meeting *that day* with Bob and Rosenstein to clear this up. He also told us that he was reaching out directly to Rosenstein, as well as FBI Director Christopher Wray, to complain about what he perceived to be going on.

With the mention of Rosenstein and the FBI director, Aaron called O'Callaghan to let him know what might be coming. Aaron explained Team 600 was waiting for answers from the president (and that the deadline was now) and that another team was dealing with counsel for Person-A. The two events were not connected. O'Callaghan said he understood.

Giuliani contacted us multiple times throughout that day, insisting on a sit-down between their team, Bob, and Rosenstein, on the most urgent of timetables. At 3:53 p.m. he sent an email to our office, writing, "As we told you and Rod Rosenstein, we would like the courtesy of a face-to-face meeting at Main Justice today or this evening." He said it was a matter of the "utmost importance and urgency." The email was signed, "Rudolph W. Giuliani, Counsel to the President."

Jim and Andrew read this together in Jim's office, shaking their heads. They concluded that, in all likelihood, Giuliani and the rest of the president's team were attempting to use this paperwork as a basis for not submitting the president's written answers. It felt like one more example of presidential delay.

Aaron walked into Bob's office. As we saw it, this was not an issue that required a principals' meeting with Bob and Rosenstein. Two minutes into the conversation, Bob raised his hand to signal that he had heard enough. "I won't be attending this séance," he said. "But you should be there—tell them we need the president's answers." Aaron confirmed with O'Callaghan that Rosenstein also would not attend.

The meeting was set. It would be Aaron, Jim, and Andrew from the SCO, and from the DOJ it would be O'Callaghan.

We arrived at Main Justice at 7:45 p.m. and were led to the DAG's conference room adjacent to Rosenstein's office. Giuliani, Sekulow, and Jane Raskin were already there, along with O'Callaghan. We took seats. The room was oddly dark. It was almost as if no lights had been turned on and there was just some low ambient glow coming from Rosenstein's empty personal office at the end of the room, only enough that we could make out who was who, but not enough to see what shade of dark suit each of us wore. In that light, we all appeared to be dressed in black—with the requisite white shirt underneath, of course—like a roomful of legal undertakers.

Giuliani began: "We were at the White House yesterday from four to eight, trying to get the questions done. We are ninety-five percent done. We had scheduled time today, from one to four this afternoon, to finish the answers, but then last night Jay received these materials." Giuliani produced a copy of the papers which had precipitated this, waving them around for effect. "We were shocked to get this. We don't know who it came from," he said. "You appear to be going after [Person-A] to get to the president." As Giuliani spoke, he got more and more worked up. "Our conclusion is you're aiming for [the president], you're going after him. This is a tremendous burden on the president. We think you should conclude the damn thing."

Jane Raskin, perhaps sensing Giuliani was being overblown, stated calmly, "Might I suggest that if we are to give you the president's answers, it should come at the very end of your investigation. You're not at the end. You're continuing."

Andrew almost blurted, "*If?*" but held his tongue. We now had a better understanding of all the fuss: it seemed they wanted to know everything they could about our investigation in order to make sure they didn't write the president's answers in a way that could ultimately be contradicted.

Aaron responded to Jane: "The deadline for responses was today. We expected to receive them. You are now saying that you won't be delivering the responses. Is that right?"

Giuliani answered: "Under these circumstances, we'd be disbarred if we gave you the responses now."

Up until then, O'Callaghan had been silent, but now he weighed in. "From the department's perspective, the questions are specifically about actions before the president took office. They are directed to an individual in his private capacity. Our position is that the questions should be answered." He added, "It is very important to get these answers. The right time to get them is now. It is in the best interest of the country."

Giuliani, now more worked up, said, "These materials show that the investigation is not coming to a conclusion. It says you interviewed this guy on September sixth—that was right when we were negotiating the president's testimony."

O'Callaghan responded again, and Aaron knew it was better to let him speak. "Your argument is that they were doing this to go after the president. That couldn't be farther from the truth. I am one hundred percent sure that there was no intent to get the president's answers and time it with this. Investigations have different avenues; they go in different directions." O'Callaghan had been a prosecutor in SDNY, as had Giuliani. The point was obvious, but it helped that it came from O'Callaghan.

The meeting ended without complete resolution, but we had delivered the intended message. We went our separate ways from Main Justice, wondering if the president's team would really hold out and not submit the written responses, contrary to what the department had insisted.

It took five more days to find out. On November 20, the president's answers to our many questions arrived via hand delivery.

As expected, they were not particularly revealing. On more than thirty occasions, Trump answered that he did "not recall" or "remember" or have an "independent recollection" of information called for by the questions. Other answers were incomplete or imprecise. We would end up including these responses, along with our questions, in an appendix to our report to formally memorialize the lack of information we had received.

We told the president's team that the answers "demonstrate the inadequacy of the written format, as we have had no opportunity to ask follow-up questions that would ensure complete answers and potentially refresh your client's recollection or clarify the extent or nature of his lack of recollection." We gave them a final opportunity for the president to sit for an in-person interview to provide his version of events. On December 12, the president's lawyers declined.

Bob had decided in September that issuing a subpoena wouldn't have been worth it, but he paused to consider it one last time. We now had evidence about Trump's conduct and state of mind from multiple sources, including real-time White House staff notes and statements from McGahn (his White House counsel), General John Kelly (his chief of staff), Steve Bannon (his adviser), Sarah Huckabee Sanders (the White House press secretary), and a range of other staff who had observed and heard President Trump on a daily basis. We doubted an interview would give us much more. We weighed the costs of a potentially lengthy constitutional challenge to a subpoena—which could mean keeping the office open for another year, and perhaps much longer—against the anticipated benefits of finally sitting down with Trump. There was little reason to think any answers he gave in person, assuming he didn't assert his Fifth Amendment right not to testify, would be better than the written responses. If we finally sat down with him after a one-year-plus battle, the number of "I don't recall" responses would probably increase.

Considering all this, Bob saw no reason to change course, and we agreed. There would be no subpoena for President Trump.

Seventeen

WRITING THE REPORT

"Have we started writing the report?" Bob asked in mid-May 2018, referring to the confidential report we were required under the regulations to submit to the attorney general at the end of our investigation.

This was classic Bob. No matter which case it happened to be, if a report were required, Bob did not want to wait until every fact had been established before starting to write. He would say, "If things change, we'll edit."

In the spring of 2018, we were in the thick of our investigation. We still had ahead of us the hack-and-dump indictment; the Manafort trial; the remainder of our investigation of the president's conduct (including deciding whether to subpoena him); and our continued pursuit of more information about Russian interactions with Manafort, Stone, and others during the 2016 campaign. No matter. Bob wanted to make sure our report was finished as soon as possible after we were done investigating. As we've written, he did not want us to be open even a single day more than necessary.

The regulations required our report to explain to the attorney general "the prosecution or declination decisions reached by the Special Counsel." In other words, we would need to explain in writing the criminal charges we had brought, as well as the matters we had investigated where we decided not to bring charges. According to the regulations, the attorney general had the authority to decide whether to release all or part of our report to the public.

By early June 2018, Aaron had drafted an outline. The report would be divided into two parts: Russian interference, which became volume I; and the president's conduct toward the Russia investigation, which became volume II. But there were many questions to consider. How much detail should we include? How should we frame the Russian interference operations? What should we say about the contacts between various Russians and the Trump campaign, and how should we characterize the willingness of the campaign to accept and benefit from Russian interference? And perhaps most difficult of all: What should we say about the president's conduct toward our investigation?

As we worked through these questions and the shape of the report, we were mindful that the attorney general could decide to release some (or perhaps all) of it publicly. The credibility of our entire endeavor could be affected by the way we drafted our findings. Bob wanted the report to be the definitive account. Every fact needed to be triple-checked. Nothing gratuitous would be included. Inferences had to be tightly bound to specific evidence. Our conclusions would be based solely on the facts and the law. It took months of writing and rewriting until we thought we had it right, and we would make changes up until the very end.

We started drafting volume I first. Scott Meisler, one of the young lawyers Dreeben had recruited for the legal team, was given the task of debriefing the leaders of Team R, Team M, and Team F in order to produce an early draft. But that task was too great for any single mortal. The team leaders had been living complicated investigations for a year; it was not possible to transmit a nuanced understanding of evidence about the many Russia-related threads to just one person.

So as the summer of 2018 wore on, we had the team leaders write initial drafts for their respective investigations. Meisler and Aaron reviewed and edited each section against grand jury transcripts and other underlying evidence to ensure that all of our factual statements and investigative conclusions were accurate, warranted, and supported. Nearly every paragraph required judgment calls. (Meanwhile, the teams were continuing their investigations and obtaining new evidence at the same time everyone was also writing and editing.)

By the end of 2018, as we drew closer to concluding the investigation and drafting the final report, it became clear that for certain events we would be unable to reach definitive conclusions. For example, we could not discern what Deripaska or Ukranian oligarchs had done with the polling data provided by Manafort, or whether George Papadopoulos had shared with anyone in the Trump campaign the Russian offer to assist with the anonymous release of information damaging to Clinton. Neither Manafort nor Papadopoulos had fully cooperated, and we had exhausted all other means of obtaining evidence on these events. This often happens in investigations. Prosecutors do everything they can under the law to hunt for evidence. At some point, when you have exhausted all lawful avenues to obtain additional evidence, you step back and assess what you are able to prove. When our report stated that we were able to establish a particular fact, that meant we had substantial, credible evidence to prove it. At other times we pointed out the absence of evidence or the conflicts between evidence. There were certain instances where we had some evidence of an event, but not enough evidence to prove it, so we did not put those events in the report.*

We also labored over how best to frame our bottom-line conclusions across the entire investigation. In the weeks before we delivered the report,

---

* Some have suggested, without knowledge of the full scope of our work, that we shied away from certain viable avenues of investigation. That is untrue. For example, while we did not conduct a wide-ranging financial investigation of all of the president's business affairs because we did not have cause to do so, we did do a rigorous investigation into the movement of money in and around the campaign, and we looked closely at every tie between Trump and the Trump Organization and Russia that we had evidence of.

we drafted an introduction and an executive summary for each volume that laid out our principal findings and conclusions. For volume I, we wanted to make sure a reader would immediately see our most important finding. We made it the first substantive line of the entire report: "The Russian government interfered in the 2016 presidential election in sweeping and systematic fashion." We also made it clear that this Russian interference was designed to favor one candidate over another—the Russians were trying to help Trump win. We wrote:

> The Special Counsel's investigation established that Russia interfered in the 2016 presidential election principally through two operations. First, a Russian entity carried out a social media campaign that favored presidential candidate Donald J. Trump and disparaged presidential candidate Hillary Clinton. Second, a Russian intelligence service conducted computer-intrusion operations against entities, employees, and volunteers working on the Clinton Campaign and then released stolen documents.

After describing the main Russian interference operations, we moved to the issue of coordination with the Trump campaign. Our introduction to volume I explained that the investigation "did not establish that members of the Trump Campaign conspired or coordinated with the Russian government in its election-interference activities." That same sentence also stated that "the investigation established that the Russian government perceived it would benefit from a Trump presidency and worked to secure that outcome, and that the [Trump] Campaign expected it would benefit electorally from information stolen and released through Russian efforts."

The introduction also explained that lies told by certain members of the Trump campaign during the course of the investigation affected our ability to get to the truth of what had occurred: "The investigation established that several individuals affiliated with the Trump Campaign lied to the

Office, and to Congress, about their interactions with Russian-affiliated individuals and related matters. Those lies materially impaired the investigation of Russian election interference." We also noted that several people associated with the Trump campaign had deleted communications or had communicated using apps that automatically deleted messages.

Volume II presented different challenges. Chief among them: we had evidence of multiple instances in which the president appeared to interfere with the Russia investigation. The regulations said that we were supposed to explain our "prosecution or declination decisions." But how should we do that when the OLC opinion said a sitting president could not be charged with a crime? Under what principles should we assess the evidence of obstruction that we had gathered? Should we assess the evidence at all?

We spent many days thinking through these issues in the fall of 2018. Andrew, working with Team 600's lead FBI agent, Michelle Taylor, organized our evidence into ten "episodes"—each involving a separate course of conduct by the president that interfered or could have interfered with the investigation. Three of the episodes took place before Bob's appointment—the Oval Office meeting where Trump asked FBI Director Comey to "let[] Flynn go"; the president's efforts, right after he learned about the FBI's Russia investigation, to have intelligence leaders Dan Coats and Mike Rogers publicly say that Trump had nothing to do with Russia; and the decision to fire Comey.

The other seven episodes took place after Bob's appointment, including Trump's outreach to White House Counsel Don McGahn to have Bob removed right after Trump learned we were investigating him for obstruction of justice; and later pressuring McGahn to deny, orally and in writing, that Trump ever tried to have Bob removed.

For each episode, we pulled together all of the relevant documentary evidence, including internal White House emails, calendars, notes, and phone records, as well as our write-ups of the relevant witness interviews, which Taylor and other agents had carefully documented throughout the investigation. Some of the most important evidence included handwritten notes we had obtained from the White House Counsel's Office, the White House staff secretary, and other senior White House staff that had been taken in real time during or immediately after meetings with the president. (The president's lawyers, knowing we had access to this information, argued that these notes were better evidence of the president's intent than anything he would tell us in an interview.)

On the morning of November 7, 2018, Team 600 held a meeting in the SCO's Maple conference room. Large black binders containing key documents and interview reports were stacked in the middle of the table; additional binders of evidence filled shelves along the side of the room. The plan going in was for Andrew and Taylor to walk through the evidence of the different episodes of potential obstruction and see if Team 600 could come to an initial consensus as to which, if any, might have crossed the line into criminal conduct.

The DOJ's Justice Manual, which sets out the policies for federal prosecutors, has a section called "Grounds for Commencing or Declining Prosecution." It states that a prosecutor should commence or recommend charges if he or she (emphasis added):

> *believes that the person's conduct constitutes a federal offense and that the admissible evidence will probably be sufficient to obtain and sustain a conviction,* unless (1) the prosecution would serve no substantial federal interest; (2) the person is subject to effective prosecution in another jurisdiction; or (3) there exists an adequate non-criminal alternative to prosecution.

The first steps in the analysis are for the prosecutor to decide if he or she "believes" that the person under investigation committed a crime, and whether the evidence is sufficient to obtain a conviction that will be upheld on appeal—that is, proof of guilt beyond a reasonable doubt. If those steps are met, a prosecutor must still evaluate whether a prosecution would serve a substantial federal interest or if there are adequate alternatives to federal prosecution.

The task in our meeting was to apply the Justice Manual's charging standard to each episode of the president's conduct. Did we believe he had committed a crime? Could we prove it in court? We started the meeting at 10:00 a.m. and were prepared for it to go all day.

Andrew began discussing the two episodes involving White House Counsel Don McGahn. Andrew viewed this conduct as the most straightforward evidence of potential obstruction. The first took place exactly one month after Bob was appointed. Soon after the president had learned for the first time that he (and not just his campaign) was under investigation, he called McGahn at home and directed him to have Bob removed as special counsel, on the purported basis of "conflicts" that multiple advisers had told Trump were not real. "Mueller has to go," Trump told McGahn. "Call me back when you do it."

The second episode took place after the press first reported that Trump had tried to get McGahn to have Bob fired. Over the course of nine days, the president tried several times and in multiple ways to get McGahn to say publicly that Trump had never told him to remove the special counsel. McGahn refused. The president also pushed McGahn to create a written record denying what McGahn had believed to be true. Because this episode involved pressure on a witness and the attempt to create a false document that could affect a grand jury proceeding, it did not implicate the same statutory and constitutional issues that had been raised by the department and the president's lawyers over the summer of 2018 when we were considering a grand jury subpoena for the president's testimony. Indeed, in the June 2018 memo Barr wrote to the department as a private citizen, he acknowledged that "if a President knowingly . . . induces a witness to change testimony . . . then he, like anyone else, commits the act of obstruction."

A few minutes into Andrew's presentation, Jim interrupted him. "What are we doing here?" he asked. "The president can't be indicted. So why are we trying to decide what's criminal? Aren't we doing exactly what the OLC opinion tells us we shouldn't do?"

These questions had been gnawing at Jim for some time. When prosecutors make the decision to bring criminal charges against someone, at the very top of mind is whether they will prevail at trial. But if we accused President Trump of committing a crime, he couldn't be indicted until after he was out of office. Our office would be closed by then—so some other prosecutor would have to decide whether to take up the case, not one of us. "That's a big frickin' deal," said Jim. "Nothing keeps a prosecutor more focused than knowing that they will have to prove their case in court." Furthermore, if we made an accusation, the president could not go to trial to try to clear his name. The accusation would just sit there, unable to be pursued by us or defended by the president.

The room went silent. For months we had been carefully gathering evidence of the president's conduct. The OLC opinion made it clear that while we couldn't indict the president, we could investigate potential wrongdoing by the president in order to assemble evidence while memories were fresh and documents were available. We had told the president's lawyers that we had deliberately held off reaching conclusions about the president's conduct during the course of the investigation. But now that we were near the end, what was the right thing to do?

Andrew understood where Jim was coming from. Prosecutors should be committed to getting to the truth and holding wrongdoers accountable— and Team 600 ran the investigation in that manner. But at the end of an investigation, prosecutors also should be willing to step back and assess the best way to move forward. We were in uncharted waters. None of us had confronted the issue now before us.

We spent the rest of our meeting, and the week that followed, discussing the questions Jim had raised. We discussed how to balance the constitutional arguments laid out in the OLC opinion with the importance of accountability and the strong view held by each of us that no person, even the president, can be above the law.

The OLC opinion is based on the president's unique position in our government and the incapacitating effect a criminal charge could have on the president. According to the opinion, only the president, and not any other public official, has a period of temporary immunity from prosecution while in office.* That is due to the president's role in our government. Under Article II of the Constitution, the "executive power shall be vested" in the president, who is charged to "take Care that the Laws be faithfully executed." The president is the country's sole representative to foreign nations and is the commander in chief of the armed forces. The president and the vice president are the only two officials elected by the entire country. The OLC opinion asks: What process or what person is permitted to make an accusation that "would unduly interfere with the ability of the executive branch to perform its constitutionally assigned duties"?

The OLC opinion answers this question by explaining that under the Constitution, the "mechanism for accusing a sitting President of wrongdoing" is through impeachment by Congress—which is comprised of "politically accountable legislative officials"—and not a prosecutor who is "only indirectly accountable to the public." The opinion cautions against "plac[ing] into the hands of a single prosecutor . . . the practical power to interfere with the ability of a popularly elected President to carry out his constitutional functions."

This constitutional analysis was central to how we approached the issue. Under the Justice Manual, the first thing a prosecutor is supposed to do at the end of an investigation is decide whether he or she believes a person is guilty of a crime. But if Bob took that step for the president, and found that any of the episodes we had investigated had crossed the line into criminal

---

* The Supreme Court's 2024 decision in *Trump v. United States* held that for certain actions the president's immunity is permanent.

conduct, wouldn't Bob then be the single prosecutor accusing a sitting president of a crime?

We also considered whether it made a difference that our findings would be submitted in a "confidential report" to the attorney general and not, at least initially, in a public forum. But the OLC opinion states that even a *sealed* indictment of the president is impermissible because it would be "difficult to preserve its secrecy." If the fact of a sealed indictment became publicly known, which would be likely given the public interest in an indictment charging the president, "the stigma and opprobrium could imperil the President's ability to govern." Similarly, we all understood that even though our report was to be submitted confidentially, it would be nearly impossible for the entire report to stay confidential given public interest in the investigation, particularly if the report included a special counsel's accusation that the president had committed a crime.

By November 16, Team 600 was ready to share its recommendations with Bob and Aaron. We met in the Sequoia conference room, and Team 600 presented two issues that Bob needed to decide.

First, was there any reason to reconsider our decision to adhere to the OLC opinion that a sitting president could not be indicted? Bob dispensed with that quickly. He had decided that issue in April and nothing had changed so dramatically since then that would warrant a different course.

Second, should we evaluate the president's conduct under the standards in the Justice Manual? We walked through the issues we had been discussing within Team 600. We focused on the language in the OLC opinion stating that "the Constitution specifies a mechanism for accusing a sitting president of wrongdoing"—that is, impeachment—not a process in the "hands of a single prosecutor." We discussed how taking the first step in the normal Justice Manual process—for Bob to decide whether he believes the president committed a crime—was inconsistent with this admonition.

To make sure Bob had the full set of considerations, Andrew presented what we believed to be the strongest counterpoint: the department had determined that extraordinary circumstances had required it to step back and for Bob to run this investigation. "The public interest requires me to place this investigation under the authority of a person who exercises a degree of independence from the normal chain of command," Rosenstein had said on May 17, 2017, the day he appointed Bob. Wasn't there a public interest in Bob saying whether he viewed the president's conduct as criminal? How else would people understand the import of what we found in our investigation?

At the end of our discussion, Bob gave his view: We would not make a traditional prosecutorial determination. We would not potentially accuse the president of a crime that he could not defend himself against. That would not be consistent with the OLC opinion. And it would not be consistent with Bob's view of our office's place in the constitutional structure. The Constitution specifies that Congress is responsible for making accusations of presidential wrongdoing.

A question remained: If we weren't going to make a charging decision, should we still assess the evidence under the obstruction-of-justice statute? Ordinarily, a prosecutor weighs the evidence of each element of a crime. Obstruction has three elements: an obstructive act; a "nexus" or connection to an official proceeding; and corrupt intent. Should we apply that analysis here even though Bob decided we would not make a traditional prosecution decision? He said yes. Bob reasoned that it was important for the people most familiar with the evidence to organize, document, and analyze it. And there was a public interest in providing a detailed recitation of the facts and our assessment as to whether or how the evidence matched up with the elements of the statute.

Bob said, "Do it. Write it up."

Eighteen

OUR ANALYSIS AND
OUR WORDS

"Who the hell are you?"

Aaron stood, facing the man who'd just spoken. It was 3:00 p.m. on March 5, 2019. Aaron had been alone in Attorney General William Barr's private conference room at Main Justice, and Barr had just walked in. Aaron and Barr had never met, and these were the first words Barr spoke to him.

Bob and Jim arrived a few minutes later. We had worked with Barr's security detail to avoid anyone knowing that the three of us, but especially Bob, were in the building. It worked almost too well—Aaron had been delivered to the attorney general's inner sanctum without even the attorney general being aware of it.

Barr had been confirmed two weeks earlier, succeeding Attorney General Jeff Sessions, who resigned at President Trump's request in early November. Because Sessions had recused himself from overseeing the Russia investigation, Rosenstein had been the acting attorney general as far as the SCO was concerned. Barr, however, had no recusal issues, so he was the person to whom Bob now reported. As such, Barr had summoned Bob to talk about where things stood.

Bob and Barr knew each other well, the two having served together at the Department of Justice during the George H. W. Bush administration.

Between 1989 and 1993, Barr had held three significant roles—first as head of the OLC, then as deputy attorney general, and finally as attorney general. But while the two men knew and respected one another, Bob was not certain about how Barr would approach our investigation.

We had some hints, however. The day before Barr's Senate confirmation hearing in early December 2018, the DOJ provided us with the nineteen-page memorandum he had authored as a private citizen in June 2018 entitled "Mueller's 'Obstruction' Theory." Among other things, Barr claimed that we were pursuing a "novel" theory of obstruction of justice against the president that was "grossly irresponsible." During Barr's confirmation hearing, Bob's name came up 134 times—many in connection to Barr's memo. Several senators at the hearing wanted to know: Had Barr prejudged the case? Would he permit Bob to finish his work? If yes, would Barr allow the public to see our report? Barr tried to address these issues in his testimony:

> I believe it is vitally important that the special counsel be allowed to complete his investigation. I have known Bob Mueller personally and professionally for thirty years. We worked closely together throughout my previous tenure at the Department of Justice under President Bush. We've been friends since. I have the utmost respect for Bob and his distinguished record of public service. When he was named special counsel, I said that his selection was good news and that, knowing him, I had confidence he would handle the matter properly. I still have that confidence today.

Barr went on to say that it was in everyone's best interest, including the president's, that Bob be allowed to complete his work.

As to whether the office's work would ever see the light of day, Barr said that he aspired to show it. "My goal will be to provide as much transparency as I can, consistent with the law," he stated. California senator

Dianne Feinstein, then the ranking member of the Judiciary Committee, pushed Barr on this topic. Barr responded, "I am going to make as much information available as I can, consistent with the rules and regulations that are part of the special counsel regulations."

As we prepared to meet with Barr on March 5, we were confident we would reach the finish line, and we also knew that would be soon. We had very few loose ends. Roger Stone had refused to speak to us after his indictment in January. We concluded we would not get any information from him that would further the investigation. Aaron met with Rhee as the leader of Team R and confirmed that she saw no remaining Russia-related leads worthy of prolonging the investigation.* Bob was up to speed on each team's work—he had met with team leaders every week throughout the life of the office. In the first days of March and before our meeting with Barr, Bob conferred with Aaron to take stock of the investigation as a whole. Bob concluded there were no additional investigative steps that could or should reasonably be undertaken by our office. The report still required work, but the bulk of it was nearly finished.

We knew that one of the main issues for our March 5 meeting with Barr would be obstruction of justice. In the days leading up to the meeting, O'Callaghan had asked Aaron how we planned to handle our obstruction findings. "Will your report be as aggressive as your legal analysis from last summer?" he asked, referring to the memo we submitted in July 2018 about a subpoena for the president's testimony. "That is a topic we want to discuss."

Aaron explained to O'Callaghan that we would not reach a judgment one way or the other about whether the president had committed a criminal act of obstruction. O'Callaghan asked, more than once, "Are you saying 'but for' the OLC opinion, you would find that the president committed a crime?"

---

* Our other teams had completed their investigative work by February 2019: Team M after Manafort breached his cooperation agreement and was sentenced, Team F after Flynn's plea and a period of attempted cooperation, and Team 600 after Stone's refusal to speak with us.

"No. We have determined not to make a decision about whether the president's conduct amounted to a crime," Aaron responded. "We are not doing a typical prosecution-declination analysis." Aaron and O'Callaghan had covered this terrain a few times, but O'Callaghan told Aaron that Barr wanted to hear directly from Bob on these issues.

And so here we were in a principal-to-principal meeting in the attorney general's conference room. We were joined by O'Callaghan and Rosenstein, both of whom appeared shortly after Aaron finished introducing himself to Barr. Barr then sat at the head of the table, and Bob sat closest to him on one side. Everyone else took seats down the length of the table.

Bob began by delivering a status report in his usual matter-of-fact staccato: "We expect to finish during the week of March 11. We're planning to deliver the report on Friday, March 15." He noted that we had referred more than a dozen cases to other components or offices in the department.* As for the Russia side of the investigation, he stated, "Our conclusions about Russian conduct are clear from the indictments," referring to the charges against Russian individuals and entities for the active-measures and hack-and-dump cases. Bob also pointed to some of our remaining questions about Russian contacts with the Trump campaign, most notably Stone's apparent foreknowledge of WikiLeaks' dumping of emails stolen by Russian military intelligence, and Manafort's transmission of polling data to Konstantin Kilimnik, the Russian national whom the FBI assessed had ties to Russian intelligence.

Aaron and Jim then explained that we were still reviewing returns from a search warrant on some of Stone's electronic media. That work had the potential to delay our plan to close the office, but that was as it should be—evidence establishing a role by Stone in Russian election interference would merit keeping the office open. (As it turned out, the search warrant returns did not yield that kind of evidence).

---

* We referred evidence of potential criminal conduct when the facts were outside the scope of authority given to Bob in his appointment order. Michael Cohen's payment of hush money to Stormy Daniels was one example.

After this, Bob addressed obstruction. We had discussed in advance what to say to Barr about the evidence of the president's efforts to alter or stop the course of the Russia investigation. Bob explained that our inquiry had been about the president's conduct and how it had "affected the integrity of our investigation." Bob did not directly address O'Callaghan's question in the days leading up to the meeting about how "aggressive" the report might be when it came to obstruction. Instead, he repeated that we would follow the OLC opinion, and that we were not ready to give the attorney general our final language.

As the meeting broke, Barr approached Bob, gave him a broad smile, and walked alongside him as we left the room. Aaron was just behind them when he heard Barr ask, "Will the report have an executive summary?"

"Yes," Bob responded. Aaron breathed a sigh of relief. He took Barr's question to mean that if Barr were to release anything in the short term, then it would be our executive summaries. Inside the SCO, we had been taking pains to distill our work into a short introduction and executive summary for each volume. The introductions explained our top-line conclusions and legal analysis, and gave a road map for how each volume was structured. The executive summaries described and analyzed our most important factual findings. Every word was being carefully weighed and reweighed before making the cut. These introductions and summaries would be the definitive distillation of our work—our analysis and our words.

The following day, O'Callaghan called Aaron. He said that Barr and Rosenstein had questions about how we might phrase our conclusion on obstruction. They had no concern with us not stating a definitive crime or no-crime conclusion in volume II. Instead, the issue was framing: Would our report come as a referral about the president's conduct, something akin to a referral to an inspector general?

Aaron was puzzled by the question, and answered with what he presumed Barr was driving at. "We can't say there was no crime," Aaron said. "Could someone evaluate the evidence later? Yes." Aaron was thinking about after the president was out of office and therefore past the period of temporary immunity from prosecution for sitting presidents described by the OLC opinion.

Over the following days, Aaron spoke further with the department about the issue of framing, and the department raised two related questions.

First, they wanted to know if our decision not to reach a prosecutorial judgment about the president's conduct was the equivalent of a declination. Our answer, which by now we were repeating, was a clear no. Based on the evidence we had obtained, we could not say that there was no crime, and our report would not be a declination.

Second, the department wanted to know whether we believed the attorney general had the authority to evaluate and reach his own judgments about the president's conduct. Aaron discussed this with Bob over the course of that week. The attorney general sits atop the entire Department of Justice and remains responsible for a special counsel's investigation—so yes, he could evaluate the president's conduct.

This raised a separate question, however, which Barr's team did not ask: whether the attorney general *should* use that authority. After all, the department had appointed a special counsel so that the attorney general would not make such decisions.

As our proposed March 15 delivery date approached, O'Callaghan called with a new issue: whether it would be clear in the report what was or was not grand jury material. This was important. We understood the question to mean that the DOJ was looking ahead to releasing the report. The Federal Rules of Criminal Procedure generally prohibit the government from disclosing "a matter occurring before the grand jury" except as part of a court proceeding. O'Callaghan was asking, in essence, whether they would be able to determine what was grand jury material (and therefore what the DOJ would have to consider redacting) from the report itself. Broadly speaking, grand jury material is something that discloses the proceedings of a grand jury, which are required by law to remain secret.

We were prepared to identify grand jury material in the report, but we wanted to be careful about how we responded—we were reluctant to be involved in decisions about precisely what the DOJ would redact or release from our confidential report. Under the special counsel regulations, decisions about what to publicly release belonged exclusively to Barr. Public releases had the potential to be politically charged, as was clear from the questions Barr had been asked at his confirmation hearing. We knew the redaction or release of any particular item could be portrayed as hiding or over-disclosing information, all in service of, or in opposition to, one political agenda or another. We had no such agenda.

The task of how to apply the rule protecting grand jury information is often in dispute—and even litigated. There are occasions when the department views the prohibition against disclosure expansively so as to avoid releasing investigative material; other times, the department views it narrowly in the interest of fuller public disclosure. For example, the DOJ could elect to redact information from telephone records (such as who called whom and when) that had been obtained through a grand jury subpoena. Alternatively, it could elect to release that information and redact only the existence of the subpoena.

To release our report, the DOJ would have to apply other redactions as well, for example, to protect sources and methods or to avoid affecting ongoing cases. Those cases included Roger Stone's, which at that point had not yet gone to trial. Some redactions would also have to protect the personal privacy of subjects of investigation whom we had explicitly contemplated charging with a crime, but had not. Like grand jury material, each of these categories required judgment calls by the attorney general.

A day or so after O'Callaghan's call, Rosenstein called Aaron to confirm that grand jury material in our report would be clearly indicated. Aaron said it would be. By then, we had footnoted every fact to make clear where information had come from. Accordingly, if the DOJ chose to release the report, it had what it needed from us to make judgment calls on redactions—including for grand jury material.

As things stood at that precise moment—with all signs being that if the attorney general were to release anything, it would be our work—it did not make sense to play a greater role in the judgments about what should or should not be redacted.

This calculation would soon change.

* * *

We missed our delivery date of March 15. The report was not ready.

Six days later, on March 21, we were still making a small number of final edits. Bob made the following morning, March 22, 2019, our deadline. From Bob's perspective, we had concluded our investigation and he knew we would always find reasons to want additional time to write. When Aaron floated the possibility of holding off for a few more days, Bob gave an answer Aaron had heard from Bob many times at the end of long assignments with an impending deadline: "Quit playing with your food."

As darkness settled on the evening of Thursday, March 21, most of Team 600 squeezed into Andrew's office. Jim holed up in his office across the hall, and Aaron was in his own office next to Jim's. Andrew's group went through the most recent draft of volume II, confirming that everything was 100 percent accurate and making last edits for clarity. When a section had been completed, they would print it for Jim so he could read it with fresh, if tiring, eyes as a final check before it went to Aaron and then to Bob.

Bob ducked out shortly after midnight for a few hours of sleep at home, and Aaron went home to shower and change clothes at 3:30 a.m. For those who lived farther from the office than Aaron, there was no time to go home. We wanted to do one final review first thing in the morning. Andrew turned off the lights in his office and struggled to sleep on the floor. Jim headed to the couch in Bob's office. A couch in your government office is a sign of status—but it is not an assurance of comfort. Moving the blue Naugahyde cushions to the floor, Jim sought and mostly failed to find a couple hours of sleep.

The next morning, we did our final review. For volume I, we discussed one last time whether the report was sufficiently clear about "coordination" with Russia. One of the sticking points: on July 27, 2016, Trump had made his "Russia, if you're listening" speech urging Russia to find Clinton's "missing" emails. Five hours later, the Russian GRU launched attacks into the Clinton team's personal email accounts. This appeared to be Russia's response to Trump's speech.

Bob had tied our work to established criminal standards. We did not view this "call and response"—Trump's publicly asking for an action and then Russia taking one—as sufficient for a criminal agreement or conspiracy. But without more explanation, we were concerned a reader might not understand why these July 27 events did not constitute "coordination." That morning, we added a paragraph to the introduction to volume I to make our reasoning clearer (emphasis added):

"Coordination" does not have a settled definition in federal criminal law. We understood coordination to require an agreement—tacit or express—between the Trump Campaign and the Russian government on election interference. That requires *more than* the two parties taking actions that were informed by or responsive to the other's actions or interests. We applied the term coordination in that sense when stating in the report that the investigation did not establish that the Trump Campaign coordinated with the Russian government in its election-interference activities.[*]

* The introduction to volume I also addressed the term "collusion," which was frequently invoked in discussions about our work. But collusion was not a specific offense or theory of liability in the statutes at issue in our investigation. In evaluating whether evidence about collective action of multiple individuals constituted a crime, we applied the framework of conspiracy law, not the concept of collusion.

While we added this new paragraph to volume I, we continued to scrutinize the introduction to volume II. We recognized the complexity of the issues in those two short pages, and we had worked to make our thinking clear. But in retrospect, it was not as clear as we had hoped. We have been explaining our thinking ever since—including in this book. The paragraph that would produce the most confusion read:

> Because we determined not to make a traditional prosecutorial judgment, we did not draw ultimate conclusions about the President's conduct. The evidence we obtained about the President's actions and intent presents difficult issues that would need to be resolved if we were making a traditional prosecutorial judgment. At the same time, if we had confidence after a thorough investigation of the facts that the President clearly did not commit obstruction of justice, we would so state. Based on the facts and the applicable legal standards, we are unable to reach that judgment. Accordingly, while this report does not conclude that the President committed a crime, it also does not exonerate him.

We tried in this paragraph to make two main points. First, we had *chosen* not to make a traditional prosecutorial judgment. This meant we did not reach "ultimate conclusions" about the president's conduct—we were not saying one way or the other whether the president had committed an obstruction offense.

Second, we could not say that our investigation exonerated the president. This is not a question typically addressed by a prosecutor—whether a crime was *not* committed. But in a case involving the president, if we had concluded that there had been no crime, it would have been essential for us to tell the attorney general.

Only we couldn't. The evidence of the president's interference with the

Russia investigation was substantial enough that we could not say there had been no crime. Taken together with our reference to impeachment (which also was in this same opening section of volume II), we were trying to convey that it was Congress's role to make judgments about a sitting president, not a lone prosecutor's. The OLC opinion pointed out that only Congress, with its unique Article I powers, had the ability to hold a sitting president to account.

Bob reviewed the final edits at around 11:00 a.m. We then printed a complete copy of the report, placed it in an unmarked filing folder, and double-wrapped it with packing tape for security. At noon, Ben Cohen, our security officer, went to the underground parking lot, climbed into his unmarked FBI SUV, and drove the report to Main Justice. None of the reporters outside our office paid any attention to him—just as they hadn't on the many occasions when he quietly drove key witnesses into or out of our building.

A short while later, Cohen handed the report to O'Callaghan in his fourth-floor office, which was connected to Rosenstein's suite of offices. It was done.

Cohen then returned to Patriots Plaza. By 4:30 p.m., everyone began to filter out. Each of us was looking forward to some sleep over the weekend.

Later that day, Barr sent a one-page letter to the chairs and ranking members of the Judiciary Committees in both the House and Senate, and then released his letter publicly. It stated, in part, that Bob had concluded his investigation and submitted his report. Barr also wrote, in accordance with the special counsel regulations that require the attorney general to notify Congress at the end of an investigation if he had overruled any of our decisions, that there were no instances "'in which the Attorney General' or acting Attorney General 'concluded that a proposed action by [the] Special Counsel was so inappropriate or unwarranted under established Departmental practices that it should not be pursued.'"

We zeroed in on one additional paragraph in Barr's letter: "I am review-ing the report and anticipate that I may be in a position to advise you of the Special Counsel's principal conclusions as soon as this weekend." We imme-diately asked ourselves, was he referring to our executive summaries that contained our "principal conclusions," or was he planning something else?

Nineteen

THE BARR REPORT

Sunday, March 24, 2019

Early on Sunday afternoon, O'Callaghan called Aaron at home.

"What would you say if offered an opportunity to look at the AG's letter to Congress about your report?" O'Callaghan asked.

Bright sunshine streamed into Aaron's home office. It had been forty-eight hours since Ben Cohen delivered our report, and O'Callaghan's phrasing stood out. The attorney general was not offering an opportunity to look at his letter—he was trying to figure out whether to make such an offer.

Aaron immediately thought that if Barr was to provide Congress with our "principal conclusions," as he had suggested on Friday, he had our executive summaries and should use those. If Barr had altered our summary, we were never going to adopt it, and we didn't want to take a step that could be claimed as an endorsement of his version.

But before answering, Aaron had to run the question by Bob. "I'll have to get back to you," he told O'Callaghan.

"It'll need to be soon," O'Callaghan responded, indicating Barr's letter was imminent.

Aaron called Bob and conferenced in Jim. He relayed O'Callaghan's question (really, the attorney general's question) and his own immediate thoughts that we should push for Barr to use our executive summaries for any letter to Congress or for public release.

Both Bob and Jim agreed. Bob commented that this was Barr's letter on Barr's schedule—no way we were going to put ourselves in a position where someone else's responsibility and schedule would drive or limit our ability to get it right. If Barr planned to release a summary of our report, our executive summaries already had it right. Barr should use those.

Aaron drove to the office so he could have access to all of our files if necessary. He then called O'Callaghan. "We would not review the letter if asked," Aaron said. He made clear that the attorney general should use our summaries. There wasn't a reason for the attorney general—or anyone else—to prepare different ones, and we weren't going to enable Barr to do so by participating. "Our report states our results and decisions," Aaron said. "Our summary is *the* summary; it was the result of extensive internal work and decision-making."

O'Callaghan thanked Aaron for the quick response and hung up.

An hour or so later, Barr sent a four-page letter to Congress; the DOJ released it publicly at the same time. The letter claimed to "summarize the principal conclusions reached by the Special Counsel and the results of his investigation."

But the letter did not accurately summarize our principal conclusions. It did not track our introductions or executive summaries. It omitted or misstated our analysis. In its discussion of volume I, the letter accurately stated our core charging decisions, but left out any reference to the intent of the Russian social media campaign to aid Trump in his bid for the White House, nor did it describe that same objective driving the hack-and-dump operation run by Russian military intelligence. There was no mention of the contacts between members of the Trump campaign and Russian officials and proxies. The letter also left out a core conclusion of volume I: that the "Russian government perceived it would benefit from a Trump presidency and worked to secure that outcome, and that the [Trump] Campaign expected it would benefit electorally from information stolen and released through Russian [military intelligence] efforts."

But our principal concern was Barr's characterization of volume II, which was further off from our actual analysis and words. Unlike our Russia investigation and its multiple public indictments, there was *no* other public explanation of our work on obstruction. Barr did not mention any of the facts of the ten potentially obstructive episodes we had examined, nor did he explain or describe our legal analysis. Without any of this, it was impossible to understand what we had done or concluded regarding the law and the president's conduct.

The letter stated that Bob's "decision to describe facts of his obstruction investigation without reaching any legal conclusions leaves it to the Attorney General whether the conduct described in the report constitutes a crime."

This was not accurate. We had reached significant legal conclusions (based on then-current law) about how the obstruction-of-justice statute applied to the president. We also had decided, based on our legal analysis of the OLC opinion and Bob's view of his role as special counsel, that we *would not* determine whether the president's conduct violated the law. However, Barr's letter suggested that we *could not* reach a judgment about the president's conduct and that we had left the decision to him. That was not what we had done. Barr had the authority to reach his own conclusions—but we certainly had not left it to him in this way.

The letter also stated that Barr and Rosenstein had reviewed the report and consulted with DOJ officials, and that they had "concluded that the evidence developed during the Special Counsel's investigation is not sufficient to establish that the President committed an obstruction-of-justice offense." Without mentioning any of the president's conduct that we had described in the report, Barr's letter said that the report "identifies no actions that . . . constitute obstructive conduct, had a nexus to a pending or contemplated proceeding, and were done with corrupt intent." This language struck us because while we had not made a final judgment or accusation about whether any of the ten episodes constituted a crime, we had concluded there was substantial evidence showing each element of obstruction in four of the episodes. In fewer than forty-eight hours, without asking us any questions, Barr had concluded the opposite.

Barr ended his letter to Congress by stating that he intended to release as much of the report as possible consistent with applicable law and DOJ policy. He also wrote that before he could release the report, the department had to identify grand jury material as well as information that could affect ongoing DOJ matters, including matters Bob had referred to other parts of the department. Barr said he was requesting Bob's assistance in making these determinations.

At 4:13 p.m., minutes after the public release of Barr's letter, the White House press secretary put out a tweet announcing: "The Special Counsel did not find any collusion and did not find any obstruction. AG Barr and DAG Rosenstein further determined there was no obstruction. The findings of the Department of Justice are a total and complete exoneration of the President of the United States."

Monday, March 25, 2019

The mood in the SCO Monday morning was a combination of shock and anger. Before that weekend, we had understood that if Barr chose to release anything, it would be our carefully worded summaries. Instead, Barr had written a new summary of our "principal conclusions" that was inaccurate and incomplete in critical ways.

Aaron spoke to the department early that morning. As he held the phone, he was surprised to discover that he was struggling to contain his anger and disappointment. Aaron got right to the point: "Our summary is *the* summary. It was difficult to get there"—meaning every word had been carefully chosen, checked, and re-weighed. Aaron said that Barr's letter failed to reflect our work and was incomplete.

The attorney general's team interjected, "Is there anything *wrong* in the letter?"

The tone and content of the question surprised Aaron—because the answer was obvious. Yes, the letter was wrong on multiple points.

Aaron began by identifying the letter's inaccurate statements about our legal analysis: "The AG's letter says our report did not reach any legal conclusions, but we did reach legal judgments about the OLC opinion and about the application of the obstruction statutes to the president." As to the facts, Aaron said, "We did an analysis of the facts and law and concluded we couldn't say the president had not committed a crime." None of that was in Barr's letter.

There was more to say, but without any recognition from the department that it needed to take immediate corrective action, Aaron ended the call. It was clear we had to take a different tack.

Aaron grabbed Jim and pulled him into Bob's office. The attorney general had put out his own analysis while withholding ours. We needed to get the department to correct course, and decided on our next steps: we would immediately scrub the introductions and executive summaries for grand jury information or anything that could potentially harm any ongoing cases. This only took about an hour. By early afternoon, these were ready for release. We simultaneously launched an office-wide effort to scrub and prepare the entire report for public release.

That afternoon, Bob sent a short letter to Barr, enclosing the ready-for-release introductions and executive summaries, explaining the redactions. Bob referred to Barr's letter and its request for our assistance in identifying such grand jury material as quickly as possible—here was exactly that assistance. The summaries were ready to go.

Ben Cohen hand-delivered all of this to O'Callaghan's office by late Monday afternoon.

Tuesday, March 26, 2019

We heard nothing from Barr.

Bob convened an all-hands meeting at 1:00 p.m. People were disappointed and confused. "I wanted to get together to tell you what's going on, and to say thank you again," Bob began. "I know you are pissed. I want to tell you what has happened."

Bob walked everyone through the timeline of the last several days, including that Barr had "completed his own analysis of the president's conduct" described in volume II. Bob then summarized our plan to move as quickly as possible to prepare the full report for release, explaining that on the previous afternoon we had "delivered copies of the introductions and executive summaries to the department with modest redactions." He expressed his hope that the department would release them imminently.

Wednesday, March 27, 2019

Congress and the media were now raising more questions and expressing greater confusion about what had already been dubbed "the Mueller Report." Some outlets interpreted Barr's letter as saying that Bob had bypassed obstruction altogether—yet we had not bypassed it; the entirety of volume II analyzed the president's conduct and reached factual and legal judgments about it.

Aaron called O'Callaghan to push for the department to release our summaries and to clear up the confusion that Barr had created. The message was unequivocal: "There is confusion. We want to release."

O'Callaghan responded, "The AG has made up his mind about release of the executive summaries." He explained that Barr was not willing to release the report in parts. "But you're free to weigh in." The call ended.

Following this, Bob wrote another letter to Barr. This time, he highlighted the damage caused by Barr's continued refusal to release our work.

The letter recounted the course of events since early March: "As we stated in our meeting of March 5 and reiterated to the Department early in the afternoon of March 24, the introductions and executive summaries of our two-volume report accurately summarize [our] work and conclusions."

Bob continued: "The summary letter the Department sent to Congress . . . did not fully capture the context, nature, and substance of this Office's work and conclusions. We communicated that concern to the Department on the morning of March 25. There is now public confusion about critical aspects of the results of our investigation." With these few sentences, Bob had summed up all that was wrong about Barr's response to our report, the harm it was causing, and what we had done to try to help Barr correct course.

As he had two days earlier, Bob enclosed ready-for-publication versions of the introductions and executive summaries. "The enclosed documents are in a form that can be released to the public consistent with legal requirements and Department policies. I am requesting that you provide these materials to Congress and authorize their public release at this time."

DOJ officials typically do not send letters to the attorney general calling on him or her to change course. By writing it down and sending it with his signature, Bob was committing the issue to paper in a way that, he believed, would force Barr to act. Bob had been crystal clear: You have caused confusion about our work. The only way to fix that is to release our summaries, and they are ready for release.

As we awaited Barr's response, we briefly considered whether to release the summaries ourselves. Such a step would have taken from the attorney general a decision that belonged to Barr by regulation. We also were concerned that a unilateral release by Bob (or a public statement by Bob requesting release) would cast our work in a political light—as though we were hoping to score points against Barr or the president.

Thursday, March 28, 2019

At 11:30 a.m., Barr's assistant called the office and asked for Bob. Connie Kozlusky (Bob's intrepid and longtime executive assistant) quietly told Aaron and Jim that the attorney general was on the line.

They joined the call in Bob's office.

As soon as Barr came on the line, he said, "What the hell is this letter, Bob?"

Bob's phone was on speaker so we all heard it. Bob responded that Barr's March 24 letter had not put the issues in their full context. "There are now mischaracterizations" of our analysis, Bob said. He added, "We need something more accurate. We worked long and hard on the introductions and executive summaries. Everyone would be best served by releasing those."

Barr paused. "I was summarizing the bottom line only," he explained. "I'd prefer to get the report all out at once, not piecemeal." Then he added, "I can see a compromise by releasing the introduction to volume II."

This didn't make a great deal of sense to us in the moment—how would that kind of compromise solve Barr's concern for piecemeal releases? But perhaps this was a start.

Bob answered, "I think that's the issue," referring to Barr's treatment of volume II as the area of greatest confusion. "I want maximum disclosure to explain our work." Bob closed by saying he was most worried about the explanation of our work on obstruction—it had been delicate and dealt with multiple factors. All of that had been lost.

As soon as the call with Barr concluded, Aaron and Jim called O'Callaghan. O'Callaghan repeated Barr's idea of releasing just the introductions—but this time he mentioned volume I in addition to volume II. Aaron then repeated a version of Bob's point to Barr: "We'd prefer they not go alone and, instead, go with the executive summaries."

Friday, March 29, 2019

Public confusion about our conclusions and reasoning continued. The media discussed obstruction as something Bob had been incapable of deciding, not something that he had determined should not be decided by a lone prosecutor. Some members of Congress were erroneously stating that volume I had found "no" evidence of Russian contacts with the Trump campaign. Some lawmakers were also asking whether any of our work had been necessary, because—as they now believed—there was "no" evidence of a connection between Trump and Russia. This was all incorrect.

In a series of calls throughout the day, we continued to press the department to release the introductions and executive summaries. That evening, Barr sent another letter to Congress, making it clear he was no longer willing to carry out the compromise he had suggested on Wednesday. He was not going to release either our introductions or executive summaries in the near term. The letter stated he would work with our office to prepare the full report for release—meaning redacting sensitive material—but added, "I do not believe it would be in the public's interest for me to attempt to summarize the full report or to release it in serial or piecemeal fashion."

Barr had purported to "summarize" our work, but did so inaccurately. He was now using a stated aversion to a release in "piecemeal fashion" to refuse what we had been requesting he do since Monday morning.

This letter from Barr also outlined his process for preparing the report for eventual release. He described four categories of redactions that would need to be applied: grand jury information (which we had already identified); materials "the intelligence community identifies as potentially compromising sensitive sources and methods"; material that could affect ongoing matters; and information that would unduly affect the privacy of uncharged persons. Barr noted that the report was "nearly 400 pages long" and that he expected the redaction process to take several weeks.*

Barr also attempted to defend his initial March 24 letter. "I am aware of some media reports and other public statements mischaracterizing my March 24, 2019 supplemental notification as a 'summary' of the Special Counsel's investigation and report," he wrote. He added that his March 24 letter "was not, and did not purport to be, an exhaustive recounting of the Special Counsel's investigation or report." Barr said his March 24 letter was intended to be "a summary of [the report's] 'principal conclusions'—that is, its bottom line," and he noted that "everyone will soon be able to read it on their own."

The result of this latest letter by Barr was that his March 24 summary letter—the words of the politically appointed attorney general, not the special counsel—would remain the only description of our obstruction work available to the public for the next several weeks. Barr's account of our report became the de facto official account for many.

*   *   *

Before our March 22 delivery of the report, we had tried to steer clear of the attorney general's decisions about what aspects of our report to release. But now, in order to correct the record, we had no choice but to sprint to identify redactions across the whole report for each of the four categories that Barr had spelled out in his March 29 letter. We finished this work on April 15.

---

* Barr did not mention in his letter a potential fifth category for potential redaction: information protected by executive privilege. When the report was ultimately released on April 18, 2019, Barr said that the president "could have asserted privilege" over aspects of the report, but after a review the president "confirmed" he would not do so.

Barr released our report three days later, at 11:00 a.m. on April 18, 2019.

That morning, Barr stepped behind a podium at Main Justice. After some introductory remarks, he said, "I would like to offer a few comments today on the report." He started with volume I, describing the Russian social media campaign. But, as he had in his March 24 letter, he omitted any mention of Russian support for Trump's election bid.

He then described the Russian military intelligence operation to steal and dump Clinton campaign emails, but again omitted the Russian government's purpose of harming Clinton's election bid in order to aid Trump. Barr also did not mention our finding that the Trump campaign expected it would benefit electorally from information stolen and released through Russian military intelligence efforts.

Regarding volume II, Barr stated that our office had examined ten episodes of conduct involving the president. He did not describe any of these episodes, each of which involved potentially obstructive conduct. He said he had concluded that the evidence was not sufficient to establish that the president had committed obstruction of justice.

He then added that "it is important to bear in mind the context" of these episodes. Barr said that the president had faced "relentless speculation in the news media" about his potential culpability and was, according to Barr, "frustrated and angered by a sincere belief that the investigation was undermining his presidency, propelled by his political opponents, and fueled by illegal leaks."

For two years, we sought to act with integrity, speed, and a commitment to the rule of law. We understood that the Russia investigation had an impact on the presidency, but Barr's words struck us as an argument a defense lawyer would have made.

Barr also said that the White House had "fully cooperated" with our investigation, and that the president "took no act" that deprived us of the "documents and witnesses" necessary to complete the investigation. But Trump himself refused to be interviewed, unlike other presidents who had faced investigation. And his private and public comments concerning cooperation with our office may have deterred subjects like Roger Stone and Paul Manafort from cooperating.

At 12:59 p.m., after Barr's press conference concluded, President Trump tweeted, "As I have been saying all along, NO COLLUSION—NO OBSTRUCTION!"

* * *

The special counsel regulations require a "confidential" report to the attorney general, and the notion of a public report that describes both prosecution and declination decisions is contrary to normal DOJ practice. Prosecutors typically do not issue public reports about wrongdoing that is not charged as a crime.

At the same time, the attorney general calls upon a special counsel only in "extraordinary circumstances," for instance, when there is a potential conflict of interest for ordinary DOJ officials to run a case. This is when it is "in the public interest to appoint an outside Special Counsel." It is precisely in these circumstances that public confidence is won and the public interest is served when the public can see the work of the special counsel—and know that it was carried out with integrity.

We have dubbed Barr's March 24 letter to Congress "the Barr Report." Once Barr made the decision to publicly release the results of our investigation, he should have used our analysis and our words—not his. The purpose of appointing a special counsel was to shield the investigation from political interference so there would be public confidence in the outcome. That required the public to see our actual analysis and conclusions, not those of the politically appointed attorney general.

Twenty

CLOSING THE OFFICE

Following Barr's press conference and the public release of our report, the one thing left to do was close the office. This was no small task. We'd handled a lot of material, much of it classified, nearly all of it sensitive, and now it had to be processed and stored. We couldn't simply turn off the lights, call it a day, and take some time off with our respective families and friends.

Some agents and prosecutors had turned in their SCO badges shortly after we delivered the report, but Bob, Aaron, Jim, and Andrew would stay to the end.

While our final days were largely dedicated to organizing and storing records and handling logistics, we also devoted significant time and energy to responding to the aftereffects of the public release of our report.

Almost immediately after its release, Congress began to make noise about Bob testifying. This did not come as a surprise.

Bob had testified before Congress at least a hundred times, nearly all as FBI director during oversight hearings. But if he had to appear this time, it would be different. Bob had just concluded two years as special counsel—as a federal prosecutor—and had delivered a confidential report to the attorney general that had now been released in redacted form. Two of the cases we had charged, which we had handed off to the US Attorney's Office for the District of Columbia, were still in litigation. One of them—against Roger Stone—would go to trial in the coming months, and the presiding judge had issued a gag order prohibiting government officials (including Bob) from commenting on case proceedings. The other, against the Russian companies involved in the active-measures interference campaign, was also proceeding in court. The court in that case had issued its own gag order, which Bob was also bound by. Additionally, we had referred more than a dozen other cases to US attorney's offices around the country, a majority of which remained ongoing criminal investigations. (Some would result in criminal charges and convictions, others would not.)

Given these circumstances, Bob could not testify without potentially violating a court's order or compromising criminal cases. But beyond this, unlike his time as FBI director when he testified as part of Congress's oversight of the bureau, it was not Bob's role as a federal prosecutor to be involved in a political process before Congress.

Moreover, there was nothing more to say. The findings and conclusions of our investigation were already stated in our report. Every word had been chosen with care and had been reviewed multiple times. If more were needed, our report had identified a long list of documents and witnesses with firsthand accounts of events. Congress had a road map for where to look.

On May 3, the Democrat-controlled House Judiciary Committee demanded Attorney General Barr comply with the committee's subpoena to deliver an unredacted report by May 6. At that moment, some in Congress and the media were talking about what the OLC opinion referred to as the "constitutional process for addressing presidential misconduct"—that is, impeachment. When Barr declined to produce the unredacted report, the Judiciary Committee voted to hold him in contempt of Congress.

Throughout May, the calls for Bob to appear before the Judiciary Committee and others grew. Bob was steadfast: the report *was* his testimony, and he would not appear before Congress. But these calls didn't fade, and, as we discussed how to handle them, we realized that over the course of two years as special counsel, no one had heard Bob utter a word. He hadn't spoken publicly once, and intentionally so. His preference was for the office's work—the indictments, the Manafort trial, the seven guilty pleas, and the report—to speak for itself.

Bob decided that on the very last day of the office, he would make one definitive public statement. We hoped that doing so would meet the demand to hear directly from him, and he could do it from behind a DOJ podium, not at a witness table in Congress. We also saw this as an opportunity to state in simpler terms our analysis in the introduction of volume II of our report, which explained why we had not made a judgment about whether the president had committed a crime.

On Wednesday, May 29, 2019, two years and twelve days from the date of his appointment, Bob, along with Aaron, Jim, and Peter Carr—the press representative who had served quietly and professionally for two years—were driven to Main Justice by Ben Cohen in his unmarked FBI SUV. Andrew and the small number of others who had stayed to the end traveled to the DOJ headquarters separately. We arrived early—Bob was never late to anything—and made our way to the greenroom on the seventh floor behind the stage where the attorney general and other senior DOJ officials briefed the press.

That morning, Bob walked down the narrow hall to the press room and took the podium. The Washington press corps was assembled. Aaron, Jim, and Andrew stayed behind and watched on the greenroom's television; Carr sat with the reporters.

Bob opened with a brief synopsis of his appointment and then said that we would be formally closing the office, after which he would resign from the Department of Justice and return to private life. When his statement moved to the substance of our report, he focused on two messages. The first, which had been lost in the way Barr had handled the report's release, was the magnitude of Russia's interference in the 2016 election.

Bob emphasized that Russian military intelligence officers had launched a concerted attack on our political system that had been designed and timed to interfere with our election and damage a presidential candidate. Running alongside this, a private Russian entity—the Internet Research Agency, headed by a close associate of Putin's, Yevgeny Prigozhin—had engaged in a social media operation in which Russians posed as Americans, also to influence our election.

Bob then addressed a different form of interference—obstruction of justice—and why it mattered. The department had established our office so that we could investigate and understand all that Russia had done to interfere in the presidential election. "The matters we investigated were of paramount importance," Bob said, which also was a reason "we investigated efforts to obstruct the investigation." Bob explained that it had been "critical for us to obtain full and accurate information from every person we questioned. When a subject of an investigation obstructs that investigation or lies to investigators, it strikes at the core of their government's effort to find the truth and hold wrongdoers accountable."

He then moved to why we decided not to make a traditional prosecutorial decision about the president's conduct. He explained that the office was bound by the OLC opinion and stated that after our "investigation, if we had had confidence that the president clearly did not commit a crime, we would have said so." He continued, "We did not, however, make a determination as to whether the president did commit a crime." As to judgments about the president's conduct, "the Constitution requires a process other than the criminal justice system to formally accuse a sitting president of wrongdoing." As our report stated, this process is impeachment, a process that Congress and Congress alone can initiate and undertake.

Bob closed by saying that these would be his only remarks on our office and the report. "No one has told me whether I can or should testify or speak further about this matter," he said. "There has been discussion about an appearance before Congress, [but] any testimony from this office would not go beyond our report." He added, as we had said among ourselves, "The report is my testimony."

In closing, he thanked the people who had worked in our office, told the reporters that he would not take questions, and then quietly left the stage.

*   *   *

A few days later, Aaron walked out of his local gym, got in his car, and started the engine. His cell phone rang as he sat there, car idling. It was a professor at the University of Virginia School of Law calling to ask whether Bob might serve as a scholar in residence for the coming semester. Bob was an alumnus and had spoken at UVA many times; perhaps he would consider spending more time there.

The call ended and Aaron called Bob to convey the request. The school had included Aaron in the offer (he was an alumnus too), but this was all about Bob: Would he be a "scholar in residence" at UVA?

"You can tell them I will be neither," Bob responded.

He spoke in jest, but he also meant it. He did not view himself as a "scholar" and he was not planning to live in Charlottesville. He planned to return to private practice at his former firm in DC. Despite Bob's initial reaction, this was the moment we began to formulate the idea for our UVA law course, which we have taught each fall since 2021.

Later that same afternoon, a staffer from the House Judiciary Committee called Aaron. He let it go to voicemail and passed word to the DOJ that Congress was reaching out.

Early the following week, Adam Schiff, the chair of the House Intelligence Committee, contacted both Bob and Aaron, requesting that Bob testify before Congress. By June 7, only ten days after Bob's press conference, the DOJ called Aaron to tell him the Intelligence Committee was trying to contact him to "work out the parameters of Bob's testimony." The Hill was not asking *whether* Bob would testify, but trying to figure *how* he would testify.

On June 17, Aaron and Jim trudged to Capitol Hill. Neither wanted to be there. (Jim had cut short a family vacation in celebration of his sister's birthday.) Aaron, in his former role as FBI chief of staff, had spent significant time in meetings with congressional members and staff negotiating witness and other evidence issues, so he knew what to expect. They met with representatives of the House Judiciary and Intelligence Committees. Aaron took the lead, telling the group that we recognized Congress had legitimate interest in the content of the report, but that Bob meant what he had said at his press conference—he did not think it was appropriate for him to testify, and he had nothing more to say.

Aaron explained that Bob was adamant that as a prosecutor, he should speak only through the public work of the office. Aaron pointed to the ongoing cases, any one of which could be affected by Bob's testimony. He also highlighted the two standing gag orders in cases our office had indicted.

We added that an appearance before Congress would be perceived as Bob participating in a political process, which would diminish Bob's work and the work of the entire SCO. The committees also had all they needed to identify fact witnesses who could provide firsthand accounts.

Aaron urged the committees' staff to accept Bob's decision. He told them that we were willing to put his position in a letter and send it to them. "Don't read this as a request for a subpoena," Aaron said. "It isn't." Bob was not being a reluctant witness; he was outright declining.

They didn't listen. We continued to refuse in follow-up meetings and calls, but the talk on the Hill soon turned to a subpoena. Bob was willing to tell Congress it should not ask him to testify, but he would not defy a subpoena. When it became clear that subpoenas were imminent, Bob knew he would have to testify. No date was initially set, but it would happen sometime in July 2019.

*   *   *

Preparing for a congressional hearing is its own special hell. You must simultaneously know the facts and the political point your questioners might be trying to score through your answers—so that you can avoid being used as a political instrument. Bob knew better than most how to do this, and his preparation had always been exceptionally rigorous. This hearing would be no different. Aaron and Jim were on board to help, but were hoping for some assistance.

Andrew and his wife were hiking in Bryce Canyon National Park in Utah when his phone rang. They were on top of a mountain, taking in the red, Mars-like landscape. Andrew had been trying not to think about work.

He saw that it was Aaron and answered. "I know you are far away," Aaron said. "But I have news. Congress decided to subpoena Bob. He is going to have to testify. Can you help us prepare?"

Andrew mouthed to his wife, *Bob's getting subpoenaed.* After a pause he answered, "Yes. I can be there in forty-eight hours."

By late June, the House Intelligence and Judiciary Committees had both subpoenaed Bob. Perhaps the only benefit of the subpoenas was they made clear to the public that this was not something Bob was choosing to do; rather, he was being legally compelled to appear.

The subpoenas required testimony on July 17, but the hearing date was later moved to July 24. The Judiciary Committee would go first and take up the full morning, concentrating on the president's conduct detailed in volume II. The Intelligence Committee would go in the afternoon and focus on the Russia-related topics of volume I.

With the arrival of the subpoenas, Aaron spoke to Rosenstein, O'Callaghan, and others about what Bob would be permitted to say in an open hearing: Could he talk about the redacted sections of the report? Could he discuss the myriad facts and prosecutorial judgments that never made it into the report? The answer, in short, was no.

On July 22, 2019, the department formalized its position in a letter to Bob. They wrote, "[A]ny testimony must remain within the boundaries of your public report because matters within the scope of your investigation were covered by executive privilege. . . . [You] should decline to address potentially privileged matters." Bob knew without asking that anything classified remained out of bounds, as did any topic relating to any of the more than a dozen ongoing cases.

What was already a significant undertaking—preparing to address questions about a 448-page report—had become more difficult. In essence, Bob had to be able to parse and respond to any aspect of the report on the spot, all while knowing what he could *not* talk about—not just the redactions, but the totality of our investigation, some elements of which did not make it into the report.

This was unreasonable, and based on our conversations with the congressional committees and the department, they recognized that too. Bob requested that Aaron—who had been his deputy and, effectively, the chief operating officer for all investigation and prosecution matters—be permitted to testify alongside him. Aaron was the one person in the office besides Bob who had read every pleading in every case in the SCO. If some detail were needed in the course of the hearing that wasn't at Bob's fingertips, then Aaron could take the question.

* * *

The morning of July 24 was hot and dry. There were no windows in the Judiciary Committee hearing room, and it was packed. Bob went to the witness table, Aaron at his side. Jim and Andrew sat behind Bob in the first row.

Between the witness table and the dais where more than forty representatives sat was a phalanx of press photographers. Bob and Aaron stood to be sworn in, and the cameras all went off at once, clacking like a hailstorm on a tin roof. Normally, after a hearing commences, the photographers stop taking pictures or largely disappear, but for these two hearings many stayed for the full seven hours and never stopped snapping photos.

Bob made his statement. He thanked the representatives, repeated much of what he had said in his press conference, set expectations about what he would and would not talk about, and once again thanked the attorneys, FBI agents, analysts, and professional staff who had worked hard and with integrity for over two years at the special counsel's office.

He closed his statement repeating what we all felt was our work's most important message, one that Congress and the American people should hear and have no confusion about:

"Over the course of my career, I've seen a number of challenges to our democracy. The Russian government's effort to interfere in our election is among the most serious. As I said on May 29, this deserves the attention of every American."

He was right.

Twenty-One

THE RULE OF LAW

Nearly every day for two years, media coverage of the SCO pitted Bob against Trump, raising hopes for some that our investigation would take down the president. At the same time, others accused us of conducting a baseless "witch hunt" aimed at bringing down Trump.

Both of these perspectives missed the point. The criminal justice system does not pit a prosecutor against the subjects of investigation in the ways longed for or feared by either of these political camps. The work and the markers of success do not depend on outcomes in this way. It was never the mission of the special counsel to bring down Trump. And the mismatch between some people's expectations and the reality of what a criminal investigation of a sitting president could and should actually do came at a real cost. Accusations that we were not aggressive enough, or that we were out to get Trump, led millions of people to discount or dismiss the results of our investigation.

One of the main purposes of a special counsel is to give the American people confidence that an investigation will be carried out fairly and thoroughly, and without undue influence from the president or an attorney general who is appointed by the president. And when the subject of an investigation is the president, as this book has discussed, there are unique constitutional and other factors to navigate—not least that the special counsel is within the executive branch, one step (by way of the attorney general) from the president. We were investigating the president using what is ultimately the president's own power.

After our report came out and Bob testified before Congress, some people concluded that he had not been the right person for the job. The critique was that Bob was too by the book, too much of an institutionalist, for an investigation of a president who bent norms and used his immense power to undermine our work.

We thought at the time, and believe just as strongly now with the benefit of five years of perspective, that this criticism has it backward. Bob was the right person for this role precisely because he understood the importance of America's institutions and because he would not put short-term expediency over principle. He took the long view of the rule of law throughout his career—and he did so here as well.

Over the last several years, we have seen attacks on America's most important institutions, and the occasional fragility of those institutions in the face of those attacks. The Department of Justice is entrusted with enforcing the law fairly and evenhandedly. Trump, first as president and then as the leading Republican candidate for the 2024 election, has repeatedly attacked the DOJ and the FBI. This started with his firing of Comey, carried through the two years of our investigation, and continues as of this writing. Trump has referred to Special Counsel Jack Smith as "Deranged Jack Smith" and the FBI as "Hacks and Thugs." These attacks erode Americans' faith in these critical institutions and harm the presidency itself. Many now perceive the DOJ and the FBI as tools that are deployed against political adversaries depending on who holds the reins of executive power. The result is deep distrust in cases brought by the DOJ, even where the evidence of wrongdoing is clear. Perhaps worse, parties who claim they were victims of past abuse say they now are willing to use the DOJ to settle scores. Many Americans accept this kind of retribution as ordinary, a downward spiral that was inconceivable until recent years.

As we see it, the best way—the only way—to push back against the erosion of faith in the DOJ is for prosecutors to show in all they do that they act in the service of justice and the rule of law, and nothing else. As Attorney General Robert H. Jackson put it in 1940, the best protection against abuse of power is a prosecutor who "seeks truth and not victims," "who serves the law" and not any "factional" purpose, and who "approaches his task with humility." That was Bob Mueller.

Bob required the office to put these principles and integrity first. We stayed within the scope of Bob's appointment order and worked quickly. We made sure there were no leaks, which would have been seen as manipulating public opinion and which we knew would have unfairly impacted innocent people who might have gotten swept up in the investigation. We did not include gratuitous details or try to land unnecessary punches in our court filings, our charging instruments, or our report, nor did Bob do any of that in his testimony before Congress.

These principles were evident in Bob's decision not to engage in a lengthy legal battle over a subpoena for President Trump's testimony—especially once it became clear that Trump was unlikely ever to testify and where we had accumulated substantial other evidence about his state of mind. Bob's instinct was correct. In August 2023, Trump asserted his Fifth Amendment right not to testify more than four hundred times during a deposition in a case brought by the New York attorney general, and in the spring of 2024, Trump declined to testify in the criminal case against him brought by the Manhattan District Attorney's Office.

It is also clear that a subpoena for the president's testimony would have raised serious legal issues requiring months if not years to litigate, and could have resulted in adverse court decisions that undermined rather than advanced presidential accountability.

The Supreme Court issued two opinions in 2024, five years after our office closed, that substantially narrowed the scope of presidential conduct that can be subject to criminal investigation. In one case, *Fischer v. United States*, the

Supreme Court held by a vote of 6–3 that the obstruction-of-justice statute that was the focus of volume II of our report applies only to actions that impair the availability or integrity of evidence used in an official proceeding. The Court held that this provision does not apply to other actions that impede an official proceeding, even if they were done for a corrupt purpose.

In the other case, *Trump v. United States*, the Supreme Court held, also by a vote of 6–3, that a president has absolute immunity from criminal prosecution when carrying out "core" constitutional functions, such as issuing pardons and removing executive officers, and has "presumptive immunity" for all "official" actions. The Court held that a president is not immune for "unofficial" actions.

These decisions sharply limit the areas of presidential conduct that can be subject to criminal investigation—permitting a president to use his or her power in wholly corrupt ways without the possibility of prosecution. And because a special counsel (or any DOJ prosecutor enforcing the criminal laws) is authorized to investigate only conduct that might constitute a crime, the Supreme Court has placed many presidential actions beyond the scope of investigation—thereby potentially preventing that conduct from ever seeing the light of day. It will likely take years for the full implications of these decisions to play out.

*   *   *

Bob's commitment to principle also was evident in his decision not to say, under the Justice Manual, whether he "believed" the president had committed a crime. Even before the Supreme Court's 2024 immunity decision, the DOJ Office of Legal Counsel issued an opinion stating it was unconstitutional to charge a *sitting* president with a crime, regardless of whether that charge were filed under seal. Making an accusation of wrongdoing against the president, OLC said, is the responsibility of Congress, not a lone prosecutor.

But if a criminal charge or accusation of Trump was not an option, what was the purpose of our investigation of the president's conduct? What, if anything, did we anticipate happening with our findings?

Bob intended our report to be the definitive account of the facts—about Russian election interference and its links to the Trump campaign, and about Trump's conduct toward that investigation. We hope we succeeded in that endeavor. There has been no serious dispute about any fact we found or sequence of events we described in our 448-page report. Bob also intended that the manner in which we conducted the investigation would stand up now and forever.

We anticipated that Congress would take steps to look at the underlying facts. Because the Constitution assigns Congress responsibility for examining potential wrongdoing by a sitting president, we expected congressional committees to follow up on the evidence—the documents and the firsthand witnesses we had laid out in our report. We did not have any expectation as to the outcome of a congressional examination of the facts, only that Congress would look at the actual underlying evidence.

We did not, however, anticipate Attorney General Barr handling our report in a manner that would make it difficult for both Congress and the American people to understand the results of our investigation. Barr used his power as attorney general to substitute his own words for ours in a way that downplayed not only Trump's conduct but also that of the Russians. His letter claiming to give our bottom line omitted several of our most important conclusions. And when he finally did release our report a month later, he held a press conference that did not speak to the facts of the case. He again omitted the Russian government's intention to harm Trump's opponent in the 2016 election. He again omitted the Trump campaign's expectation that it would benefit from Russian actions to affect the US election, some of which were publicly known at that time to have been undertaken by Russian military intelligence. And he omitted any discussion of Trump's efforts to interfere in our investigation, other than to provide his own defense of Trump's mental state at the time.

It is true that Barr had the authority to stage the release of our report and to reach his own determination about whether Trump committed a crime. But his decision to use that authority as he had—to hold back the facts while also mischaracterizing our work in a way that protected the president—turned our independent and apolitical work into a political exercise. That fundamentally undermined the purpose of appointing Bob in the first place, and made it more difficult for Congress and the American people to judge for themselves the facts we had uncovered.

It is impossible to know what would have happened if our words, instead of Barr's, had been released to the public on March 24, 2019, but at least the public would have known the real results of our investigation at the moment everyone was paying closest attention.

*　*　*

Perhaps the most significant casualty of Barr's handling of the report was the truth about Russia's attack on the United States during the 2016 election. The Russian government interfered in our democracy in sweeping and systematic fashion. Those are the first substantive words of our report. This statement is beyond dispute, and yet many in America do not know that, and still others deny it.

As detailed in volume I of our report, Russian operatives working for the Internet Research Agency visited the United States in 2014 to gather intelligence for what they called "information warfare" against the United States. They returned to Russia and—sitting at their desks in Saint Petersburg—planned and advertised rallies to support Trump at specific US locations, invited Americans to attend, provided banners for Americans to wave, and then handed off logistical responsibilities for the events to real Americans. The goal of these activities, along with their yearslong campaign of false-name social media accounts, was to further divide Americans and cause them to think and behave in particular ways—including at the voting booth in 2016.

Meanwhile, Russian military intelligence hacked into email accounts belonging to the Democratic team supporting Hillary Clinton in 2016, and then dumped emails and other documents they had stolen at specific times during the campaign to harm Clinton and bolster Trump. The Russians also leveraged WikiLeaks to release the stolen information, and, like the Russians, WikiLeaks timed its releases to favor Trump's candidacy.

While these operations were underway, Russian government officials and their proxies reached out to multiple Trump campaign officials. George Papadopoulos was one example. A month after Trump appointed him as a foreign policy adviser in March 2016, Papadopoulos received word about a Russian government offer to assist the Trump campaign through the anonymous release of information damaging to Clinton—"dirt" in the form of "thousands of emails." This offer coincided with the Russian military's then secret hack-and-dump operation.

It is beyond dispute that the Russians interfered in the 2016 election to support Trump—that was no hoax. They worked to secure his win. Our investigation of this work was no witch hunt.

It is impossible to quantify the effect, if any, the Russians had on the election's outcome. But it is undeniable that they affected Trump's campaign activities. Trump's team organized a press strategy around emails stolen and dumped by Russian military intelligence. And Trump's own Facebook page contained photos of rallies in the United States organized by Russian IRA operatives working from inside Russia.

As Bob repeated both when we closed the office and in his testimony before Congress, Russia's interference in our democracy should be of paramount concern to every American. When a foreign adversary launches an attack on our country, Americans of all parties, and the government at every level, should mobilize to defend America's interests. But instead Russian interference has become a partisan issue.

It has not seemed to matter, for instance, that our hack-and-dump indictment, which was backed by financial, email, and other records, demonstrated irrefutably that the Russian military executed this operation. Three days after the indictment came out, Trump dismissed it all in a press conference in Helsinki, Finland, after Putin—standing a few feet to Trump's left—told him, "It's not Russia." Trump and his advocates declared it all a hoax, taking Putin's word over the plain facts. And millions of Americans have taken this as truth, siding with Kremlin propaganda over the US Department of Justice.

We are now heading into another election. Russia interfered before, Russia is emboldened, and Russia is interfering again. Bob described Russia's actions as one of the most serious attacks on democracy he has seen in his career—chilling words from the person who helped lead America's fight against terrorism following the 9/11 attacks. As he put it in his 2019 testimony, the Russians are interfering in our democracy "as we sit here, and they expect to do it during the next campaign."

* * *

Our justice system has no traditional or obvious way to address criminal conduct by a sitting president. And yet, the president cannot be above the law.

The special counsel system was designed to bridge some gaps. It provides for an investigation by a person with a measure of day-to-day independence from the Department of Justice. But a special counsel remains in the president's chain of command. For cases involving elected public officials other than the president, prosecutors face challenges and hard judgments, but, eventually, a viable path to prosecution or declination will emerge. There is no such path for a criminal investigation of the commander in chief. The Constitution limits the possible solutions, and there is obvious tension inherent in having a special counsel within the executive branch investigate the head of the executive branch.

Bob charted his path through these obstacles with two key ideas in mind. First, the office would stick to the rules and the department's core principles. We were to be deliberate and principled in every decision, every pleading, every inference. Second, the office would deliver a report on the president's conduct that outlined the facts in unassailable fashion.

Precisely because there was no straightforward way to address Trump's conduct as a sitting president, it was important that we provide an account of his actions in plain terms. Prosecutors typically do not issue public reports about conduct that is not charged as a crime—and we are not suggesting changing that core principle for the DOJ. At the same time, when it came to a president who (under the OLC opinion) could not be charged with a crime while in office, there needed to be some path to accountability. A written report of the president's conduct, authored by a person outside the political chain of command, can provide a measure of accountability. It can allow Congress and the American people to judge the facts for themselves.

However, for the publication of a report—or at least some portion of it—to work as a solution to the problem of presidential accountability, two things must happen. First, a special counsel must be exceptionally careful and deliberate about the information included in his or her report. A report that includes gratuitous details about the president that are unnecessary to impartial decision-making about the conduct under investigation can do real damage to the presidency and the DOJ.

Second, the attorney general should not replace a special counsel's findings with his or her own. There are good reasons for the attorney general to have the authority to decide whether and what aspects of a special counsel's report to release; and there are good reasons for the attorney general to have the ability to overrule a special counsel who takes steps that are inappropriate under DOJ policy or practice. That authority can ensure accountability within the criminal justice system. But once the attorney general decides it is in the public interest to release information from a special counsel's investigation, it is essential for Americans to see the actual findings and analysis of the special counsel—not just the attorney general's take on it. It is one thing to make appropriate redactions of information in a report; it is something else for an attorney general to withhold the special counsel's findings and replace those findings with his or her own. Doing so could defeat the purpose of appointing a special counsel and prevent the president from answering for his conduct.

We formulated these ideas before the Supreme Court's 2024 immunity decision, and we believe they still hold. However, the Court's decision dramatically reduces the range of conduct that a special counsel can investigate.

* * *

What can Americans do about the attacks on our institutions and the threat to the rule of law?

We think at least part of the answer can be found in the federal oath of office to "support and defend the Constitution." We believe that means Americans should support and defend the constitutional order, its institutions, and the accompanying rule of law that have developed over the last 250 years. Only federal officials take the oath, but every citizen—no matter what kind of work you do, where you live, or where you went to school—can honor it. Every citizen can defend the institutions that enable our democracy to function.

In a speech Bob gave in 2012, he said: "It is not enough to catch the criminal. We must do so while upholding his civil rights. It is not enough to stop the terrorist. We must do so while maintaining his civil liberties. It is not enough to prevent foreign countries from stealing our secrets. We must do so while upholding the rule of law. It is not a question of conflict; it is a question of balance. The rule of law, civil liberties, and civil rights—these are not our burdens. These are what make all of us safer and stronger."

We can't take these things for granted. The rule of law is ours, but only if we can keep it.

ACKNOWLEDGMENTS

This book would not have been possible without the support of our respective spouses, Kate Easterly, Sharon Quarles, and Julie Rawe. Julie also moonlighted as our toughest editor.

We also want to thank Ronald Baldwin, Bruce Berman, Preet Bharara, Jon Goldstein, Matt Kutcher, Bill Lee, Tim Neely, and Tom Strickland for reading our early drafts and providing invaluable feedback; Nils Johnson-Shelton for helping us translate lawyer talk into readable prose; Emily Berman and Hutton Marshall for their first-rate research assistance from their law-firm posts; our brilliant editor, Priscilla Painton, and her outstanding team at Simon & Schuster; and our colleagues and friends from our two years in the SCO, whose hard work, dedication, and integrity we tried to capture in these pages.

INDEX

ABOUT THE AUTHORS

Robert S. Mueller, III, who wrote the book's preface, was appointed special counsel in May 2017 with the instruction to investigate the Russian government's efforts to interfere in the 2016 US presidential election as well as any links or coordination between the Russian government and individuals associated with the Trump campaign. Prior to this, Mueller held several prominent government posts. He served as FBI director from September 2001 to September 2013; US attorney for the Northern District of California from August 1998 to August 2001; acting US deputy attorney general from January 2001 to May 2001; US assistant attorney general for the Criminal Division from August 1990 to January 1993; and acting US attorney for the District of Massachusetts from October 1986 to April 1987. He also served as an officer in the US Marine Corps from 1968 to 1970. While in the Marines, he led a combat platoon in Vietnam and received a Purple Heart and Bronze Star with Valor.

Aaron Zebley was Mueller's deputy in the special counsel's office. Before serving in this role, Zebley held multiple positions at the US Department of Justice and the FBI, including FBI chief of staff, senior counselor in the Department of Justice's National Security Division, assistant US attorney for the Eastern District of Virginia in the national security and terrorism unit, and FBI team leader and case agent in the 9/11 investigation. Zebley is in private legal practice in Washington, DC.

James "Jim" Quarles was Mueller's senior counselor in the special counsel's office. Before serving in this role, Quarles practiced as a trial lawyer for more than four decades, with a primary focus on representing technology companies. Prior to his long career in private legal practice, Quarles served as an assistant special prosecutor on the Watergate Special Prosecution Force from 1973 to 1975.

Andrew Goldstein was one of Mueller's lead prosecutors investigating obstruction of justice and Russian interference. Before serving in this role, Goldstein was chief of the public corruption unit at the US attorney's office for the Southern District of New York, where he prosecuted numerous high-profile cases. Earlier in his career, Goldstein was a staff writer at *Time*. He chairs the white collar defense and investigations practice at Cooley LLP.

Mueller, Zebley, Quarles, and Goldstein developed the concept for this book while co-teaching an annual seminar titled The Mueller Report and the Role of the Special Counsel at the University of Virginia School of Law.